21世纪 全国高职高专国际商务专业规划教材

外贸函电（第二版）

BUSINESS CORRESPONDENCE

王慧敏 主编

北京大学出版社
PEKING UNIVERSITY PRESS

图书在版编目(CIP)数据

外贸函电/王慧敏主编. —2 版. —北京:北京大学出版社,2013.3
(21 世纪全国高职高专国际商务专业规划教材)
ISBN 978 − 7 − 301 − 21739 − 9

Ⅰ. ①外… Ⅱ. ①王… Ⅲ. ①对外贸易 − 英语 − 电报信函 − 写作 − 高等职业教育 − 教材 Ⅳ. ①H315

中国版本图书馆 CIP 数据核字(2012)第 295190 号

书　　　名：外贸函电(第二版)
著作责任者：王慧敏　主编
策 划 编 辑：叶　楠
责 任 编 辑：周　莹
标 准 书 号：ISBN 978 − 7 − 301 − 21739 − 9/F · 3429
出 版 发 行：北京大学出版社
地　　　址：北京市海淀区成府路 205 号　100871
网　　　址：http://www.pup.cn
电 子 信 箱：em@ pup.cn　　　QQ:552063295
新 浪 微 博：@北京大学出版社　　@北京大学出版社经管图书
电　　　话：邮购部 62752015　发行部 62750672　编辑部 62752926
　　　　　　出版部 62754962
印 刷 者：北京虎彩文化传播有限公司
经 销 者：新华书店
　　　　　730 毫米×980 毫米　16 开本　20.75 印张　329 千字
　　　　　2005 年 4 月第 1 版
　　　　　2013 年 3 月第 2 版　2019 年 4 月第 3 次印刷
印　　　数：6001—7000 册
定　　　价：36.00 元

未经许可,不得以任何方式复制或抄袭本书之部分或全部内容。
版权所有,侵权必究
举报电话:010 − 62752024　电子信箱:fd@ pup.pku.edu.cn

内容简介

本教材是依据外贸业务员这一工作岗位对从业人员的书面沟通知识、能力与素质的要求编写的。本教材是以培养学生的实际运用语言能力为目标，突出内容的针对性和实用性，将语言能力与职业能力的培养有机结合，并融合了相关职业资格证书对函电知识和技能的要求。

本教材内容可以分为两个部分：第一部分是第一单元的内容，主要介绍外贸函电的文体特点和行文格式；第二部分是第二至第十三单元，是按照外贸业务流程分别介绍各个业务环节进出口双方需要进行函电沟通时所需掌握的写作要领和写作技巧。通过大量的模板式范例讲解，帮助学生掌握各个业务环节需要写作的函电的结构框架、常用的表达和句型；再通过样信分析、阅读材料学习以及实训练习等内容方便学生反复训练，举一反三，提高学生业务函电的写作能力。

本教材内容丰富生动，不仅适合教学需要，任何从事外贸业务的工作者都可以根据个人工作需要有针对性地选学相关内容，并按照范文模式，更换具体内容，迅速完成一封高质量的业务函电的写作。

作者简介

王慧敏,女,副教授,毕业于中国人民大学。现任教于北京经济管理职业学院商学院,研究方向为国际贸易理论与实践、跨国公司战略管理;长期从事国际贸易理论与实务相关领域的教学与研究工作;编著有《国际贸易实务》《报关实务》《外贸函电》《商务沟通》等八本教材;翻译了《市场营销》《零售企业经营管理》《组织行为学》等六本国外教材。

编写说明

高等职业教育是我国高等教育体系的重要组成部分。深化高职教育改革，以服务为宗旨，以就业为导向，以培养高技能人才为目标，是满足社会发展和经济建设需要，促进高职教育持续健康发展的关键环节。为此，教育部启动了"新世纪高等教育教学改革工程"，在高职高专教育中开展专业教学改革试点工作，并分两批组织实施了《新世纪高职高专人才培养模式和教学内容体系改革与建设项目计划》。北京市经济管理干部学院的国际商务专业是北京市高职高专教育教学改革试点专业，也是教育部《新世纪高职高专教育人才培养模式和教学内容体系改革与建设项目计划》第二批批准立项的《高职高专教育财经类专业人才培养规格和课程体系改革、建设的研究与实践》（Ⅱ15—1）项目中重点研究和推广的优秀专业。"21世纪全国高职高专国际商务专业规划教材"正是几年来该试点专业根据高职教育培养目标的要求，在实践中进行教学内容和课程体系改革的成果。

《21世纪全国高职高专国际商务专业规划教材》的编写，坚持以就业为导向，以职业能力为本位，按照岗位要求设置课程、整合教学内容的指导思想，力求在建立完善的基本理论知识体系的同时，强化智能结构、知识结构对开发学生潜能的影响。该系列教材涵盖了国际商务及相关专业的骨干课程，旨在构建以核心职业能力培养为主线的理论与实务相结合的特色鲜明的课程教材体系。该系列教材在体例上力图新颖，各章前设"导读"，中间设"思一思"、"议一议"，章后设"本章小结"、"案例分析"、"思考与练习"、"技能实训"；在内容上，充分反映时代特点及国外同类教材之优点，并将学习、探究、实训、拓展有机结合，使大学生在学习知识的同时，自主学习能力得到提高。

《21世纪全国高职高专国际商务专业规划教材》是身处教学改革第一线的教师们，在深入研究高职教育思想，广泛汲取国内外优秀教材精华的基础上，以创新的意识和大胆改革、勇于实践的精神，经过集体研讨、反复试验而编写完成的。我们期待着这一成果能为推动高职教改作出贡献。我们国际商务高职试点专业的教学改革还在不断深入进行，这一系列教材能否得到广大老师和学生的认可，还有待在实践中检验。我们真诚地欢迎老师和同学们提出宝贵意见。

本系列教材不仅可作为高职高专财经类专业的教材，也可作为高职高专财经类大学生的自学用书。

课题组

2005 年 8 月

前言

中国现已成为世界第二大经济体,对外贸易已成为我国经济发展的重要组成部分,随之而来的是对国际商务人才需求的激增。所谓国际商务人才不仅要有国际化的视野,熟悉国际规则和惯例,更要掌握国际商务语言能够进行涉外的沟通。所以,国际商务人才培养的一个重要内容就是语言能力的培养。外贸函电课程也就成为国内各高校国际商务或国际贸易等专业的核心主干课程。2005 年第一版的《外贸函电》教材畅销数年恰恰反映了这一社会现实。广大读者和同行对第一版教材给予了肯定和赞誉,也提出了进一步完善的宝贵意见。我们集思广益,在广泛听取一线教师和众多读者的意见基础上进行了教材的修订,力求为大家提供一本更高质量的教材。

本次修订依然贯彻"让学生在外贸业务操作过程中学习函电写作"的编写理念,以及让学生在了解、掌握外贸业务中常用的英文商务函电的文法知识的基础上培养英语写作和交流能力的编写目的。本次修订的重点体现在以下几个方面:

1. 出于方便学生自学的考虑,增加了课文内容的中文注释以及生词及专业术语的讲解注释。

2. 为了体现现代商务英语语言简洁、书面表达口语化的特点,进一步凝练信函的语言,删除了一些不符合目前函电写作发展特点的信函。

3. 进一步丰富练习题型,提高学生的学习兴趣,改善其学习效果。

经过修订,本教材形成如下特点:第一,内容全面、实例丰富、涵盖面广,系统介绍外贸业务中常用函件的标准格式、基本术语、书写技巧和常用表达,具体包括建立业务关系、询盘、报盘、订购、装运、支付、保险、销售合同、申诉索赔等业务环节;第二,注重实用性和可操作性。本书选择简洁的实际业务信函作为范文,每一章列出学习目标,之后对业务背景知识、重点掌握内容、书信示例、常用表达进行介绍;第三,每篇范文附有生词及短语注释,并列出各种情境下的常用表达;第四,提供更多的信函并设置需要分析回答的问题,让学生独立思考并真正掌握函电的文体结构和用词特点;第五,章后设置练习，便于学生提高实际运用能力。

　　本书由王慧敏主编，参与编写的还有魏彩慧、张彦欣、韩玉珍、陈丕西。本书的编写得到了北京京海航物流有限公司李红军经理、北京安惠达科技有限公司高奉涛经理、成都凌天通讯网络有限公司杨竣杰经理等企业外贸业务专家的指导和帮助；北京大学出版社的叶楠编辑和周莹编辑也给予了大力支持和帮助；另外，我们还参考了国内外专家的一些研究成果和教材。在此，一并向诸位表示衷心的感谢。

　　限于作者水平，书中难免有疏漏和不妥之处，敬请读者不吝批评指正。

目录

Unit 1　Introduction to Business Correspondence …………………（1）
Unit 2　Establishing Business Relations ……………………………（33）
Unit 3　Inquiries and Replies …………………………………………（56）
Unit 4　Quotations and Offers …………………………………………（77）
Unit 5　Counter Offers …………………………………………………（100）
Unit 6　Order ……………………………………………………………（121）
Unit 7　Foreign Sales Contracts ………………………………………（148）
Unit 8　Terms of Payment ……………………………………………（176）
Unit 9　Establishment, Extension and Amendment of L/C …………（200）
Unit 10　Packing ………………………………………………………（228）
Unit 11　Insurance ……………………………………………………（248）
Unit 12　Shipment ……………………………………………………（272）
Unit 13　Claim …………………………………………………………（295）

Unit 1　Introduction to Business Correspondence

💡 Learning Objectives

After studying this unit, you should:
- ✍ Know principles of business-letter writing(了解信函写作原则)
- ✍ Know the parts of a business letter(了解信函内容组成)
- ✍ Know the format of a business letter(了解信函格式)
- ✍ Know how to address an envelope(了解信封的写法)
- ✍ Know the general tips of e-mail writing(了解电子邮件的写作技巧)

1. Introduction to Business Letter Writing

A business letter is written for the purpose of requesting or conveying information, making arrangements for business activities or dealing with matters concerning business negotiations. What one writes should be free from grammatical blemishes, and also be free from the slightest possibility of being misunderstood. Clarity, conciseness and courtesy are the essential qualities of business letters. Moreover, complete contents, correct information and language, concrete ideas and consideration for the customers' needs are also important.

Although a less conventional and friendly style is preferred nowadays in business letter writing, it is still better to follow a set standard determined by customs as the business world has become accustomed to such established practices.

商务信函的写作目的是索要或传达信息、安排商务活动或者处理与商务磋商有关的事宜。商务信函中不应该出现语法错误，也不应该引起任何误解。所以，清晰、简洁和礼节是商务信函的基本特质。此外，写作内容完整、信息和语言准确、观点具体明晰以及为顾客着想也是非常重要的。

现代商务信函中使用得较为普遍的是更随意、友好的体例，但因为商界人士已经习惯于一些写作惯例，所以还是应该遵循一些约定俗成的标准。

1.1 Parts of a Business Letter

A business letter consists of seven principal parts:

1. The letterhead(信头)
2. The reference and date line(参考编号和日期行)
3. The inside name and address(封内地址行)
4. The salutation(称谓)
5. The body of the letter(正文)
6. The complimentary close(结尾敬语)
7. The signature(签名)

Some letters may contain miscellaneous matters, which are optional parts as shown below:

8. The attention line(经办人)
9. The subject line(事由行)
10. The reference notation, or the identifying initials(主办人代号)
11. The enclosure(附件)
12. The carbon copy notation(抄送)
13. The postscript(附言)

The following sample letter illustrates the position of each part mentioned above.

Example 1　Parts of a Business Letter

1. China National Cereals, Oils and Foodstuffs Imp & Exp Corp.
   8 Jianguomen Nei Street
   Beijing 100005, China
   Tel: 86-10-6526-8888
   Fax: 86-10-6527-6028
   E-mail: carl@ cofco. com. cn
2. Our Ref.
   Your Ref.
   Date: 15th November, 20××

3. Messrs H. Ronald & Co.
   556 Eastcheap
   London, E. C. 3, England
8. Attention: Import Dept.
4. Dear Sirs,
9. Aquatic Products
5. We thank you for your enquiry of 5 November.

   In compliance with your request, we are sending you herewith a copy of our illustrated catalogue and a quotation sheet for your reference.

   All prices are subject to our confirmation for our aquatic products have been selling well this season. Therefore, we would suggest that you advise us by a fax in case of interest.

   We await your early favorable reply.
6. Yours truly,
   China National Cereals, Oils and Foodstuffs Imp & Exp Corp.
7. Sig. _____
              (Manager)
10. QS/AN
11. Enclosures
12. cc our Shanghai Branch Office
13. P.S. We require payment by L/C for a total value not exceeding USD50,000.

1.1.1 The Letterhead (The Heading)

This part, often already in printing, expresses the personality of a company that writes the letter, and contains the name of the company, its business type and addresses (postal address, telephone number, fax number, telex number and e-mail address). Sometimes, even the logo, names of chief executives or icon of the products are printed in the heading.

信头部分一般是已经印在信纸上的,表明写信公司的身份,一般包括公司名称、业务类型和地址(邮寄地址、电话号码、传真号、电传号和电子邮件地址)。有时,也将公司标识、总裁名字或者产品标志印在上面。

It is important to note that a postal address in English is written from the specific to the general。

注意,英文中邮寄地址的书写顺序是从具体到一般。

Example 2　A UK address

```
                2076 West Main Street
                   Devon, EX14 0RA
                        U. K.
```

Example 3　A USA address

```
                The Betty Mills Company
                  60 East 3rd Avenue
                       Suite 230
                 San Mateo, CA 94401
                       U. S. A.
```

Example 4　A Chinese address in English

```
        Sinochem Jiangsu Import and Export Corporation
           Jiangsu International Business Mansion,
                 50 Zhonghua Road, Nanjing
                    210001, P. R. China
```

Sometimes the telephone number, fax number and e-mail address are put at the left margin below the postal address. Usually the reference and date are put in the same lines but at the right margin to build a neat appearance.

有时,电话号码、传真号和电子邮件地址放在邮寄地址的左下方。通常,参考编号和日期与电话号码、传真号和电子邮件地址在同一行,但靠近信纸右侧,这样,纸面外观整洁。

Good quality stationery and a neat, well-balanced letterhead will enhance the prestige of the writer's company.

质感好的信纸再加上整洁、分布合理的信头会大大提升写信公司的形象。

1.1.2 The Reference and Date

Most letterheads provide for reference letters and numbers. When one firm writes to another, each will give a reference to avoid confusion. References are quoted to indicate what the letter refers to (Your Ref.) and the correspondence to refer to when replying (Our Ref.).

The date line is usually typed between the letterhead and the inside name and address. In British letter style, however, it is normal to put two-line spaces below the inside address and above the salutation.

大部分信头中都写参考字母和数字。当一家公司写信给其他公司时,双方都提供参考编号以避免混淆。写信时,写上对方的参考编号(Your Ref.)以表明信函内容所指,而对方回复时也写上来信人的信函编号(Our Ref.)。

日期行通常写在信头和封内地址之间。但在英式信函体例中,日期通常写在封内地址和称谓之间,间隔两行。

Example 5 Date line of American style

Interstate Products, Inc.

511 Interstate Court

Sarasota, FL 34240

U.S.A.

　　　　　　　　　　　　　　　　　　　　　　Date: April 4, 20—

Shandong Foreign Trade (Holdings) Corporation Limited

51, Taiping Road

Qingdao, 266001

China

Example 6　Date line of British style

<div style="text-align:center">OFFICE SYSTEMS PTY. LTD.</div>	
124 Oak Street	Tel：(61-2)419 3209
Chatswood	Fax：(61-2)419 4011
England	E-mail：info@os.com.uk
Aqueous Technologies 291 Caxton Street Sante Fe U.S.A. 18 November, 20—	

The date should be typed in full; either in British style—D/M/Y (i.e. the order of day, month, then year) or in American style—M/D/Y (i.e. the order of month, day, then year). Figures like 11/12/20- may easily cause confusion. Either cardinal or ordinal numbers can be used. A comma must be put before the year with American style.

拼写日期要完整,英式日期写法顺序是日、月、年,美式日期写法顺序是月、日、年。只写数字容易引起误解。日期既可以写基数词也可以写序数词。美式日期拼写中,在年份前需要点逗号。

Example 7　Dates

1. 2nd May, 20××
2. 2 May, 20××
3. 2 May 20×× (Comma can be omitted)
4. September 21st, 20××
5. September 21, 20××

1.1.3　The Inside Name and Address

This is the name and address of the person to whom the letter is written. It is usually put at the left-hand margin, which helps to give the letter a tidy appearance.

封内地址行是收信人的名称和地址，一般写在左侧以保证页面的整洁。

Courtesy titles used for addressing correspondence are Mr., Mrs., Miss and Messrs.. Messrs., an abbreviation for the French word "Messieurs", is used occasionally for two or more men (Messrs. Holmes & O. Hardy) but more commonly forms part of the name of a firm with a person's name (Messrs. Laurel & Co.).

称呼收信方的敬称有 Mr., Mrs., Miss 和 Messrs.。Messrs. 是法语 "Messieurs" 的缩写，有时用来指两个以上的人，但更多的是用在以人名命名的公司名称前。

Like the address in the letter head, an inside name and address should also be written from the specific to the general.

封内地址与信头地址的写法一样，从具体到一般。

1.1.4 The Salutation

The salutation is a complimentary greeting with which the writer opens his or her letter. Its particular form depends on the relationship between the writer and his or her correspondent. To some extent, it settles the form of the complimentary close. The two must always be in keeping.

称谓是写信人信函开头的一种礼节性的称呼方式。具体形式取决于双方的关系。一定程度上，称谓也决定了结尾敬语的形式，这两者一般是要保持一致的。

Dear Sir is used to address a man and ***Dear Madam*** to a woman, whether single or married. ***Dear Sir or Madam*** (***Dear Sir/Madam***) can be used to address a person of whom you know neither the name nor the sex.

Dear Sir 称呼男士，***Dear Madam*** 称呼已婚或未婚的女士。如果不知道对方的姓名和性别，可以用 ***Dear Sir or Madam*** (***Dear Sir/Madam***)。

Dear Sirs, ***Dear Sirs or Mmes***, while the most common ones in the British letters and ***Gentlemen*** in the U.S., are used for addressing two or more, as where a letter is addressed to a firm.

英式信函中的 ***Dear Sirs***，***Dear Sirs or Mmes*** 或美式信函中的 ***Gentlemen*** 通常用于致信给两个以上的人，比如致信给一家公司。

When you know the name of the person, the salutation takes the form of Dear followed by a courtesy title and the person's surname. Initials or first names are not generally used in salutation: ***Dear Mr. Johnson***, not Dear Mr. R. Johnson or Dear Mr. Richard Johnson.

如果知道对方的名字,可以在 Dear 后加敬称及对方的姓氏,一般不能写对方名字的首字母或名字,比如可以写 ***Dear Mr. Johnson***,但不可以写 Dear Mr. R. Johnson 或者 Dear Mr. Richard Johnson.。

When you and your correspondent have become friendly to each other, you may address him or her by first name, e.g. ***Dear Jacky***.

如果和对方关系密切了,也可以称呼对方名字,如 ***Dear Jacky***。

Usually, the salutation is followed by a comma for Dear Sirs and a colon for Gentlemen. Now it is also popular not to use any punctuation mark here.

通常,Dear Sirs 称谓后面接逗号,而 Gentlemen 称谓后面接冒号。但现在不使用任何标点符号的情况也很常见。

1.1.5 The Body of the Letter

This is the subject matter or message of any business letter, and is its most important section.

正文是信函的主题内容,也是最重要的部分。

It is wise to streamline your letters to make them more effective, keep them brief and flowing with short sentences and short paragraphs. To achieve your purpose, you must consider your aim in writing the letter and the best way to go about it. The following serves as reminders:

对信函的内容要进行合理安排以使信函更有效地传递信息,并且用简短的句子和段落以使信函内容简洁流畅。为了达到这样的效果,必须考虑自己的写作目的以及达到这一目的的最好方式。提醒注意下面几点:

(1) Write simply, clearly, courteously, grammatically correctly, and to the point, avoiding stereotyped phrases.

写作需简单、清晰、礼貌、语法正确、切中要点、避免陈词滥调。

(2) Confine each paragraph to one point you wish to stress and arrange them in a logical order.

每一段只表达一个观点,并合理安排顺序。

The opening sentence of the first paragraph usually indicates the subject and intention. The closing sentence of the last paragraph shows friendliness and good will. You may finish the letter with present participles, phrases or a complete sentence. e. g.

第一段的第一句通常表明主题和意图。最后一段的结束句表明友善的态度和良好的愿望。信函结束可以用现在分词、短语或者句子。例如:

Awaiting your good news.

Looking forward to your early reply.

We hope to receive your early reply.

Using a complete sentence to close the letter is now preferred.

但现在更倾向于使用完整的句子结束信函。

1.1.6 The Complimentary Close

The complimentary close is simply a matter of custom or a polite way of bringing a letter to a close. The expression used must suit the occasion and match the salutation. The following are the salutations with their matching close most commonly used.

结尾敬语只是一种习惯或是礼貌地结束信函的方式。表达方式需要适合语境以及开头称谓。下面是称谓以及与之对应的结尾敬语。

Salutation	Close	Occasion
Dear Sir(s) Dear Sir or Madam (Mmes)	Yours faithfully Faithfully yours	Standard and formal closure
Gentlemen Ladies/Gentlemen	Yours (very) truly Very truly yours	Used by Americans
Dear Mr. Malone	Yours sincerely/ Sincerely Best wishes (U. K.) Best regards/ Regards (U. S. A.)	Less formal and between persons known to each other

(1) Sometimes the expression of "***Best regards***" or "***Best wishes***" is used as the closing sentence in the last paragraph and followed by complimentary close like "***Yours Sincerely***" at the same time.

有时,信函内容最后一段的结束语是"*Best regards*"或"*Best wishes*",结尾敬语就写"*Yours Sincerely*"。

Example 8 Complimentary Closes

Best regards. Sincerely, ***Brian*** Brian	Best regards. ***J. Houta*** J. Houtas	Thanks and regards. Truly yours, ***Maria Salgado*** Maria Salgado

(2) If no punctuation is used in the salutation, the complimentary close will not be punctuated either. Otherwise, a comma is needed.

如果称谓中没用标点,结尾敬语也不用,否则用逗号。

(3) The complimentary close must never be separated from the substance of a letter by being carried to a separate sheet. Re-arrange the spaces to keep it on the same sheet with the body of the letter or carry some portions of the letter to the next sheet. When using continuation sheets, always type a heading to show:

结尾敬语一定不能放在单独一页,和信函内容分开。出现这种情况时,要调整行距把内容放在一张纸上,或者把信函一部分内容转到下一页来。如果用纸超过一页,要在纸上打上标题(第二页的标题,不是指信函本身的标题),内容为:

① the number of the sheet (in the upper center of the page);

页码(纸张上端中间部分);

② the name of your correspondent (on the left-hand side);

收信人名称(左侧);

③ the date of the letter (on the right-hand side).

日期(右侧)。

e.g.

例如:

-2-

Goodcare Medical Apparatus Co. Ltd.   1st March, 20—

1.1.7 The Signature

In the signature area you can include the name of your company, your signature, your typed name and your business title. Every letter should be signed by hand, in black or blue (not red) ink below the complimentary close.

签名处可以写公司的名称、个人的签名、打印的个人名字以及职位。每封信都应该手签,在结尾敬语下面以蓝色或黑色墨水签名。

The signature, however, should not vary from one letter to another, because a signature is the distinguishing mark of the one who uses it. The same style must always be adopted and the written signature and the printed signature must correspond exactly.

因为签名是区别写信人的一种标记符号,所以在不同的信中签名应该保持一致,始终采用同样字体风格的签名,并且打印的名字要与手签签名一致。

Sometimes the company name may follow the preposition "For", indicating that the writer works and types the letter for this company (sender's company). If the writer types the letter for someone else, add the person's position and name to "For".

有时,在介词"For"后面写上公司名称,表明写信人是在此公司工作并代表此公司写作此信函。如果写信人是替别人打印信函,那么就在"For"后面写明这个人的名字和职位。

Example 9   Signatures

Yours faithfully, Ciba-Geigy Chemicals Co. ***Pam Lotis*** Pam Lotis Inspection coordinator	Yours faithfully, ***Pam Lotis*** Pam Lotis Inspection coordinator For Ciba-Geigy Chemicals Co.	Yours faithfully, ***L. Van Linde*** L. Van Linde Manager, QAD Software Co.

1.1.8 The Attention Line

This line may be used if you wish to address the letter to a particular member of a department of the company, but perhaps you only know the surname of the member and thus cannot write the name in the Inside Address (which needs a complete name), or you expect your letter to be promptly attended to by any other member of the company who takes care of the business of the addressee in case the latter is absent from the office.

It is typed two-line spaces above the salutation, underlined and centered over the body of the letter, except with the fully blocked letter style.

如果信是写给公司某个部门的某个具体的人的,但你又只知道此人的姓氏而不能在封内地址中写此人的名字(封内地址应该写对方的全名),这时就可以使用经办人行。如果收信人不在公司时,你希望自己的信函能够得到对方公司的任何其他人及时处理,也可以使用经办人行。

经办人行通常在开头称谓上面,间隔两行,用下划线标示,在非齐头式格式中,一般是放在中间位置。

Example 10　Attention Line

1. Attention: Mr. H. A. Donnan, Export Manager
2. Attention of Mr. Cave
3. To the attention of Mr. Liu Ming

1.1.9　The Subject Line

The subject line gives a brief indication of the content of the letter. It is placed two lines below the salutation and above the body of the letter. The line may begin with or without the Latin preposition-Re: (which means "regarding"), and is usually underlined.

主题行是简明地说明信函内容。主题行位于称谓和正文之间,间隔两行,主题行开头可以写 Re:(意思是关于),也可以不写,通常画下划线。

Example 11　Subject Line

1. Re: Your Order No. 463 for 1,000 Wide-screen TV Sets
2. **SHEEP WOOL**

1.1.10　The Reference Notation

The reference notation, also called identifying initials or identification marks, is made up of the initials of the typist, sometimes with the initials of the dictator if not typed in the signature area. Usually the reference notation is typed two spaces below the typed signature.

主办人代号是打字员名字的首字母,有时如果信函内容口述者没有在签名处签名的话,也可以将他的名字的首字母打在此行。通常主办人代号放在打印的签名下方,间隔两行。

Example 12 Reference Notations

1. ASB hu   2. ASB/HU   3. ASB/hu   4. ASB:hu

1.1.11 The Enclosure

When there is something enclosed with the letter, type the word "Enclosure", or an abbreviation of it on the bottom left-hand, two-line spaces under the reference notation. Here are some examples:

如果随函附寄了东西,则在信纸左下角打上"Enclosure"或它的缩写,位于主办人代号下方,间隔两行。

Example 13 Enclosures

1. Enclosure
2. Enc.
3. Encl. As Stated
4. Enclosure: Brochure
5. Enclosures: Bill of Lading (6 copies)
   Commercial Invoice (4 copies)

1.1.12 The Carbon Copy Notation

There are two types of carbon copy notation—cc and bcc (Blind Carbon Copy). The former is followed by the names of the persons who will receive copies of the letters and this notation is typed on both the originals and the copies. The latter, bcc, is followed by the names of the recipients of the copies and is specified on the copies only. You and the recipients of the "bcc" are the only persons that know that the letter is blind copied.

有两种抄送形式——抄送和盲抄。前者是在信件的原件和复件上 cc 后面打上收到复件的所有人的名字。盲抄是只在复件上 cc 后面打上收到复件的所有人的名字。只有写信人和盲抄的复件的收信人知道此信是盲抄的。

Example 14　Carbon Copies

1. cc Marketing Department
2. bcc Mr. Simpson

1.1.13　The Postscript

The postscript is used when you wish to add something you forgot to mention. However, the adding of P. S. should be avoided as much as possible as it is usually considered as a sign of poor planning.

如果忘记说的事情要加到信函里,可以用附言。但要尽量避免用附言,因为这被视为缺乏统筹规划。

Example 15　Postscript

P. S. When replying to this letter, please enclose a copy of your survey report.

1.2　Layout of a Business Letter

There are two main templates for layout. The conventional indented style (See Example 16) takes in five or six spaces in the first line of each paragraph, which makes the letter easy to read. The blocked style (See Example 17) now appeals to most readers for all the typing lines begin at the left-hand margin. To make the letter compact and tidy, the spaces between paragraphs should be increased.

常用的信函格式有两种。传统的缩进式(例 16),每段开头缩进 5 或 6 个字符,使得信函内容一目了然。齐头式(例 17)则是所有内容都从左侧顶格开始。段落之间间距要增加以保持信函的整洁。

However, now there is a third template for layout. The modified blocked style (See Example 18) avoids the inconvenience of paragraph indentations in the indented form and the loss of clarity occasioned by the absence of indentation in the blocked style.

第三种格式就是改良的齐头式(例18),这种格式避免了缩进式中段落缩进的麻烦,也避免了齐头式中有时出现的段落划分不清的问题。

Whichever style is used, it is a good plan to adopt one form of layout and to stick to it.

无论采用什么信函格式,最好就是选择以后坚持用同一格式。

Example 16　Indented Form

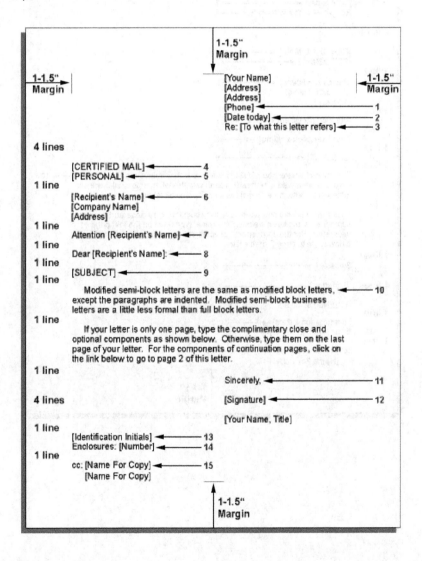

Example 17   Blocked Form

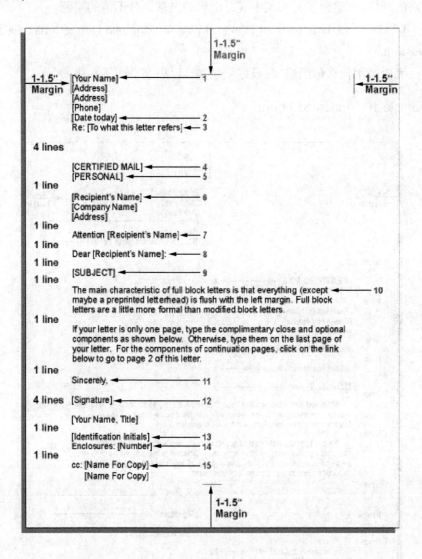

Example 18   Modified Blocked Form

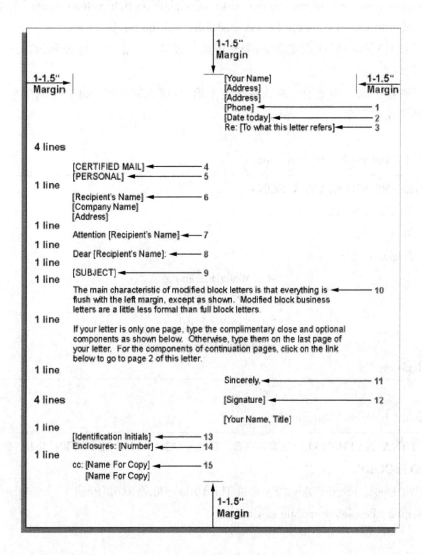

1.3 Envelope Addressing

Envelope addressing calls for accuracy, legibility and good appearance. The address on the envelope and the inside address on the letter should be in the same style and present the same information.

The sender's name and address are always put on the top left corner and the receiver's name and address in the center or slightly on right bottom corner. Here are some examples showing the indented form and the blocked form.

信封写作中要注意准确、清晰易辨和外观整洁。信封的地址和封内地址应该保持一致。

寄信人名字地址通常在信封的左上角,收信人的名字地址在信封的中间或略微偏右下角。

1.3.1 Indented Form Envelope

MESSRS WILLIAM & SONS	
76 Lancaster House	stamp
Manchester,	
England	
Mr. Wang Kai-ming	
China National Transport Co.	
120 Nanjing Road	
Shanghai, China	
Registered	

1.3.2 Blocked Form Envelope

CHINA NATIONAL CEREALS, OILS AND FOODSTUFFS IMP & EXP CORP.	
11th Floor, Jingxin Bldg. 2A East Third Ring Road North Rood	stamp
Beijing, People's Republic of China	
El Mar Packing Company	
12 Main Street, Fresno	
California, USA	
Confidential	
Par Avion	

The following are some suggestions on addressing an envelope:

(1) Post road may be mentioned and put on the left bottom corner. e. g.

信封左下角可以写邮寄方式,如:

Per S/S "Empress of Canada"

Via Cape Town

Via Air Mail (By Airmail, or Par Avion)

Registered

Parcel Post

Express

Samples Post

(2) If it is a personal letter of a confidential one, put the words on the left bottom corner. e. g.

如果是私人信函或密函,可以在信封左下角写:

Private

Personal

Confidential

(3) If a letter is to be taken from you by someone to the addressee, no address is needed. Just put his name below the addressee's with "Kindness of (Politeness of, Favored by, Through the Courtesy of, Per Kindness of, Forwarded by, With Favor of, Per Favor of)" in front of it. e. g.

如果是某人从你这取走信并带给收信人,那信封上就不用写地址了。只要在收信人名字下面写上"Kindness of (Politeness of, Favored by, Through the Courtesy of, Per Kindness of, Forwarded by, With Favor of, Per Favor of)",然后加上取信人的名字,如:

   Mr. Charles Wood

  Kindness of Mr. J. W. Smith

(4) When a letter is mailed to a third person (or company) who is bound to pass it on to the addressee, write a person's name down below the addressee's with the words "care of (c/o)" in front of it. For example:

如果信是寄给第三方,并由其转交给收信人,那么在收信人名字下面写上"care of (c/o)"然后写转送人的名字。如:

Mr. Part Davis c/o Mr. Harold Bean 32 Bright Street Rangoon, Burma	Mr. Brian Tories c/o Overseas Trading Co. 153 Market Street London

2. Layout of E-mails

E-mails have many advantages over the traditional methods such as postal service, telephone and fax. It is cheaper and faster than a letter, less intrusive than a phone call. Besides, it is more effective and safe. Messages can be sent or picked up anywhere in the world, thus avoiding the inconvenience in differences in location and time zone. Therefore, with e-mail documents, your recipient can ask questions immediately. Messages are stored in a mailbox until they are retrieved. Important messages may be printed out and kept for reference or file. Being more conversational and speedy, e-mail has become a popular medium in business circles.

电子邮件与传统的通信方式相比有许多优点。它比信函更快捷、成本更低，也不像电话那样容易打扰别人，而且更有效、更安全。在世界的任何地方都可以发送或接收邮件，这样就避免了由于区域差异或时差而造成的不便。所以，利用电子邮件，你的收信人可以立即向你提出问题。邮件可以在邮箱里存储，需要时就从邮箱里调出。重要的邮件可以打印出来并存档。因为邮件内容更像谈话而且速度更快，所以在商界已经成为广泛使用的沟通媒介。

Layouts of e-mails vary from website to website, but the essentials are all similar. In fact, there is not much to be done by you to lay out an e-mail, because it is already a fixed form for you to just fill in. It is usually made up of the heading (receiver's e-mail address, subject, attachment, carbon copy and so on) and the body (where there is a blank space for you to key in your message).

不同网站的邮件格式有所不同，但本质内容都是相近的。实际上，我们不需要对邮件格式进行太多设计，因为它都是要求你填一些固定的空格。邮件的构成一般是信头（收件人的邮件地址、主题、附件、抄送等）和正文（也是一个空白处，可以在这里键入信息）。

Example: An outgoing e-mail

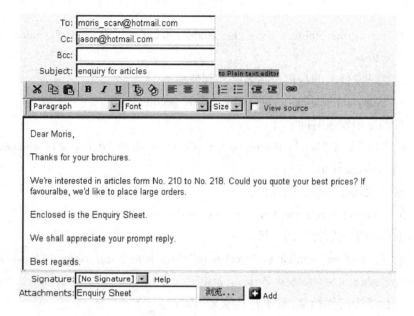

Example: An incoming e-mail

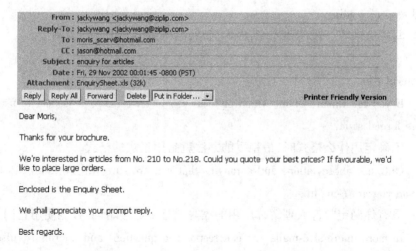

1. To: this column includes the recipient's email address. The information should be correct, otherwise the letter may be sent incorrectly or be returned from

a non-existing address.

这栏是写收件人的邮件地址。地址信息要准确,否则会发给他人或者被退回。

2. From: this column gives the sender's identity—the sender's name and e-mail address.

这栏是发件人的身份包括名字和邮件地址。

3. Date: automatically shows the time of sending.

自动显示发送时间。

4. "Cc" and "bcc": the two columns contain email addresses of whomever this mail is copied to.

这两栏是邮件抄送的地址。

5. Subject: serves the same purpose as the Subject Line in a letter.

和信函中主题行作用一样。

6. Attachment: similar to "Enclosure" in a letter, this column shows that there are other files attached to this e-mail.

与信函中附件相似,表明有其他文档附寄。

7. Body of the e-mail: where you write your message. Using short paragraphs, fewer lines and sentences can provide your audience with a clear layout and ease of reading.

写邮件内容。段落要简短,内容简洁,结构清晰便于收件人阅读。

General tips

If you are unsure about which style to use in an e-mail, it is best to use a more formal style.

不确定用什么格式时,最稳妥的办法就是用正式的格式。

Only use abbreviations and acronyms that you are sure will be known to the person you are e-mailing.

只有你确定收件人理解你所用的缩写或首字母缩略词,方能使用它们。

In more informal e-mails you can respond to questions and queries by inserting your answers into the original message, which is then sent back to the original writer.

在非正式的邮件中,如果回答问题或调查问卷你可以直接将答案插入原始邮件中然后返回给发件人。

In summary, remember to follow these main guidelines when composing e-mail messages:

Try to keep to one subject per message—don't cover various issues in a single e-mail;

Use a descriptive and informative subject heading;

Be concise—keep messages short and to the point;

Write short sentences;

Use bulleted lists to break up complicated text;

Quote from the original e-mail if replying to a message;

Conclude your message with actions required and target dates.

总之,记住下面几个主要原则:

一个邮件中阐述一个主题,不要在一个邮件中涉及多个问题;

主题内容是描述性的、可以反映邮件内容的;

简洁,信息要言简意赅;

写短句;

利用带记号的目录将复杂的邮件内容断开;

回复邮件时要引用原邮件的内容;

邮件结束时要表明你要采取的行动和目标期限。

3. Useful Expressions

1. We have (take) pleasure in informing you that...

兹欣告你方……

2. We have the pleasure of informing you that...

兹欣告你方……

3. We are pleased (glad) to inform you that...

兹欣告你方……

4. Further to our letter of yesterday, we now have (the) pleasure in informing you that...

续谈我方昨日函,现告你方……

5. We confirm telegrams/fax messages recently exchanged between us and are pleased to say that...

我方确认近来双方往来电报/传真,并欣告……

6. We have the pleasure in acknowledging the receipt of your letter dated...

欣获你方×月×日来信。

7. We acknowledge with thanks the receipt of your letter of...

谢谢你方×月×日来信。

8. We have duly received your letter of...

刚刚收悉你方×月×日来信。

9. We thank you for your letter of... contents of which have been noted.

谢谢你方×月×日来信,内容已悉。

10. Referring to your letter of... we are pleased to...

关于你方×月×日来信,我们很高兴……

11. Reverting to your letter of... we wish to say that...

再洽你方×月×日来信,令通知……

12. In reply to your letter of..., we...

兹复你方×月×日来函,我方……

13. We wish to refer to your letter of... concerning...

现复你方×月×日关于……的来信。

14. If you require any further information, feel free to contact me.

如果你方需要更多信息,请随时与我联系。

15. I look forward to your reply.

期待你方答复。

16. I look forward to hearing from you.

期待收到你方回信。

Exercises

I. Identify the style each following letter adopts.

Letter 1

Institute of Language Education
    28 Ashby Road
    SYDNEY NSW 2001
    Tel: (612) 2110388   Fax: (612) 2115237
18 February 2004
The director
Supreme Holdings Co. Ltd.
83 Crystal Street
PERTH WA 6000
Attn. : Mr Ray Taylor
Dear Sir

Hints on Business Letter Writing

    Thank you for your letter of 18 February asking about hints on writing business letters.

    You may be interested to learn that our Institute has adopted the five key points listed below over the past ten years and found them very helpful.

    (1) Plan what you wish to write according to your objectives and sequence it logically.

    (2) Break the sequence into parts; use one paragraph for each part.

    (3) Specify the topic of the letter at the beginning and state your intended action at the end.

    (4) Keep your sentences and paragraphs short; use appropriate punctuation; use columns and sub-paragraphs where necessary.

    (5) Use simple words and write in ordinary language; always keep a sincere and friendly tone by thinking of your reader.

    I hope the above will help you and your staff write better business letters.

Please write to me again if you need further information.

Yours faithfully

Letter 2

MACEETOSH COMPANY

20 Arthur St, SINGAPORE, 1088
Tel: (65) 744 8433   Fax: (65) 7442108

23 July 2004

Mr Stephen Young
John Hill Motors Ltd.
321 King St.
London
LN1 EC2, England

Dear Mr Young

Solar Powered Cars (Model No. SP-7)

Further to our telephone conversation on 20 July regarding the above vehicles, I am writing to confirm the delivery details as follows:

Colour: Blue
Number of vehicles: 6
Delivery address: 123 Queen St., London
Date of dispatch: 1 August 2004
Couriers: via London Express

I hope you will find the above arrangements satisfactory. Please feel free to contact us if you have any queries.

It has been a great pleasure conducting business with you. We shall be glad to hear from you again if we can be of further assistance to you.

Yours sincerely

Letter 3

 The Electrolux Group

St. Gangsgatan 143 Stockholm, 105 45 Sweden

Telex: 53892 SHELEC SS   Our Reference: No. H/W—T008
Tel: 46-8-738-6000   Your Reference: No.
Fax: 46-8-738-6016
E-mail: hwlee@ electrolux. com

Date: 30th March, 20 × ×

Messrs. William & Warner
105 Roller Road
Sydney, Australia

Attention: Mr. Donnason, Marketing Dept.

Dear Sir,

Re: Shipping Advice of Freezers

With reference to your order No. F256 of February 5 for 1 000 sets of Freezers, we're pleased to inform you that the goods have been loaded on board the S/S "Peace", which is sailing for your port on April 1st.

We've sent a telex to the above effect this morning. Please insure the goods as contracted and make preparation for taking the delivery. We are now making out the necessary documents for negotiation.

We assure you that our goods will be found satisfactory upon arrival at your port. We also hope that we can close more business with you in the future.

Yours faithfully,
The Electrolux Corp.

Horis De Wolley
Horis De Wolley
(Manager)

Letter 4

Johnson & Johnson

1 J&J Plaza New Brunswick,
NJ 089333 U.S.A.
Tel: 732-524-0400
Fax: 732-525-0622
E-mail: carrie@jnj.com

Date: 22nd July, 20××

Soft Health Care Product Corp.

Room 2301 Yili BLD,

35 Nanjing Road,

Shanghai, China

Attention: Mr. Wang, Import Dept.

Dear Sir,

Re: SHAMPOO

 We've received your letter of July 10th enquiring about our JOHNSON'S (r) Baby Shampoo With Natural Lavender, but unfortunately, the stock of this product is running low due to the heavy demand. But we will inform you as soon as the new supplies come up.

 We sell a wide variety of Baby's Shampoo. All of them are made of the NO MORE TEARS formula. For your reference, we enclose an illustrated catalogue of our shampoos and we hope you will find it interesting.

 We hope that we can close business to our mutual advantage in the future.

Yours faithfully

Johnson & Johnson

Doris Fergoson

Doris Fergoson

(Manager)

Letter 5

SAMSUNG ELECTRONICS

310 Taepyung-ro 2-ga, Chung-gu
Seoul, 100-102, Korea
Tel: 82-2-3706-1114
E-mail: qsl@ samsungcorp. com

Our Reference: No. ODL-11
Your Reference: No.
Date: 23rd December, 20—

Shandong Science & Technology Co. Ltd.
21/F Bright Plaza
138 Jinni Road, Jinan
Shandong, China
Attention: Mr. Zhou Jun, Import Dept.

Dear Sir,

Re: Our Offer for PDA Type III-H

 Thank you for your interest in our latest Personal Digital Assistant Type III-H.

 As requested, we offer you 500 sets of PDA at USD 140 per set FOB Inchon for shipment in February, 20—. We require payment by L/C.

 Because there is an increasing demand for this product, our price is non-negotiable. We look forward to your reply.

            Yours truly

            Samsung Electronics
            Lavis Kim
            Lavis Kim
            (Manager)

II. Put the following titles into Chinese.

1. Chairman of the Board (of Directors)
2. President (General Manager)
3. Managing Director
4. Deputy or Vice President
5. Standing (Executive) Director
6. Director
7. (Standing) Auditor
8. Finance Manager
9. Administration Manager
10. Acting Manager
11. Section Chief

III. Rewrite the following sentences, to make them more concise and effective.

1. Plant A is successful in terms of production.

2. There appears to be a tendency on the part of investment bankers to become more cautious.

3. It was her last argument that finally persuaded me.

4. There are likely to be many researchers raising questions about this methodological approach.

5. It is inevitable that oil prices will rise.

6. Central to our understanding of the problem of the organizational structure in the XYZ division of the ABC Company is the chain of command between the position of the division vice president and the subordinate departments, because although all of them are under this office, none of them are directly connected up with it.

7. We plan to give consideration to the idea at our meeting.

8. There is a need for more careful inspection of all welds.

9. My final comment is that this construction job has progressed very satisfactorily up to present time and it will be adversely affected by the prolonged strike of the electric trades.

10. It should be noted that this is the best price we can offer in this season.

IV. Arrange the following parts in a proper form as they should be set out in a letter.

1. Writer's name: The Wharton Business School, University of Pennsylvania
2. Writer's address: Pennsylvania, USA, Tel: 8981776
3. Date: 4 May 2007
4. Receiver's name: Hudson Foodstuff Co. Ltd.
5. Receiver's address: 26 High Street, Barnes, Yorkshire, Britain
6. Subject: Executive Education
7. The message:

Dear Entrepreneurs

To successfully drive your business, you must be competitively focused and customer focused. It is a lesson too many people forget.

George Day, marketing professor of The Wharton Business School, University of Pennsylvania has introduced "market-driven strategy" to be the business vocabulary—only one of the many innovative ideas developed by our world-class faculty.

As the oldest business school in the world, Wharton has been at the frontier of finance, international business, management, strategy and marketing. Driven by a faculty with unparalleled depth and breadth, Wharton continues to help organizations negotiate the tricky turns of our increasingly global environment.

This rich tradition of innovation is the foundation of our executive programs, which incorporate a unique blend of scholarly excellence and real world pragmatism. These insightful, dynamic courses offer the opportunity to refocus and refuel.

Are you running low on new ideas? Come to Wharton Executive Education. You will put what you learn into action and quickly pull away from the field.

Visit us on the web-site http://wh-execed. Wharton. upenn. edu/2463. cfm or call us at 1-215-898-1776.

(1) Sender's name: Beijing ITT Hardware Products Imp& Exp Corp. .
(2) Sender's address: 82 Dong An Men Street.
(3) Sender's telephone number: 86-010-62536891.
(4) Sender's email: davy_qi@ itthw. inf. com.

(5) Date: April 25, 20××.

(6) Receiver's name: Compaq Computers.

(7) Receiver's address: 20555 SH 249, Houston TX77070, U.S.A..

(8) Attention of Marketing Department II.

(9) Salutation: Dear Sirs.

(10) Subject: Key Boards.

(11) The message:

Thanks for your offer for "Compaq" Brand Key Boards.

We feel regretful that our buyers find your price a little high. If a 10% reduction can be reached, we can assure you that substantial business will materialize.

We look forward to receiving your kind comments.

(12) Complimentary close: Yours faithfully.

Unit 2　Establishing Business Relations

Learning Objectives

After studying this unit, you should be able to:

✎ Know how to obtain the information about a potential trade partner in foreign countries(了解获取海外潜在贸易伙伴信息的方法)

✎ Know the essential components of a letter to establish business relations (了解建交函内容的基本组成要素)

✎ Master useful expressions in writing such letters(掌握建交函中常用表达方式)

2.1　Introduction

To seek prospective clients and establish business relations is one of the most important undertakings for a newly established firm or an old one that wishes to expand its market and enlarge its business scope and turnover.

对于新创建的企业或者是希望扩大市场、业务范围和营业收入的老企业来说,寻找潜在的客户以及建立业务关系是最重要的一项工作。

Opportunities for establishing business relations in international trade can be found in the information from the following sources:

Specialized magazines and newspaper advertisements;

Recommendations by a business friend or a client;

Market research;

Chambers of Commerce both at home and abroad;

Enquiries from foreign merchants;

Commercial Counselor's office;

Trade directory;

Exhibitions and trade fairs;

The internet.

在国际贸易活动中,可以通过以下渠道获得建立业务关系机会的信息:

专业报刊上的广告;

生意伙伴或客户的推荐;

市场调研;

国内外的商会;

外商的询函;

商务参赞处;

行业名录;

展览与贸易交易会;

互联网。

When writing a letter to start business with another company, you are supposed to tell your reader how you get his name and address and what your business line is, then state your purpose and request and finally express your sincere wish to cooperate in future business and your hope to get a favorable reply soon.

在写作建交函时,信件中应该说明你是如何获悉收信人公司名称和地址的,本公司所从事的业务范围,还要说明写作意图和具体请求,最后表达在未来开展业务合作的诚挚愿望以及对对方尽快给予肯定答复的期望。

Any letter of this nature received must be answered in full without the least delay and with courtesy for the sake of creating goodwill and leaving a good impression on the party who hopes to start business.

为了建立良好的关系,并给提出开展业务往来愿望的一方留下一个美好印象,对于任何一封建交函都必须全面、及时、礼貌地答复。

2.2 Model Letters Comments

2.2.1 an Importer Write to a Manufacture (First enquiry)

The Elegant Leather Products Inc.

9 Green Street

Manchester

England

Tel:234759

Fax:234890

22 March 2003

Granford Leather Stores
23 Western Highway
New York
U. S. A.

Dear sirs

　　We have learned from Messrs Armstrong & Smith of Liverpool that you manufacture a range of high-fashion handbags in a variety of leathers. As we are one of the leading dealers of leather handbags in this area and believe there is a promising market here for handbags of high quality, we would like you to send us details of your various ranges, including sizes, colors and prices, and also samples of the different qualities of skins used.

　　When replying, please state your terms of payment and discount you would allow on purchases of large quantities of individual items. Prices quoted should include insurance and freight to Liverpool.

　　Should prices be found reasonable and suitable for our market, we shall be pleased to place regular orders with you.

　　We hope that will meet your prompt attention.

Yours sincerely

Notes

　　1. We have learned from... that you... 承蒙……的介绍,获悉贵公司……
类似的表达方法有:

　　We have obtained (learned, come to know) your name and address from the Commercial Counselor's Office of your embassy in Beijing.

　　我们从贵国驻京使馆商务参赞处得悉贵公司行名及地址。

　　We owe your name and address to China Council for the Promotion of International Trade in Beijing.

　　我们从设在北京的中国国际贸易促进委员会得悉贵公司行名及地址。

　　Through the courtesy of Mr. Green, we learn (understand) that you are one of the leading exporters of Chinese textile in your country.

承蒙格林先生介绍,我们得知贵公司是贵国中国纺织品的主要出口商之一。

Your firm has been recommended (introduced, given, suggested) to us by Bank of China, Shenzhen.

中国银行深圳分行已把贵公司介绍给我们了。

Having had your name and address from the Commercial Counselor's Office of the Embassy of the People's Republic of China in Washington, we now avail ourselves of this opportunity to write to you and see if we can establish business relations by a start of some practical transactions.

从中华人民共和国驻华盛顿大使馆商务参赞处获悉贵公司名称和地址,现借此机会与贵方通信,意在达成一些实际交易为开端,以建立业务关系。

2. leading (a.),意为主要的,意思相同的词还有 chief, main 等

Having been a leading importer of tobacco machinery for 20 years, we think that we are in a position of concluding considerable business transactions with you.

20多年来,我们一直都是烟草机械的主要进口商,因此,有信心能够与贵司达成大量交易。

We write to introduce ourselves as one of the chief exporters of first class cotton goods, enjoying an excellent reputation.

现具函自我介绍,本公司是优质棉织品的主要出口商之一,享有极高声誉。

3. sample 样品

original sample 原样　　　　duplicate sample 复样
counter sample 对等样品　　representative sample 代表性样品
reference sample 参考样品　　sealed sample 封样

4. terms of payment, payment terms 支付条件,付款条件,付款方式

Our company may consider more favorable payment terms after we have done more business.

待我们做了更多的业务后,我方会考虑更有利的付款方式。

We are prepared to accept D/P at sight and sincerely hope that this payment term will be acceptable to you.

我们愿意接受即期付款交单的托收方式并真诚地希望你方也能接受这一支付条件。

5. discount,意指折扣,意思相同的词还有 reduction,allowance

We are ready to grant (allow) you a discount of 10% on the original price.

我们愿意在原来价格的基础上给你方10%的折扣。

We give you the same goods at a discount of 3% off our last prices.

同样的货物,我们在上次价格基础上给你们打3%的折扣。

Instead of 10% reduction, we suggest a reduction of 5% on orders of over USD 4000.

我们建议对于订购额超过4000美元的订单给予5%的折扣,而非10%。

We make this allowance because we should like to do business with you, but we must stress that it is the furthest we can go to help you.

我们给予该折扣是因为我们愿意与你方做生意,但是要强调一点,这是我们能作出的最大让步。

6. quote 报价

This is the lowest price we can quote.

这是我们可以报出的最低价格。

We shall be pleased if you will quote on a CIF basis.

惠请贵司报 CIF 价格。

Please quote us your best price.

请报给我方你们的最优惠价格。

Will you please quote for the following items?

请报出下列商品的价格。

7. order 订单

Upon checking, we found your samples satisfactory and are very pleased to place an order with you by the quality of the samples you sent us.

经检查,我们认为你方所寄的样品令人满意,现按所寄样品的质量向你方下订单。

Through your full cooperation, we have been able to confirm our order with you as follows:

经你方通力合作,我方终于能够向你方确认订货如下:

8. Should prices be found reasonable and suitable for our market, we shall be pleased to place regular orders with you.

如果价格公道、适合我们的市场需求,我司愿长期向你方订购。

该句是"if"引导的条件句,省略了"if",所以主谓倒装。

Should this trial order prove satisfactory to our customer, we can assure you that repeat orders will be placed.

如果这次试订货我方客户感到满意,我们可以保证将重复订货。

Should you not agree to our proposal, we would like to settle by arbitration.

如果你们不接受我们的建议,我们愿仲裁解决。

9. reasonable (*a*.)(价格)合理的、公道的,意思相近的词有:attractive, workable, realistic, moderate

You certainly will note that the prices we quote are very attractive which are made possible by our mass production and cost control.

贵司应能注意到我们所报的价格非常合理,这是我们大量生产和成本控制的结果。

We feel sure you will quote us realistic prices to help us initiate our business.

我们深信贵司会向我们报出公道的价格以协助我们启动业务。

10. We hope that will meet your prompt attention. 盼早复。通常我们以"盼早复"、"盼佳音"等来结束此类信件。

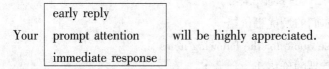 will be highly appreciated.

We should be grateful if you would reply at an early date.

敬请早日答复,不胜感激。

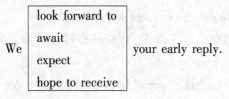 your early reply.

盼早复。

Comments

Paragraph1: say how you obtained the company's address, introduce yourself and state the enquiry clearly

Paragraph 2: state additional requests

Paragraph 3: encourage the potential supplier to quote competitive prices

Paragraph 4: ask for a quick response

The enquiry is brief and to the point, telling the reader exactly what the enquiry is about. It makes it clear that the prospective purchaser wishes to buy top quality products at very competitive prices.

2.2.2 a Manufacturer Write to an Importer

Dear Sirs

We owe your name and address to the Chamber of Commerce, London, who informed us that you are in the market for garden tools.

We are one of the largest garden tools manufacturers in our country and have been handling various kinds of garden tools for about 20 years. We approach you today in the hope of establishing business relations with you and expect, by our joint efforts, to enlarge our business scope.

In order to acquaint you with our business lines, we enclose a copy of our illustrated catalogue covering the main items suppliable at present. If you are interested in any of the items, please tell us by fax. We will give you our lowest quotations and try our best to comply with your requirements.

Our customers are always satisfied with our products and the service after the sale. We believe that you will be, too, after we do business together.

Our banker is the Bank of Westminster, London. They can provide you with information about our business and finances.

We are looking forward to your early reply.

Yours faithfully

Notes

1. chamber of commerce 商会

Your firm has been recommended to us by the Chamber of Commerce in Tokyo, Japan.

日本东京商会已把你行介绍给我们。

2. in the market for 欲购，求购

You are in the market for chemicals.

你公司要购买化工产品。

We have heard from China Council for the Promotion of International Trade that you are in the market for electric appliances.

从中国国际贸易促进会获悉，你们有意采购电器用具。

3. handle 经营，同义词 deal in

We are informed that this company handles Chinese textiles.

我们得知这家公司经营中国纺织品。

As you may be well aware, we are a state-operated corporation handling such items as fertilizer in both import and export business.

也许你们已有所知，我们是国营公司，经营化肥的进出口业务。

4. in the hope of 希望

We understand that you are interested in both the import and export of textiles and it is on this subject that we wish to introduce ourselves in the hope of establishing mutually beneficial business relations between our two corporations.

了解到你们对纺织品的进口和出口都感兴趣，故愿自荐，希望在我们两公司间建立互利的业务关系。

Through your trade delegation that recently paid a visit to this country, we learned that you are well-established importers of silk garments and are writing to you in the hope of receiving your orders from time to time.

通过贵国最近来访的贸易代表团，我们了解到你们是信誉良好的真丝服装进口商，现发信给你们，盼能不断地接到你们的订单。

5. establish business relations with... 与……建立业务关系

注意：relations 必用复数；business 可用 trade 替代。

to establish
```
direct(直接的)
pleasant(愉快的)
friendly(友好的)
good(良好的)
mutually beneficial(互利的)
close(密切的)
```
relations with...

类似的表达方式:

business association(业务联系,交往)

business connection(业务联系)

business contact(业务关系)

to establish(build up, enter into, set up)business relationship(建立业务关系)

to continue business relationship(继续业务关系)

to keep up business relationship(保持业务关系)

to improve business relationship(改善业务关系)

to promote business relationship(促进业务关系)

to speed up business relationship(加快业务关系的发展)

to enlarge (widen) business relationship(扩大业务关系)

to restore (resume) business relationship(恢复业务关系)

to interrupt business relationship(中断业务关系)

to cement business relationship(巩固业务关系)

6. by our joint efforts 通过我们的共同努力

It is hoped that by our joint efforts we can promote business as well as friendship.

希望通过我们共同努力,既可以促进我们之间的贸易又能增进友谊。

7. business scope 经营范围

类似表达方式:line of business, business line, frame of business

As the goods you ordered are out of our business scope, we are reluctantly compelled to decline your order for the time being.

由于你方所订购之物不属于我公司经营范围,所以我们不得不暂时拒绝你方订单。

Specializing in the export of Chinese Art & Craft Goods we express our desire to trade with you in this line.

我们专门经营中国美术工艺品出口,愿与你们进行交易。

We have been in this line of business for many years.

我们经营这项业务已有多年。

We are given to understand that you are potential buyers of Chinese soybean which comes within the frame of our business activities.

据了解,你们是中国大豆有潜力的买主,而该商品正属我们的业务经营范围。

8. acquaint

acquaint sb. with sth. 使某人熟悉(了解)某事(物),意思相同的短语有 inform sb of sth; tell sb sth.

Will you please send us your samples so as to acquaint us with the material and workmanship of your supplies?

请将你方样品寄给我们以便我公司熟悉你方供货的质地和工艺。

We are sending you by courier our product brochures to inform you of our product lines.

为使你方了解我们的产品线,现快递给你方我们的产品手册。

9. business lines 经营范围 (见注释7)

line 可以表示行当,货色的意思

We have been for many years in the textile line.

我们经营纺织品已有多年。

Their chief line is the import of cotton.

他们主要经营棉花进口。

This is a low priced line in woolen underwear.

这是一种低价的毛织内衣。

10. enclose 随函附寄,把……附在信中

We enclose a copy of our price list.

随函寄去我方价目表一份。

Enclosed please find our revised quotation.

随函附上我方修改后的报价。

Please refer to the price list enclosed in our letter dated June 2.

请查阅 6 月 2 日去信所附的价目表。

过去分词 enclosed 前面加定冠词可作名词：

We believe you will find the enclosed interesting. 我们相信你们对所附之件会感兴趣。

11. illustrated catalogue

catalogue (n.) 目录(本)，适用于一般商品，列名详细规格及商品号码等；有绘画、照片或图表者，称为 illustrated catalogue；单页的商品说明书称为 leaflet。

sample books 样品本把布匹、纸张等各种花样、图案的小块剪样(sample cuttings)装订成一本，注明商品号码，称为样品本，供客户选购之用。

12. covering 关于，有关的

Please see to it that the covering L/C should reach us one month before shipment.

请注意，有关信用证应在装船前一个月开到我方。

13. comply with 遵照，按照，与……一致、吻合，同义词有 conform with, agree with

We sincerely hope that both quality and quantity comply with the contract stipulations.

我们真诚希望质量、数量都与合同规定相吻合。

We found the goods didn't agree with the original patterns.

我们发现货物与原式样不符。

As your complaint does not conform with the results of our own test, we suggest that another thorough examination be conducted by you to show whether there is any ground for claim.

你们的意见与我们的测试结果不符，因此建议你方再进行一次彻底的检查，以证明你方是否有索赔的根据。

Comments

Paragraph 1: state the source from which you get the company's name and address

Paragraph 2: introduce yourself and state the hope of doing business

Paragraph 3: provide reference to the company and express willingness to provide more

Paragraph 4: assure the company of pleasant trade experience

Paragraph 5: provide the source where the company can learn about your financial status

Paragraph 6: state the wish for an early reply

The manufacturer writes this letter to the possible buyer to recommend sales of their products. Such letters are considered the most effective and least expensive means in winning buyers.

2.2.3 Reply to First Enquiry

Granford Leather Stores
23 Western Highway
New York
U.S.A.
Telephone: 456734
Fax: 459876

3 April 2003

The Elegant Leather Products Inc.
9 Green Street
Manchester
England

Dear sirs

We are very pleased to receive your enquiry of 22nd March and hear that you are interested in our products.

We are sending you our illustrated catalogue and price list under separate cover, together with samples of some of the skins we regularly use in the manufacture of our products. You may rest assured that the quality of materials used and the high standard of craftsmanship will appeal to the most selective buyer.

On regular purchases in quantities of not less than 100 dozen of individual items we would allow you a discount of 3%. Payment is to be made by irrevocable L/C at sight.

We also manufacture a wide range of leather gloves and wallets in which you may be interested. They are fully illustrated in our catalogue and are of the same high quality as our handbags.

We look forward to receiving an order from you.

Yours sincerely

Notes

1. We are very pleased to receive your enquiry of 22nd March. 很高兴收到你方3月22日发出的询盘函。

回复函开头常用的表达方式：

We are in receipt of your enquiry of 22nd March.

We thank you for your enquiry of 22nd March.

We acknowledge receipt of your enquiry of 22nd March.

In reply to your enquiry of 22nd March, we are...

2. to be interested in... 对(某种商品)有兴趣,常常用以表示有意购买某种商品。

We have customers who are interested in Chinese silk neckties.

我方现有客户有意购买中国生产的真丝领带。

类似的表达：

We are in the market for chemical fertilizer.

欲求购化肥。

We are sourcing in the market for men's shirts.

觅购男式衬衫。

We are potential buyers of color pens.

欲购彩笔。

3. illustrated (a.) 附有插图的

Accordingly, we introduce ourselves to you by sending you our illustrated catalogs and price lists.

为此,我们现在寄去附有插图的商品目录和价目单,用以向你公司毛遂自荐。

illustrate (*vt.*)(用事例或图表)解释和说明

This little girl tends to illustrate problems with pictures.

这个小姑娘常常用图画来说明问题。

4. under separate cover 另封邮寄

除了 under separate cover 还可以用 by separate mail, by separate post;或 by another mail, by another post

We are sending you under separate cover by airmail a copy of the latest catalogue.

现另封航邮寄去最新产品目录一份。

We are sending by separate post a statement of account, from which you will observe that there is a balance in our favor of USD 3 400. An early settlement would be appreciated.

我们现另封邮寄去账目明细表一份,你们从中可以看到你方尚欠我方 3400 美元未付。若早日结付,不胜感激。

5. rest assured 放心

You may rest assured that the dependable quality of the material will give you every satisfaction.

请放心,料子的质量可靠,一定会令你方满意。

You may rest assured that our quotation will prove to your satisfaction.

请放心,所报价格包您满意。

6. appeal to 对……有吸引力,引起兴趣,投其所好

We are confident that its design and color will appeal to your market.

我们相信其花样和色彩会受到你方市场欢迎。

We think the superb workmanship as well as the novel design will appeal to your customers.

我们认为其高超的工艺及新颖的设计会对你方客户具有吸引力。

7. irrevocable L/C at sight 不可撤消即期信用证

Comments

Paragraph 1: make the reference clear and respond

Paragraph 2: state what actions you are taking

Paragraph 3: state the proposed method of payment and quantity discount allowed

Paragraph 4: broaden the customer's interest, hoping to sell additional products

This is a concise, yet full, response to the enquiry. It demonstrates the efficiency and dynamism of the company's approach.

2.3 Reading Comprehension

2.3.1 First Enquiry

Dear sirs

We have seen your advertisement in the July issue of "International trade". We would like you to send us details of your various ranges, including sizes, colors and prices, and also samples of the different qualities of material used.

We are large dealers in textiles and believe there is a promising market in our area for moderately priced goods of the kind mentioned.

When replying, please state your terms of payment and discount you would allow on purchases of quantities of not less than 100 dozen of individual items.

Yours faithfully

● **Activities for comprehension**

1. What is a first enquiry?
2. In your first enquiry, what information about yourself should you provide?
3. How to attract a potential supplier's attention to your enquiry?
4. How to conclude your first enquiry?

2.3.2　Reply to First Enquiry

Dear sirs

　　We are very pleased to receive your enquiry of 15th June and enclose our illustrated catalogue and price list giving the details you ask for. Also by separate post we are sending you some samples and feel confident that when you have examined them you will agree that the goods are both excellent in quality and reasonable in price.

　　On regular purchases in quantities of not less than 100 dozen of individual items we would allow you a discount of 2%. Payment is to be made by irrevocable L/C at sight.

　　Because of their softness and durability, our all cotton bed-sheets and pillowcases are rapidly becoming popular and after studying our prices you will not be surprised to learn that we are finding it difficult to meet the demand. But if you place your order not later than the end of this month, we would ensure prompt shipment.

　　We invite your attention to our other products such as table-cloth and table napkins, details of which you will find in the catalogue, and look forward to receiving your first order.

Yours faithfully

● **Activities for comprehension**

　　1. In response to first enquiry, what information should you provide first?

　　2. In addition to meet the requests made in the enquiry, what else effects could the reply letter achieve?

2.4　Summary

　　Generally speaking, communication in writing is the most commonly used approach in establishing business relations. This type of letter should include the sources of information related to the addressee, e.g. how you know his name and address; your intention, i.e. why you are writing to him; a brief introduction of your firm, e.g. your business scope; references as to your firm's financial standing, etc. if you are in the market for the goods the addressee can export, you may also request for samples, price list, catalogues, etc. Response to the letter of such nature should be prompt and courteous so as to create goodwill and leave a good impression on the reader.

在建立业务关系过程中,信函沟通通常是最普遍使用的手段。这类信函的内容应该包括,信息渠道,即如何获知收信人的公司名称和地址的;写信的意图,也就是为什么给收信人写这封信;对自己的公司进行简单介绍,如公司的经营范围;以及提供自己公司的资信状况的证明人,等等。如果你现在欲购收信人公司可出口的货物,你也可以在信中索要样品、价目表和商品目录等。对这类建交函必须及时、礼貌地回复以便能够建立良好的关系并给收信人留下美好的印象。

2.5 Useful Expressions

1. We have seen your advertisement in the Textile Journal and should be glad if you would send us by return patterns and prices of good and medium quality cotton tablecloths available from stock.

我们在《纺织》杂志上看到了贵公司的广告,如果你们能够回复我方,寄给我们可以现货供应的中上品质纯棉桌布的样品和价格,我们将不胜感激。

2. Through the courtesy of Mr. Smith of Brent Company, we are given to understand that you are the leading manufacturers of fax machines in Europe. The demand for fax machines in our area is brisk. We shall appreciate your sending us particulars about your products.

经 Brent 公司的史密斯先生介绍,我们了解到贵公司是欧洲地区传真机的主要制造商。我地对传真机的需求旺盛。如果你能将贵司产品的详细情况说明寄给我们,我们将不胜感激。

3. We learn from Granford Corporation that you are exporting PU artificial leather Ladies' slippers. There is a steady demand here for the above-mentioned commodity of high quality at moderate prices. We should be grateful if you would send us a copy of your catalogue and price list.

我们从 Granford 公司那儿得知贵公司正欲出口 PU 人造皮革的女拖鞋。

对于物美价廉的上述商品我们这儿有稳定的需求。如果你们能寄一份产品目录和价目表,我们将十分感激。

4. As we are in the market for waterproof coats, we should be pleased if you would send us your catalogues and best quotations.

我们现需求防雨服,如果你们能寄来你们的产品目录和最优惠的报价,我们将十分感激。

5. We have a considerable demand in our market for portable sewing machines and should welcome your catalogues and price lists.

我地市场现大量需求便携式缝纫机,非常希望你们能寄来你们的产品目录和价目表。

6. We request you to furnish us with a full range of samples, in assorted patterns together with your lowest quotations.

请你方为我们提供花色搭配的全套样品以及最优惠的报价。

7. If you can assure us of workable prices, excellent quality and prompt delivery, we shall be able to deal in these goods on a substantial scale.

如果你方能够保证价格合理、品质优良、即刻交货,我们愿意大规模经销这种商品。

8. We take the liberty of writing to you with a view to establishing business relations with you.

冒昧地给你方写信以图与你们建立业务关系。

9. We write to introduce ourselves as one of the leading exporters of first class cotton goods in China and are enjoying an excellent reputation through 30 years' business experience.

现具函自我介绍,本公司是中国一家优质棉织品的主要出口商之一,30年的实践使我们在业内享有极高的声誉。

10. Our products enjoy a great popularity at home and abroad due to their high quality and reasonable prices.

我们的产品品质优良、价格合理,深受国内外用户欢迎。

11. We trust that many of the items in our catalogue will be of interest to you. We would be pleased to serve you if you like them.

我们相信目录中的许多商品会让你们感兴趣。若喜欢,我们愿竭诚为您服务。

12. If any of our products are of interest to you, please send us your inquiry sheet.

若对任何产品感兴趣,请寄询价单。

2.6　Reading Materials

2.6.1

Dear sirs

On the recommendation of China Chamber of Commerce and Industry, we have learned that you are manufacturers of handmade embroidery tablecloth. Now we are particularly interested in importing various range of handmade embroidery tablecloth.

If the quality of the goods comes up to our expectation and the delivery date is acceptable, we can probably let you have regular orders. With this in mind, we think it would also be helpful if you can furnish us with some illustrated catalogues together with your lowest quotation.

As to our credit standing, please refer to the Bank of Communication, Shanghai Branch. Your immediate attention is appreciated.

Yours sincerely

2.6.2

Dear Sir or Madam

Thanks to Ms. Mary Chen, one of our business friends, we have come to know your name and address. She recommends you as one of the leading exporters of garments in China.

We are interested in buying 100% cotton ladies' blouses. We would like you to send us details of your blouses, including colors and prices, and also samples of the different colors.

We have a very good connection with leading chain stores in Japan. If your price and quality are attractive, you may expect a large order from us.

Our banker is the Tokyo Bank, Ltd., Osaka, from whom you can have any reference regarding our financial standing.

We are looking forward to hearing from you very soon.

Yours faithfully

2.6.3

Dear Sir or Madam

We were impressed by the selection of sweaters that were displayed on your stand at the Men's Wear Exhibition that was held in Chicago last month.

We are a large chain of retailers and looking for a manufacturer who could supply us with a wide range of sweaters for the teenage market. As we usually place very large orders, we would expect a quantity discount in addition to a 20% trade discount off net list prices, and our terms of payment are normally 30 days bill of exchange, documents against payment.

If these conditions interest you, and you can meet orders of over 1 000 garments at one time, please send us your current catalogue and price-list.

We hope to hear from you soon.

Yours faithfully

2.6.4

Dear sir

We have received your letter of 9th April showing your interest in our complete product information.

Our product lines mainly include high quality textile products. To give you a general idea of the various kinds of textiles now available for export, we have enclosed a catalogue and a price list. You may also visit our online company introduction at Http://xxxxxxx.alibaba.com which includes our latest product line.

We look forward to your specific enquiries and hope to have the opportunity to work together with you in the future.

Yours faithfully

Exercises

I. Fill in the blanks with your choices.

1. Your name _____ us by the Chamber of Commerce in New york.
   a) has been recommended   b) has recommended to
   c) has been recommending   d) has been recommended to

2. Our market survey informs us that you are _____ Audio and Electronic Equipment.
   a) in the market for   b) for the market of
   c) on the market about   d) inside the market to

3. We would be pleased to receive your _____ catalogue and price list
   a) illustrated   b) illustrating   c) illustrate   d) illustrates

4. We are _____ exporters of all kinds of Chinese goods.
   a) better-established   b) well-established
   c) good-establishing   d) best-establishment

5. If your prices are competitive, we are confident _____ the goods in great quantities in this market.
   a) to sell   b) to be selling   c) in being sold   d) in selling

6. We shall appreciate _____ us FOB Sydney.
   a) you quoting   b) your quoting
   c) you to quote   d) your being quoted

7. As we are one of the leading importers in this line, we are _____ to handle large quantities.
   a) at a position   b) in a position   c) on a position   d) of a position

8. We shall be much _____ of your effort in pushing the sales of our products on your market.
   a) appreciate   b) appreciative   c) appreciation   d) appreciated

9. We are seeking with keen interest to _____ direct business activities with you.
   a) establish   b) enter   c) enter into   d) build up

10. For our business and financial standing, we may _____ you to our bankers.

a) inform　　　b) refer　　　c) tell　　　d) lead

11. We wish to introduce ourselves _____ a state-run corporation dealing _____ textiles.

a) as, with　　b) for, in　　c) as, in　　d) with, with

12. As the item the _____ scope of our business activities, we shall be pleased to establish direct trade relations with you.

a) lies within　　b) fall within　　c) come under　　d) be within

13. We owe your name and address _____ Italian Commercial Bank who has informed us that you are in the market _____ table-cloths.

a) from, for　　b) to, with　　c) from, with　　d) to, for

14. In order to obtain the needed information, the inquirer should simply, clearly and concisely write _____ he wants to know.

a) that　　　b) so　　　c) what　　　d) because of

15. Your letter of May 9th addressed to our Wuhan Branch Office has _____ to us for attention and reply.

a) been passed on　　　　　　b) passed

c) passed on　　　　　　　　d) been past through

16. We are willing to enter into business relations with you _____ on the of equality and mutual benefit.

a) base　　　b) basis　　　c) bases　　　d) based

17. The Guangzhou Export Commodities Fair, sometimes known as the Canton Fair, has _____ to offer that you can find almost everything.

a) so many　　b) more　　c) so much　　d) most

II. Identify errors in the following sentences.

1. We have established here for over twenty years as general exporters.

2. We look forward to receive your favorable reply at an early date.

3. We would be most grateful whether you could provide us with a list of reliable business connections in your area.

4. Some copies of our latest catalogues are being airmailed to you on a separate cover.

5. We will send you a complete range of samples upon the receipt of your reply.

6. We are enclosed a catalogue which may be of some help to you in selecting items.

7. In compliance with your request, we send you our brochures together with the late price list.

8. We take the liberty of write to you with a view to establish business relations with you.

III. Fill in the blanks with proper prepositions.

Dear sir

We understand from your information posted on Alibaba. com that you are _____ the market for textiles. We would like to take this opportunity to introduce our company and products, _____ the hope that we may work with Bright Ideas Imports in the future.

We are a joint venture specializing _____ the manufacture and export of textiles. We have enclosed our catalog, which introduces our company _____ detail and covers the main products we supply _____ present. You may also visit our online company introduction at http://www. pili. com which includes our latest product line.

Should any of these items be _____ interest to you, please let us know. We will be happy to give you a quotation _____ receipt of your detailed requirements.

We look forward _____ receiving your enquires soon.

Yours faithfully

● **Skills Practice**

北京雅馨益智玩具有限公司海外销售部经理王英女士通过阿里巴巴网站获悉澳大利亚 Bell 公司有意购买各类电控玩具(telecontrol toy),希望与该公司建立业务联系并发去产品目录。

请以海外销售部经理王英女士的身份,向 Bell 公司发出一封建交函。

Unit 3　Inquiries and Replies

Learning Objectives

After learning this unit, you should:

✍ Know what and how to inquire about the goods an importer intends to buy(作为进口商知道对于自己有意购买的商品如何进行询盘)

✍ Know the essential components of an inquiry letter(了解询盘函的基本组成部分)

✍ Master typical sentences and expressions in writing such letters(掌握写作询盘函的典型句型和短语)

✍ Know how to make a reply to a general inquiry(了解回复一般性询盘函的方法)

3.1　Introduction

An inquiry is a request for information. In foreign trade, enquiries are usually made by the buyers without engagement to get information about the goods to be ordered, such as price, catalogue, the quantity which the seller can provide, the payment terms, delivery date and other terms. The inquiries are among the most frequent letters people write in their business transactions. One may write an inquiry after coming back from a trade fair or seeing or hearing an advertisement from the mass media or being told of a product by a friend. Some companies may start their business by writing inquiries and others may promote business relations between old business partners by writing inquiries.

询盘函是索要信息的请求函。对外贸易活动中,通常是买方发出询盘,询问欲订购的产品的详细情况,如价格、商品目录、可供数量、付款条件、交货期及其他交易条件,但发出询盘的买方没有订约的义务。询盘函是商务活动中最常撰写的一种信函。当我们参加完贸易博览会后可能需要写询盘函,或者当我们在媒体上听到或看到广告后可能需要写询盘函,甚至朋友向我们推荐了一种产品后我们也要写询盘函。有的公司可能通过发出询盘函启动业务,而有的公司通过发出询盘函推动与以往业务伙伴的业务关系的发展。

An importer may send a specific inquiry, inviting a quotation or an offer for the goods he wishes to buy, or just a general inquiry, asking for some general information about the goods, such as catalogue, brochure or price list.

进口商可能发出具体的询盘,要求卖方对其欲订购的产品做出报价或报盘,也可能发出的是一般询盘,只是要求有关产品的一般信息,如手册、目录或价目表。

Normally a letter of enquiry can be divided into three parts. The first part announces the topic or subject of the enquiry. The second part specifies details of the enquiry. Depending on the nature of the enquiry, this could take one or more paragraphs. Enquiries should be specific to enable the supplier to answer the questions completely. Finally, in the third part you should not forget to remind the supplier of making an early reply to your enquiry letter.

通常,询盘函内容分为三个部分。第一部分说明要了解的是什么产品的信息。第二部分说明具体索要哪些信息。根据询盘的性质,这部分内容可能是一段文字,也可能是很多段文字。询盘函内容要具体,卖方才能完整地回答你的问题。最后,提醒卖方及时回复你的询盘。

An effective inquiry letter must be reasonable, specific, brief and polite.

When you are making an inquiry, you need to justify it and make the reader feel obliged to provide what you want. To make a decision about a purchase, it is reasonable to ask for the catalogue or brochure of the product. If the samples of a product are advertised as "free of charge", it is justifiable to ask for one. Request for detailed information such as price and quality is also justified. But request for such confidential information as profit or market occupancy will not be honored.

有效的询盘函必须合理、具体、简洁、礼貌。

当你询盘时,一定要说明合理的原因,从而使收信人觉得必须满足你的要求。为了做出购买决定,索要产品目录或手册是完全合理的。如果在广告中提到"样品免费",也可以索要样品。索要具体信息,如价格、品质等,都是合理的请求。但是询问像利润、市场份额等可能对方就不会答复了。

Secondly, an inquiry letter should be as specific as possible. An unclear inquiry might be misunderstood or confusing and is naturally not likely to get expected response. For example, in an inquiry, if the buyer makes such a request "would you please send us some information about your Golden Ring rechargeable battery?" The seller will find it difficult to respond to such a vague inquiry.

其次,询盘函应尽可能具体。内容含糊的询盘函可能引起误解或令对方困惑,当然也就不可能得到你想要的答复。例如,在询盘函中,买方提出这样的请求"请为我方提供有关金环牌充电电池的信息",这时,对这样模糊的请求卖方很难答复。

An inquiry letter in business must be brief and concise. Any unnecessary and unrelated material will make the inquiry less effective.

商务中的询盘函务必简洁。任何不必要和无关的内容都会降低效率。

Finally, an inquiry letter should be polite. Although as a potential buyer you may bring benefits to the receiver, your writing must be courteous. This would make your request more pleasant and quickly honored. Such polite words such as "thank you", " please", "kindly", "grateful", and "appreciative" help produce desired effect.

最后,询盘函应该讲究礼貌。尽管作为潜在的买主,你可能会给收信人带来利益,但信中还是要表现出礼貌。这样,你的请求会让对方更容易接受,会更快地答复你。类似"谢谢您"、"请"、"惠请"、"感激"和"感谢"这样的礼貌用语能够产生良好的效果。

Replies to enquiries which mean potential business should be prompt and courteous and cover all the information asked for. A lot of general inquiries come for catalogues and price lists every day due to advertisement and promotion. It is all right to make a reply by sending the prepared material and a printed "with compliment" slip. However, when an inquiry suggests possible large or regular orders, you should make use of the opportunity to publicize your products. When a customer asks for goods that are not available, or special requests impossible to meet, you need answer it with care and avoid making direct refusal which may offend the customer.

询盘函意味着可能的贸易往来,所以回复函应该迅速、礼貌、内容全面。

因为广告和促销活动,出口商每天都会收到许多索要目录和价目表的一般询盘函。对此可用事先准备好的资料和印制好的"致意"函回复。但如果询盘函暗示可能大量或长期订购,应利用这个机会推销自己的商品。如果客户询问目前不能供应的产品,或是提出一些不能满足的特殊要求,回复时要谨慎,不要直接拒绝以免得罪客户。

3.2 Model Letter Comments

3.2.1 General Inquiry

Granford Fashion Stores
23 Western Highway
New York, U.S.A.
May 20, 2007

SWEET Garment Import and Export Company
2 Dalian West Rd, Shanghai
P. R. China

Dear Sir

  We visited your stand at the Paris Fashion Exhibition last month, and we were very interested in your display of ladies' silk garments. We are thinking about adding a silk garment line to our business, which we find after market investigation will be very popular in our city.

  We should be grateful if you would send us your catalogue of your complete range of this type of garments and also your export price list. We should find it most helpful if you could also supply some samples.

  We shall appreciate it very much if you will reply at your earliest convenience.

Yours faithfully

Comments

Paragraph 1: refer to the subject of the inquiry and inform the seller of a promising market

Paragraph 2: request for some information

Paragraph 3: thanks in advance for early reply

This is a general inquiry made after a visit to an exhibition to get more information about the products of market potential.

Notes

1. be interested in... 对……感兴趣

If you happen to be interested in some of the patterns, we suggest that you place a trial order to see whether they will fit your requirement.

如果你碰巧对其中某些样式有兴趣，你可以试订一些看看它们是否符合你的要求。

We are particularly interested in this type of product, and would like to have more detailed information on the above item.

我们对这一类型的产品特别感兴趣，希望了解更详细的信息。

2. stand 展位

The Chinese stand at Hanover Fair attracted so many visitors.

汉诺威博览会上的中国展位吸引了很多参观者。

We would like you to visit our stand No. 34 at London Toy Fair which starts on June 3rd.

诚邀贵公司参观本公司6月3日开始的设在伦敦玩具商品交易会的34号展位。

3. display (v. n.) 展示、陈列

Department stores display their goods in the windows.

百货商店在橱窗里陈列商品。

This delay has caused us great inconvenience, for the toys are, of course, required for sale during the Christmas Season, and our shop display is being held up by this delay.

这次到货延迟给我们带来很大麻烦，因为这些玩具是要在圣诞节销售旺

季销售的,但到货延迟使我们现在不能进行店内展示。

New styles are on display now and we need the clients' feedback.
新款式正在展出,我们需要客户的反馈意见。

4. market investigation 市场调查,同义的短语 market survey

Our market investigation informs us that there is great market potential for this product.
通过市场调查我们了解到这一产品的市场潜力巨大。

Without market survey, we could not make a competitive offer.
不经过市场调查,我们不可能做出有竞争力的报盘。

We wish to leave the question of your commission for future discussion. First of all, we wish to hear from you about the results of your market survey for our merchandise itself.
我们稍后谈论贵公司代理的问题。首先,我们想知道贵公司为我们的商品所做的市场调查结果如何。

5. We should be grateful if you would send us... 惠请寄来……

也可以用这样的表达方式:We shall be very grateful if you provide us with...

We shall be very grateful if you provide us with an illustrated catalog, together with a price list, showing your best terms and lowest quotations.
惠请寄来有图片的产品目录、价目表,并给出你方最优惠的条件和价格。

询盘时请求卖方提供一些资料信息,还可以用下面这些表达方式:

We would like to receive (the latest catalog covering your products).

Please let us have your (latest catalogue of...).

We should be glad to receive (a copy of each of your latest catalog).

We shall appreciate receiving (your sending us)...

We should be obliged if you would send us...

Please send us (the latest catalog of your manufactures).

Will You please send us samples of...?

Kindly send us your...

At present we are particularly interested in receiving your...

6. at your earliest convenience 在方便的时候尽快

Please send us your pro forma invoice at your earliest convenience.
方便时尽快将你方的形式发票寄过来。

We shall appreciate it if you reply at your earliest convenience.
早日答复不胜感激。

Can you make an offer, C & F London, at your earliest convenience?
你方能尽快报一个伦敦港成本加运费价格吗?

3.2.2　Reply to General Inquiry

SWEET Garment Import and Export Company
2 Dalian West Rd, Shanghai
P. R. China
Tel: 86 021 84536754
June 10, 2007

Granford Fashion Stores
23 Western Highway
New York, U.S.A.

Dear sir

　　We thank you very much for your enquiry of June 2 and are happy to learn that you are interested in our garments.

　　The enclosed price list and illustrated catalog will give you details of the products you may be interested in. If there is any other information you may need, please let us know.

　　We are also sending you separately, by airmail, some samples of our best selling garments. We trust that your close examination of the samples will show that the quality of our goods is superb and our prices are competitive.

　　All orders entrusted to us are given our careful and prompt attention. We sincerely desire to have the pleasure of receiving an order from you.

Yours faithfully

Comments

Paragraph 1: refer to the inquiry

Paragraph 2: tell the customer you are sending the information he requests

Paragraph 3: tell the customer the samples are on their way to him

Paragraph 4: express the hope for order

This reply to the general inquiry explains what the exporter has done to help the prospective customer to learn about the products of interest to him and express sincere wish to serve him.

Notes

1. Be happy to learn that you are interested in....
很高兴得知你们对……感兴趣
类似的表达方式:

We are happy (pleased, glad) to hear from you that you are particularly interested in...

We are glad to have been informed of your interest in...

We take pleasure in learning that you have a special interest in...

2. The enclosed price list and illustrated catalog will give you details of the products you may be interested in. If there is any other information you may need, please let us know. 随函寄去价目表和有图片的产品目录会为你提供你们感兴趣的产品的详细信息。如果需要其他信息,请告知。

类似的表达方式:

You will find the enclosed price list and illustrated catalog informative about details of the products in which you may be interested. We will be glad to supply you with any other information you may require.

3. best selling 最畅销的, best-seller 最畅销的商品

Our cell phones, superior in quality and moderate in price, are sure to be the best selling products in your market.

我们的手机质优价廉一定会成为你地市场最畅销的产品。

His new novel is one of the season's best-sellers.

他的新小说是本季畅销书之一。

It has proved a best-seller and it would be impossible for your customers to obtain better value anywhere.

这个产品被证明是最畅销的商品,你们的顾客不可能在别处买到比这更货真价实的。

4. close examination 仔细检查,认真检查

We, therefore, enclose the cuttings for your close examination which we trust will convince you of the quality of our products.

所以,我们附寄上剪样以便你方认真查验,我们相信这样你方就一定会相信我们产品品质了。

Upon receipt of your shipping documents, we made a close examination and found some discrepancies.

一收到你方的运输单据,我们就立即进行了认真核查,发现了一些不符点。

5. entrust 委托,托付

entrust something to somebody

entrust somebody with something

We entrust this large order to your careful attention.

我们将此大订单交给你们,请慎重办理。

We entrust you with the sole agency for our products in New York.

我们委托你方在纽约独家代理我公司的产品。

3.2.3 Specific Inquiry

Granford Fashion Stores
23 Western Highway
New York
USA
Tel: 456734
Fax: 459876
June 2, 2007

SWEET Garment Import and Export Company

2 Dalian West Rd, Shanghai
P. R. China

Dear Sir

Thank you for your e-mail of March 8, 2007, in which you express your wish to establish business relations with us in the line of garment.

After careful study of your catalogue and visits to your websites, we find your styles No. SL11, SS13 and WL21 of special interests to us. Please quote us for the supply of these items, giving your lowest possible CIF New York prices, stating your earliest shipment, terms of payment and discount for regular purchases. Please also indicate any NEW items not yet mentioned on your web pages.

If the quality is satisfactory and prices are reasonable, you may expect a large order from us.

Look forward to your early and favorable reply.

              Truly yours

Comments

 Paragraph 1: identify the reference and state the details of the e-mail
 Paragraph 2: state the items of interest and ask for offer
 Paragraph 3: urge the seller to make a competitive offer
 Paragraph 4: express hope for reply

This is a specific inquiry to get more detailed information on the styles of interest to the writer. The writer may just in the stage of gathering market information.

Notes

1. of special interest to sb 令某人特别感兴趣

Since we do not know what particular items are of special interest to you, we are unable to submit quotations along with our brochures.

因为我们不知道贵公司对何种品种感兴趣,故未能与此手册一并呈送报价单。

We have circled the items of special interest to us in the catalogue.

我们在产品目录上将我们感兴趣的品目圈上了。

2. lowest possible CIF New York price 可能的最低 CIF 纽约价

或可表达为 rock-bottom CIF New York price, keenest CIF New York price, best CIF New York price

We have quoted our lowest possible price and there is no room for any reduction.

我们已经报出了最低价格,没有让价空间了。

On the enclosed price list you will note our rock-bottom quotations CIF Rotterdam.

在我方附寄的价目表上你会看到我们报出了最低的 CIF 鹿特丹价。

As requested, we are enclosing herewith three copies of our Pro forma Invoice No. 870, on which you will find our keenest CIF Hongkong price.

现根据贵方请求随函寄去 870 号形式发票一式三份,已报最低的 CIF 香港价。

We have offered you the very best CIF New York price with the soonest possible delivery. Should you miss this nice chance, we are afraid you might not be able to get the same quality at this level.

我们已经报出了最低的 CIF 纽约价和最早的交货期。如果你们错过这个好机会,恐怕你们不能再以这样的价格买到同样品质的货物了。

3. 提出具体询盘请求的表达方式:

Please send us a copy of your illustrated catalog, informing us of your best terms and lowest prices on CIF New York basis.

At present, we are interested in receiving your samples and quotations in US currency on CFR Liverpool basis of the following goods:

Now we should like to receive your samples of the following goods and their prices quoted in US dollars CFR Seattle.

We appreciate your quoting the lowest possible CIF Pusan prices, delivery time and mode of payment.

We should like to receive for these products your best possible prices in US $ CFR quotation.

Please send us, by return air mail, your samples of these types of gloves with your best prices delivered FAS Huangpu.

4. regular 经常的,定期的

If your prices are competitive and your goods suit our trade, we shall be able to give you regular orders.

如果你们的价格有竞争力,产品符合我们的贸易要求,我们将长期订购。

We give 5% discount to those customers who make regular purchases in our store.

经常在我店购物的顾客可以享受5%的折扣。

5. If the quality is satisfactory and prices are reasonable, you may expect a large order from us.

如果品质令人满意、价格公道,我们会大量订购。

类似的表达方式:

If your prices and quality meet with our approval (are satisfactory) we shall be able to give you a large order.

If you give us a really competitive quotation, we may place a substantial order.

If you can supply us with goods of superior quality at reasonable prices, considerable business will result.

We shall take quantities if your goods prove best sellers and your prices admit of a reasonable margin of profit.

3.3　Specimen Letters

3.3.1　Specific Inquiry

Dear Sirs

We have attempted to get in contact with you by fax, but till now we were still unable to reach you.

I know that it's been some time since we contacted you, but this is due to the fact that we've still got plentiful stock. Please kindly quote a price for 1 000 and 2 500 units galvanized fruit and vegetable box crowbar openers as you have shipped to us before. Also, if you are in a position to quote a price on Coconut

Milk packed 24 by 150 oz units, FDA approved, we would be interested in hearing your best offer.

Truly yours

3.3.2 General Inquiry

Dear sirs

We have recently received many inquiries about your sweaters from retailers in Northeast area and are sure that demands would be very brisk on our side.

We would be obliged if you would send us details of your woolen sweaters including sizes and colours, and also samples of the different qualities of materials used.

When quoting, please state terms of payment. Should your prices be competitive, we will place large orders with you.

We look forward to hearing from you by return.

Yours truly

● **Activities for comprehension**

1. Can you tell the difference between the general enquiry and the specific enquiry?

2. Can you give some other phrases expressing the meaning that demand is great?

3.3.3 Reply to General Inquiry

Dear sir

Your letter of inquiry regarding our product line has been brought to my attention and I would like to thank you for your interest in our earthmoving equipment.

I have enclosed a price list and data sheets which describe our full line of products that serve the construction industry. This should help to familiarize you with our family of products and the high quality of our equipment.

If you have any further questions about our earthmoving equipment, please call us at our toll-free number, (800) 820-0000.

Thank you again for your interest.

Yours faithfully

3.3.4 Reply to General Inquiry

Dear sir

Thank you for your recent inquiry about our carpets.

We are enclosing our catalog and price list for your review and are confident that this literature will provide many of the answers you have requested.

If there is additional information you would like to have regarding our products, please do not hesitate to contact us.

We will be most happy to be of assistance.

Thank you for the very kind words you used to describe our line of products.

Yours faithfully

● **Activities for comprehension**

1. What are the main contents of a reply to a general inquiry?

3.3.5 Unable to Supply the Product Inquired about

Dear sir

Your letter inquiring about earthmoving equipment was brought to my attention.

While we manufacture a vast assortment of earthmoving equipment, none of our models fit the description which you provided.

We have never manufactured such model.

You may wish to direct an inquiry to the following distributor, whose firm has been in existence for many years and who may have the answer you are seeking:

Great Wall Co. Ltd

23 Western Highway, New York

I am sorry that I am unable to be of more assistance to you. Best of luck!

Yours faithfully

● Activities for comprehension

1. How to reply to an inquiry under the circumstances that you are unable to supply what they request?

3.4 Summary

Inquires for information about goods are sent and received in business all the time. A potential buyer may send an inquiry letter to the supplier asking for information on prices, quantities available and other relative details of a certain product. An enquiry letter must be replied earnestly and enthusiastically.

发送和接收关于商品信息的询问一直是商务活动的重要内容。潜在的买主可能向供应商发出询盘函，了解某种商品的价格、可供数量和其他有关详细信息。必须认真积极地对询盘函做出答复。

3.5 Useful Expressions

1. You are kindly requested to update us on the prices and availability for the following products.

请将下列商品的最新价格和供货情况告诉我们。

2. Prices quoted should include insurance and freight to Vancouver.

所报价格需包括到温哥华的保险费和运费。

3. I would like to have your lowest quotations CIF Vancouver.

希望您报成本加运费、保险费到温哥华的最低价格。

4. Will you please send us your catalogue together with a detailed offer?

请寄样品目录和详细报价。

5. We would appreciate your sending us the latest samples with their best prices.

请把贵公司的最新样品及最优惠的价格寄给我们,不胜感激。

6. Your ad in today's China Daily interests us and we will be glad to receive samples with your prices.

对你们刊登在今天《中国日报》上的广告,我们很感兴趣。如能寄来样品和价格,不胜感激。

7. Will you please inform us of the prices at which you can supply?

请告知我们贵方能供货的价格。

8. If your prices are reasonable, we may place a large order with you.

若贵方价格合理,我们可能向你们大量订货。

9. If your quality is good and the price is suitable for our market, we would consider signing a long-term contract with you.

若质量好且价格适合我方市场的话,我们愿意考虑与你方签署一项长期合同。

10. As there is a growing demand for this article, we have to ask you for a special discount.

鉴于我方市场对此货的需求日增,务请你们考虑给予特别折扣。

11. We would appreciate your letting us know what discount you can grant if we give you a long-term regular order.

若我方向你们长期订货,请告知能给予多少折扣,不甚感激。

12. Please quote your lowest price CIF Seattle for each of the following items, including our 5% commission.

请就下列每项货物向我方报成本加运费、保险费到西雅图的最低价格,其中包括我们百分之五的佣金。

13. Please keep us informed of the latest quotation for the following items.

请告知我方下列货物的最低价格。

14. Mr. Smith is making an inquiry for green tea.

史密斯先生正在对绿茶进行询价。

15. Now that we have already made an inquiry on your articles, will you please make an offer before the end of this month?

既然我们已经对你们的产品进行了询价,请在月底前报价。

3.6 Reading Materials

3.6.1

Dear Sir or Madam

  We know that you are exporters of textile fabrics. We would like you to send us details of your various ranges, including colors and prices, and also samples of the different qualities of material used.

  We are volume dealers in textiles and believe there is a promising market in our area for moderately priced goods of this kind mentioned.

  When quoting, please state your terms of payment and discount you would allow on purchases of quantities of not less than 1 000 meters of individual items. Prices quoted should include insurance and freight to San Francisco.

Yours faithfully

3.6.2

Dear sir

  Seeing your ad in "Good Housekeeper", we become interested in your silver wares of court styles. Please quote us for the supply of the items listed on the enclosed query form and give your prices CIF Shanghai.

  It would be appreciated if you include your earliest delivery date, terms of payment, and discounts for regular purchases.

Yours faithfully

3.6.3

Dear sir

  Some years ago we bought from you a consignment of handy paint brushes in 3 different qualities. Please let us know whether you are still manufacturing brushes in these qualities and quote your lowest price CIF Karachi.

We should require delivery within 4 weeks of placing the order.

Yours faithfully

3.6.4

Dear Mr. Jones

Thank you for your enquiry of 12 March cate 9 cable.

We appreciate your efforts in marketing our products and regret very much that we are unable to supply the desired goods due to excessive demand.

We would, however, like to take this opportunity to offer the following material as a close substitute:

Cate 5, US $50 per meter FOB Shanghai, including your commission 2%.

Please visit our catalog at http://www.NXP.com for more information on this item. If you find the product acceptable, please email us as soon as possible.

Yours sincerely

Exercises

I. Choose the right answer.

1. As the selling season is approaching, please ship the goods with the least _____ delay.

   a) possible   b) profitable   c) impossible   d) portable

2. _____ your terms and conditions be accepted by our clients, we will place a large order with you.

   a) Should   b) If   c) Unless   d) That

3. We hope to receive your quotation with details _____ the possible time of shipment.

   a) to include
   c) including
   b) to be included
   d) being included

4. We shall appreciate _____ us FOB Shanghai.

a) you quoting b) your quoting

c) you to quote d) your being quoted

5. We are confident that we could place regular orders with you _____ your prices are competitive.

a) providing b) provided c) provision d) provide

6. We are interested in your new digital clock radios and should be glad if you would send us by return prices of clock radios _____.

a) by stock b) out of stock

c) available from stock d) of stock

7. As we are one of the leading bicycle dealers in North China, we are in a position to _____ large quantities.

a) deal b) handle c) deal with d) handle in

8. When replying, please state the discounts _____ and the terms of payment.

a) allowable b) allowing c) to allow d) allow

9. Please quote us your lowest price for the _____, CIF New York, and the earliest shipment.

a) under-mentioned b) under

c) under goods d) mentioned

10. To enable us to apply for the import license, we should like you to airmail your pro forma invoice _____.

a) of two b) in duplicate c) two copies d) in two

11. We thank you for your letter of May 13 and the _____ catalogue.

a) sent b) enclosed c) given d) presented

12. While _____ an enquiry, you ought to enquire into quality specification and price etc.

a) making b) offering c) sending d) giving

II. Translate the following sentences into Chinese.

1. We are interested in your Haier air-conditioners and should be glad if you would send us your quotation sheet.

2. The articles we require should be durable in quality, bright and attractive

in colour.

3. So long as you can maintain moderate prices, your products should have a ready sale here.

4. If you can guarantee regular supplies, we may place considerable orders with you.

5. If your prices are competitive, we may place regular orders for large quantities.

6. Since competition of these fabrics is very keen here, it is necessary for you to quote us the most favorable prices.

7. Kindly let us know at what price you are able to deliver quantities of best refined sugar.

8. We should appreciate it very much if you would send us an illustrated catalog and a price list indicating your best terms and quotations.

9. We are considering buying 100 bicycles of German make, and shall be glad if you quote the best discount off your list price for this quantity.

10. If you prices are favorably competitive and your products are suitable enough to be well received here, we may place substantial orders.

III. Fill in the blanks with proper prepositions.

Dear sir

We thank you for your letter dated April 8 inquiring _____ our leather handbags. As requested, we take pleasure _____ offering you, subject _____ our final confirmation, 300 dozen deerskin handbags style No. MS190 _____ $124.00 per dozen CIF Hamburg. Shipment will be effected within 20 days after receipt of the relevant L/C issued by your first class bank _____ our favor upon signing Sales Contract.

We are manufacturing various kinds of leather purses and waist belts for exportation, and enclosed a brochure of products _____ your reference. We hope some of them meet your taste and needs.

If we can be _____ any further help, please feel free to let us know. Customers' inquiries always meet _____ our careful attention.

Yours faithfully

IV. Fill in each blank space in the letter below with a word that fits naturally.

Dear Sir or Madam

I am delighted to _____ you that we are _____ in the drainage system accessories _____ in China Daily.

Will you _____ send us a free copy _____ the brochure of the latest models of your products? Also, we would _____ to have a price list.

We are looking _____ to your prompt reply.

Yours sincerely

V. Rearrange the following statements taken from a letter in a correct order.

1. Ours is a leading travel service organization in Singapore.

2. Before making a decision, we'd like to know how much discount you can offer us.

3. Every year we bring over 3 000 tourists to Yunan and Guizhou Provinces in China.

4. I am pleased to tell you that we are considering establishing a long-term co-operation with your hotel.

5. We believe that we will be able to co-operate well.

● **Skills Practice**

澳大利亚 Bell 公司 Tony 先生收到北京雅馨益智玩具有限公司海外销售部经理王英女士的来函后，查阅了产品目录及网上资料，对该公司部分产品感兴趣，于是发出询盘函。

请以 Tony 先生的身份，写一封询盘函，询盘函中提出要求提供 CIF Adelaide 价格。

Unit 4   Quotations and Offers

Learning Objectives

After learning this unit, you should:

✍ Know the differences between quotation and offer(了解报盘和报价的区别)

✍ Know the essential components of an offer(了解报盘的主要内容)

✍ Master typical sentences and expressions in writing offers and quotations(掌握报盘和报价的典型句式和短语)

4.1   Introduction

Many export transactions, particularly initial export transactions, begin with the receipt of an inquiry from abroad that is followed by a request for a quotation or an offer. When making a reply to such inquiry, it is very important to know who your competitors are and their selling price and sales' strategy. Quite often, the price competitiveness overrides all other considerations in the initial contact with the buyer. How a product is priced is crucial in getting the buyer's attention, before the buyer becomes familiar with the quality of the product, delivery and service. Rarely is an exporter able to offer a product to all customers at the same price. When dealing with a large importer like chain store, quoting a high price may cause the buyer to lose interest, unless a business relationship already exists between exporter and buyer, or unless the exporter has a new product where there is no competition.

许多出口业务,特别是第一笔出口业务,往往都是因为收到国外的询盘函而开始的。在回复这样的询盘时,最重要的是要先了解你的竞争对手是谁,他们的售价和销售战略是什么。通常,在与买方初次接触时,价格竞争力的影响力可能超过其他所有因素。在买方了解产品品质、交货条件和服务水平之前,产品的定价是吸引买方的最重要的因素之一。卖方很少以统一的价格向所有客户销售产品。一般向大的进口商(如连锁商店)销售时,过高的定价会让他们失去对产品的兴趣,除非买卖双方之间有稳定的业务关系或者还没有能够和出口商的产品竞争的产品。

Sellers may send a quotation to buyers in response to their inquiries. A quotation, which includes all the necessary information requested in the inquiry, is an offer in simple form, but in no legal sense. That is, the seller is not bound to sell what has been previously quoted if he later decides not to do. No strict form is used in the quotation. Using the company letterhead for a general quotation is quite common. An efficient quotation letter includes the following parts:

1. thanks for the inquiry.
2. details about the terms and conditions of the business.
3. hope for the acceptance of the quotation by the buyer.

对于买方的询盘,卖方可以报价单回复。报价单中包括了询盘中所要求的所有信息,是一种内容简化了的报盘,但并不具有法律约束力。也就是说,虽然卖方已做出报价,但如果后来决定不卖,他有权利不卖。报价并没有严格的形式。将报价内容写在公司的信笺纸上是很常见的做法。好的报价信包括以下内容:

1. 感谢买方的询盘。
2. 详细说明交易条件。
3. 希望买方能够接受报价。

The preferred method for export quotation is a pro forma invoice, which is a quotation prepared in invoice format. Pro forma invoices are not used for payment purposes, but are models that the buyer uses when applying for an import license, opening a letter of credit or arranging for funds. In fact, it is a good practice to include a pro forma invoice with any international quotation, regardless of whether it has been requested or not. In addition to the items relevant to trade terms, a pro forma invoice should include two statements. One that certifies the pro forma invoice is true and correct and another that gives the country of origin of the goods. The invoice should also be clearly marked "pro forma invoice".

更好的出口报价方式是用形式发票,这是一种以发票的形式做出的报价。形式发票并不是用于结算的,而是买方可以用以申请进口许可证、开立信用证或安排资金融通的证明。实际上,不管买方要求与否,在对外贸易中采用形式发票报价是一种很好的做法。形式发票中除了要写明关于交易条件的内容外,还应该有两个内容。一个是证明形式发票的内容真实无误,另一个是写明货物的原产国。当然,上面还要写明"形式发票"字样。

An offer refers to a promise to supply goods on the terms and conditions stated. It is a contractual obligation, so once it has been accepted unconditionally within the term of validity, it cannot be withdrawn. An offer should meet with two major requirements. First, in an offer the seller includes complete, affirmative, specific terms of business. That is, it should describe the product, state a price for it, set the time of shipment, and specify the terms of the sale and terms of the payment. The description should include the following points:

Seller's and buyer's names and addresses.

Buyer's reference number and date of inquiry.

Listing of requested products and brief description.

Price of each item.

Appropriate gross and net shipping weight (in metric units where appropriate).

Appropriate total cubic volume and dimensions packed for export (in metric units where appropriate).

Trade discount (if applicable).

Delivery point.

Terms of sale.

Terms of payment.

Insurance and shipping costs.

Total charges to be paid by customer.

Estimated shipping date.

Second, the validity period is indispensable to an offer. The precise period during which the offer remains valid should be specified.

报盘是卖方做出的按照所说的条件出售商品的承诺。做出了报盘就要承担订立合约的义务,如果买方在有效期内无条件地接受了报盘,卖方就不能撤回报盘。报盘需要满足两个要求：

第一，报盘中各项交易条件必须完整、肯定、明确，即应该有对产品的描述，有价格条款、装船时间以及其他交易条件和支付方式规定。具体内容应该包括：买卖双方的名称、地址；买方的询盘时间和参考编号；询盘商品的简单说明；每种商品的价格；交付货物的毛重和净重(适当的情况下采用公制单位)；交付货物的总体积和尺码(适当的情况下采用公制单位)；贸易折扣(如果有的话)；交货地点；贸易术语；支付方式；保险和运输费用；买方需支付的总费用；以及预计的装船时间。

第二，报盘必须有有效期条款。应该在报盘中规定报盘的有效期。

4.2 Model Letters Comments

4.2.1 Firm Offer

Dear Sirs

Subject: Super White Crystal Sugar

We are in receipt of your e-mail dated July 7, 2007 asking us to offer 1 000 metric tons of the subject sugar for shipment to Japan and appreciate very much your interest in our product.

To comply with your request, we are offering you the following, valid until September 1:

1. Commodity: Qingdao Superior White Crystal Sugar.

2. Packing: To be packed in new gunny bag of 100kgs. Each.

3. Quantity: One thousand (1 000) metric tons.

4. Price: US dollars one hundred and five (US $105.00) per metric ton, FOB Qingdao.

5. Payment: 100% by irrevocable and confirmed letter of credit to be opened in our favor through Bank of China in Qingdao and to be drawn at sight.

6. Shipment: Three or four weeks after receipt of letter of credit by the first available boat sailing to Yokohama direct.

Please note that we do not have much ready stock on hand. Therefore, it is important that, in order to enable us to effect early shipment, your letter of credit should be opened in time if our price meets with your approval.

We are awaiting your reply.

                                                    Yours faithfully

Comments

Paragraph 1: identify the reference and the products

Paragraph 2: give details of the offer, with the time limit on the firm price

Paragraph 3: encourage the customer to make a quick decision

This offer contains all the necessary information in a concise form and is designed to get a quick response.

Notes

1. We are in receipt of your e-mail dated July 7, 2007 贵公司 7 月 7 日电子邮件,敬悉

在回复函的开头我们一般要说明此函是对对方哪封函电的回复,也就是表达"贵公司某月某日函电,敬悉"。可以选用下面这些表达方式:

We have pleasure in acknowledging receipt of your esteemed favour of May 3rd.

We are pleased to acknowledge receipt of your favour of June 7.

We have to acknowledge receipt of your favour of the 5th July.

Your letter of May 5 was very welcome.

Your letter of April 1 gave me much pleasure.

Your esteemed favour of 7th May was duly received by us.

Your favour of June 5th is duly to (at) hand.

We are in due receipt of your favour dated the 7th June.

We are in receipt of your letter of the 7th July.

We are in possession of your letter of 5th April.

We have duly received your favour of the 5th March.

Your esteemed communication of yesterday's date is just to (at) hand.

We thank you for your favour of 5th May.

We are obliged for your letter of the 5th May.

Many thanks for your latter of 5th June.

In acknowledging receipt of your letter of the 5th June,…

Your favour of the 5th May has just reached me.

Your favour of the 5th May is duly received.

2. subject sugar subject 在这里表示"标题行中所列的"，同义词有 captioned

You would be pleased to know that we have stocks on hand of the subject goods which can be shipped by the first available vessel sailing to New York.

你方定欣然获悉，标题货物我们手边都有存货，而且能以最早开往纽约的船载运该货。

It has been a long time since the last time you ordered the captioned goods.

你们上次订购标题货物是在很长时间以前了。

3. valid 有效的，同义词有 effective, open, firm, available, good

This offer will remain valid until March 4.

此发盘有效期至3月4日。

We believe that you will accept our offer, which will be kept open against your telegraphic reply.

我们相信贵公司将会接受我方发盘，此发盘至来电回复止有效。

We must stress that this offer is firm for three days only because of the heavy demand for the limited supplies of this material.

我们必须强调一点，此报盘有效期仅三天，这是因为此材料供给有限，而需求旺盛。

4. 合同中的单价条款包括4个部分:计价货币、计量单位、贸易术语、单位价格金额。报价时，这4个部分一定要完整，缺一不可。贸易术语包括：

组别	术语缩写	术语英文名称	术语中文名称
E 组发货	EXW	EX Works	工厂交货(……指定地点)
F 组主要运费未付	FCA	Free Carrier	交至承运人(……指定地点)
	FAS	Free Alongside Ship	船边交货(……指定装运港)
	FOB	Free On Board	船上交货(……指定装运港)

(续表)

组别	术语缩写	术语英文名称	术语中文名称
C 组主要运费已付	CFR	Cost and Freight	成本加运费（……指定目的港）
	CIF	Cost, Insurance and Freight	成本、保险费加运费付至（……指定目的港）
	CPT	Carriage Paid to	运费付至（……指定目的港）
	CIP	Carriage and Insurance Paid to	运费、保险费付至（……指定目的地）
D 组货到	DAF	Delivered at Frontier	边境交货（……指定地点）
	DES	Delivered EX Ship	目的港船上交货（……指定目的港）
	DEQ	Delivered EX Quay	目的港码头交货（……指定目的港）
	DDU	Delivered Duty Unpaid	未完税交货（……指定目的地）
	DDP	Delivered Duty Paid	完税后交货（……指定目的地）

5. irrevocable and confirmed letter of credit 保兑的、不可撤消信用证

6. in our favor 以我方为受益人，也可以表述为 in favor of us

Enclosed we hand you a statement of account to date, showing a balance of USD2 000 in our favor, which we trust will be found in order.

迄今为止，贵公司欠我方款项为 2000 美元。兹附上账目说明一份，请查收。

We are glad to advise you that a letter of credit in your favor has been issued by Bank of China and you may have it in one week.

很高兴通知贵公司中国银行已经开出以你方为受益人的信用证，你们在一周内应该可以收到。

7. the first available boat 第一艘可以订到舱位的船，最早的船

We shall ship your order by the first available boat sailing direct to your port immediately after receipt of your letter of credit.

一收到你方信用证后，我们将以最早直航你方港口的船装运你方订购的货物。

8. on hand 手头有

We have a large stock on hand to meet the surging demand.

我们手头有大量存货可以满足增长的需求。

So many orders on hand compel us to decline any new incoming orders.
手头订单太多,我们不得不拒绝新的订单。

You would be pleased to know that we have stocks on hand of the first four qualities which can be shipped by the first available vessel sailing to New York direct approximately one week after receipt of your irrevocable and confirmed letter of credit.

贵公司必乐于知道,上述前四项品质的产品我们手头都有存货。只要收到贵方保兑的、不可撤消信用证约一周后,我们就能以最早直往纽约的船运送该货。

9. meet with your approval 得到你方的同意

We hope the compensations we suggest will meet with your approval.
我们希望你方能够同意我们提出的赔偿建议。

If this counter offer meets with your approval, we shall send you our orders immediately.
如果你方同意我们的还盘,我们将立即寄去我方的订单。

4.2.2　Make a Firm Offer

China National Import& Export Co.
12 Hedong Road
Shanghai
China
Tel：2178490
Fax：324575

2 June 2003

The United Import Co. Ltd.
21 Fenton Street
Singapore

Dear sirs

This is to confirm your fax of 23 May, asking us to make you firm offers for rice and soybeans C&F Singapore.

We phoned you this morning offering you 3 000 metric tons of polished rice at US $300 per metric ton, C&F Singapore, for shipment during July/August. This offer is firm, subject to the receipt of your reply before 15 June.

Please note that we have quoted our most favorable price and are unable to entertain any counter offer.

With regard to soybeans, we advise you that the few lots we have at present are under offer elsewhere. If, however, you were to make us a suitable offer, there is a possibility of our supplying them.

As you know, of late, it has been a heavy demand for these commodities and this has resulted in increased prices. You may, however, take advantage of the strengthening market if you send an immediate reply.

Yours sincerely

Comments

  Paragraph 1: identify the reference and the products
  Paragraph 2: give details of the offer, with the time limit on the firm price
  Paragraph 3: reject any counter offer in advance
  Paragraph 4: in times of short supply, maximize the price by inviting higher bids
  Paragraph 5: encourage the customer to make a quick decision

  This offer contains all the necessary information in a concise form. The writer has carefully precluded any counter offer or problems due to a change in market prices. The letter is designed to get a quick response and a possible premium on the soybeans.

Notes

  1. firm offer 实盘,实盘必须满足两个条件:第一,实盘中各项条款必须完整、肯定、明确;第二,有效期是实盘的必有内容。

2. subject to 以……为条件,以……为准,这个短语在报盘函电中极为常见。

We confirm having cabled you a firm offer, subject to your reply reaching here by the end of this week.

现确认已向贵方电开实盘,本周末前复到有效。

We confirm having cabled you a firm offer, subject to your acceptance reaching us not later than June 10.

现确认已向贵方电开实盘,以你方接受的复函不迟于6月10日到达我处为条件。

3. entertain 接受,考虑

We are too heavily committed to be able to entertain any fresh orders.

我们承约过多,不能再接受新订货。

We shall be glad to entertain any constructive suggestion you may make.

我方乐于考虑你方可能提出的任何建设性的建议。

Buyers entertain the idea that these two types should be similarly priced.

买方认为这两种型号的价格应该差不多。

There is a considerable demand for your products here, and we would do our utmost to push the sale on your behalf if you are disposed to entertain our commission rate.

最近本地对贵公司产品需求很大,如果贵公司愿意考虑我们的佣金比率要求,我们乐于倾力推销。

4. with regard to 关于,可以和 in regard to, as regards, regarding, with reference to 换用

With regard to Purchase Confirmation No. 84, please ship the goods as soon as possible.

关于第84号购货确认书,请尽快装船。

With regard to the balance, we will advise you the position in a few days.

关于剩余数量的情况,将于数日内告知。

In regard to S/C No. 403, please ship the goods without delay.

关于403号售货确认书的货物,请你方立即装运。

As regards your suggestions, we shall revert to it later.

关于你的建议,我们一会儿回过头来再谈。

As regards commission, 3% is the maximum we can allow.

关于佣金问题,我们最多只能给3%。

As regards packing, we shall have a further discussion with you.

关于包装问题,我方将与你们做进一步讨论。

We know nothing regarding the market conditions there.

关于那边的市场情况我们一无所知。

We are in receipt of your letter dated August 2nd regarding shipment of your order No. 2132.

我方已收到你方8月2日来函,事关2132号订单货物的装运问题。

With reference to your letter of the 6th inst., we are glad to inform you that there has been a great demand for the articles.

关于本月6日的来信,我们高兴地告知,该商品的需求量甚大。

5. advise 通知,告知

advise sb of sth

Please advise us of your specific requirement.

请将你的具体需要通知我们。

We will advise you of developments.

有何进展,定将奉告。

advise sth

Please advise the name of the steamer.

请告知船名。

advise sb noun clause

Please advise us whether you are interested.

请告知你方是否感兴趣。

Please be advised 与 we advise you 意思相同

Please be advised that business has been done at USD100 per metric ton.

现通知你方已有业务按每公吨100美元成交。

6. demand 需求

There is little or no demand at present for this article.

这种商品目前很少或没有需求。

As the demand has become softer, interest is cooling off.

由于需求已减少,兴趣渐冷。

The goods are in large demand.

这货销路很畅。

7. take advantage of 利用

We wish to take advantage of this opportunity to write you about the exclusive agency.

我们愿借此机会与你联系独家代理事宜。

We regret we cannot take advantage of your offer.

很遗憾,我们无法接受你们的报盘。

Buyers are trying to take advantage of the present market condition to buy at cheap prices.

买方想利用当前市场情况低价买入。

4.2.3 Send a Pro Forma Invoice

China National Import& Export Co.
12 Hedong Road
Shanghai
China
Tel:2178490
Fax:324575

24 June 2003

The United Import Co. Ltd.
21 Fenton Street
Singapore

Dear sirs

Thank you for your letter dated May 4. As requested, we are sending you herewith our pro forma invoice COL-91-14 in quadruplicate.

The above-mentioned invoice, however, does not imply unreserved acceptance of your order as both prices and quantities must be further confirmed by us.

As soon as you have obtained the necessary import licence, please let us know by fax so that we may confirm our offer. In the meantime, if there is any change in price or delivery, we shall contact you.

We look forward to receiving further news from you.

Yours truly

Comments

Paragraph 1: identify the reference

Paragraph 2: remind the customer it is a non-firm offer

Paragraph 3: encourage the customer to act immediately

This letter informs the potential customer the offer made in pro forma invoice. This is also a polite reminder that the offer is still open.

Notes

1. herewith = with this (*adv.*) 与此一道，随函附上

Thank you for your order for Chinaware which we confirm herewith as follows:

感谢你方订购我们的瓷器，在此确认如下：

We are sending you herewith a draft for USD6 000 in settlement of the outstanding account.

现随函附上金额为 6 000 美元的汇票一张以结清欠款。

Due to the increase in raw material costs, we must unfortunately raise the cost of our merchandise to you. And we are sending you herewith our new price list for your review which goes into effect on June 1.

由于原材料成本上涨，我们不得已要提高商品价格，现随函附上新价目表供你方参考，新价目表 6 月 1 日生效。

2. pro forma invoice 形式发票

3. in quadruplicate 一式四份

类似的短语有：in duplicate 一式两份

　　　　　　　in triplicate 一式三份

4. above-mentioned 上述的，前面提到的；反义词 below-mentioned, under-mentioned 下面提到的，下述的

We would remind you that the above-mentioned claim is still outstanding, and we shall be glad to receive settlement as early as possible.

我们需要提醒你方，上述索赔依然未得到处理，我们希望尽快得到赔偿。

We should be obliged if you would furnish us with your opinion on the financial status of the above-mentioned company.

如果你方能够就上述公司的财务状况提供一些意见我们将不胜感激。

We inform you that we are sending by the "Virgin" the under-mentioned goods and enclose a copy of the bill of lading for same.

现通知你方，本公司已将下述货物装上"维真"号运输，同函附寄该货提单一份。

5. confirm ($v.$) 确认，证实

We acknowledge receipt of your order No. 2120 for textiles and confirm that every effort will be made to arrange early completion.

敬谢贵公司 2120 号纺织品订单并确认将尽全力早日处理完毕。

We should be grateful if you would confirm your order on the revised conditions.

惠请确认条款已更改过的订单。

We are glad to confirm your order which we have accepted on the terms.

我方很高兴确认贵方的订单并已接受贵方的条件。

confirmation ($n.$) 确认

Your immediate confirmation of our offer is appreciated.

感谢你方迅速确认我们的发盘。

Enclosed is a copy of our Sales Confirmation No. 965.

随信附上我方的 965 号销售确认书一份。

4.3 Specimen Letters

4.3.1 Send a Pro Forma Invoice

Dear Sirs

We are in receipt of your letter of July 21st. As requested, we are enclosing herewith three copies of our Pro forma Invoice No. 870, on which you will find our keenest quotation CIF Hongkong. Please note that this offer is subject to your reply being received not later than August 15th.

Shipment can be made during September if your L/C reaches us by August 20th. As it is almost certain that the market price is rising steadily, we think it advisable for you to place your order without delay.

Yours faithfully

● **Activities for comprehension**

1. What is to be included in a pro forma invoice?

2. What is the main difference between a pro forma invoice and an ordinary invoice?

3. What is the function of a pro forma invoice?

4.3.2 Make a Firm Offer

Dear sirs

We are in receipt of your enquiry of May 6 for which we thank you.

In reply, we have pleasure in offering you 200 tons tin foiled sheets for shipment in July/August at US $150 per ton CFR Seattle, please note that any further increase in freight will be for buyer's account.

It is no doubt you have observed an upward tendency in price, which has every indication of being maintained. Besides, you may also have been aware that there has been of late a great demand for this commodity everywhere. This explains why fresh enquiries and orders have been pouring in while we are busy executing the back orders. Apparently the supply position is now keenly felt in the international market, frankly speaking, we are now in a great bustle and can not successfully and satisfactorily arrange the falling supply to meet the growing demand.

If you are able to close with this offer, please fax us immediately your acceptance, which is to reach here before 16:00 o'clock today of our time. As it is quite clear to you that this commodity is now much-sought-after, we are unable to hold offer open for too long. Any hesitation on your part will only create a chance for other buyers who are also in urgent need of the goods and whose names happen to be after yours in the waiting list.

In the meantime if you require other products, please do not hesitate to let us have your specific enquiry and you can count on us to give it our best and prompt attention.

Yours truly

- **Activities for comprehension**

    1. In making a firm offer, what should be mentioned?
    2. Give a brief description of a firm offer.

4.3.3 Price Adjustment Notice

Dear sir

Rarely do we have the opportunity to inform our customers of such good news. The legislature's tariff ruling which was handed down on May 1st, 2007, has made it possible for our company to reduce our list price for Egyptian cotton. Effective as of June 1, 2007. All firm orders received for six week delivery will be billed as follows:

STOCK	OLD PRICE	NEW PRICE
#0134	$57.00	$51.30
#0135	$53.00	$47.70
#0136	$49.00	$44.10

We are very pleased to be able to pass this savings directly on to you. These prices do not include the additional 2 per cent discount that is offered to our customers who pay within the 10 day discount period.

Yours faithfully

4.4 Summary

A quotation is a promise to supply goods on the terms stated. It is taken as a non-firm offer. A seller may use a pro forma invoice to serve as a formal quotation or price reference. A firm offer is made by a seller or buyer when he makes a proposal of the trade terms and promises to sell or buy at a stated price and within a stated period of time. Once it has been accepted within the term of validity, it cannot be withdrawn. An offer is usually made by the seller. Those made by the buyer are usually referred to as bid. An offer is usually the reply made by a seller to the inquiry by a buyer. It has also been the practice that a seller voluntarily makes an offer without waiting for an enquiry to his regular customers and new customers who may have interest in his products.

报价是一种按约定条件供货的承诺,被认为是一种虚盘。卖方可以用形式发票作为正式的报价或价格参考。实盘是买方或卖方向对方提出各项交易条件,并承诺愿意按照这些条件在规定的时间内出售或购买商品。一旦在有效期内被接受就不可以撤回。通常都是由卖方向买方提出的。若是由买方向卖方提出习称为递盘。一般情况下,报盘是卖方对买方询盘的回复。对于老客户或对商品有兴趣的新客户,卖方为销售自己的商品可以不等对方询盘即发出报盘,这也是常见的做法。

4.5 Useful Expressions

1. At your request we make you an offer as follows:
按你方要求现报盘如下:

2. We take pleasure in making you an offer as required by you some time ago, subject to our final confirmation.
很高兴现按你方前一段时间提出的要求做出报盘,此报盘以我方最后确认为准。

3. We thank you for your enquiry of May 5 and are pleased to enclose our quotation sheet.

感谢你方 5 月 5 日的询盘,现随函附上我们的报价单。

4. Attached to this letter you will find our pro forma invoice in triplicate covering 5 000 shirts.

随函附上我们的关于那 5000 件衬衫的形式发票一式三份,请查收。

5. Owing to the recent considerable advance in prices of raw materials, the cost of the product has been unfavorably affected. However, we have kept the prices down to secure your orders.

由于近来原材料价格大幅上扬,产品成本上升。但是,为了得到你方的订单我们还是保持原来的低价。

6. The offer is good subject to the goods being available when the order is received.

此发盘以订单收到时货未售出为准。

7. This offer is firm, subject to the receipt of reply by us before 25th January.

此发盘是实盘,以 1 月 25 日之前复到为准。

8. Although our prices do not allow us any further discount, we will grant you a special 2% discount. We have done this because we want to assist you in extending your sales.

尽管我们的价格已经没有再打折扣的空间了,但是我们还是愿意给你们 2% 的折扣。这是因为我们想帮助你方扩大销售。

9. We are glad to know that you are very interested in our cell phones, and appreciate this opportunity of providing a quotation on this product as follows:

很高兴得知你方对我们的手机产品感兴趣,并有这样的机会就此产品向你方做出如下报价。

10. Our offer will be revoked if not accepted within 14 days.

如果 14 天内没有接受,我方将撤消发盘。

11. You may profit from the advancing market if you place an immediate order with us.

若立刻订购,你方可从上涨的行市中获利。

12. As for the above offer, it is most possible that the price will rise still

more, and it would therefore be to your interest to place your order without delay.

至于上述报价,很有可能还会持续走高,因此,为了你方利益,建议立刻订购。

13. This offer is made without engagement.

此报价无约束力。

14. If you decide to take advantage of our offer, please kindly fax us your acceptance.

若你方决定接受我方报价,请回传真接受。

4.6 Reading Materials

4.6.1

Dear sirs

Thank you for your letter dated 5 March, in which you express your interest in our men's jackets. At your request, we take pleasure in making you the following offer, subject to our final confirmation:

Commodity: men's jackets

Quantity: 500 dozen

Size: L/XL/XXL

Color: blue, black

Price: At US$200 per dozen CIF Karachi

Shipment: One month after receipt of L/C

Payment: By a confirmed, irrevocable L/C in our favor payable by draft at sight to reach the sellers one month before shipment and remain valid for negotiation in China till the 15 days after shipment.

As you know, our stock is limited and the demand is brisk. Your early decision is necessary. We are confident that you can do some profitable business.

We look forward to your prompt reply.

Yours sincerely

4.6.2

Dear sirs

　　We have received your sample with thanks. If you can accept our price US $ 13 per piece FOB Tianjin, please send us your pro forma invoice and we shall be ready to place an order for 100 dozen of your handmade cotton embroidered tablecloths.

　　There is no question about our getting the necessary import license from our authorities. After the license is approved, we shall establish an irrevocable letter of credit in your favor.

　　We hope that this will be the first of many orders we will be placing with you.

　　　　　　　　　　　　　　　　　　　　　　　　　　Yours sincerely

4.6.3

Dear sirs

　　We refer to our quotation of 2 June and our mail offer of 12 June regarding the supply of polished rice.

　　We are prepared to keep our offer open until the end of this month.

　　As this product is in great demand and the supply is limited, we would recommend that you accept this offer as soon as possible.

　　　　　　　　　　　　　　　　　　　　　　　　　　Yours sincerely

4.6.4

Dear Sirs

　　Thank you for your letter inquiring for our Forever Brand Bicycles. Based on your requirement, we are glad to inform you that we can supply YE803 26′ and TE600 24′ bicycles with the favorable quotation as below:

　　FOREVER BRAND BICYCLE:

　　　　YE803　26′　USD69.17　per set　CIFC5　Copenhagen 600 sets
　　　　TE600　24′　USD74.49　per set　CIFC5　Copenhagen 600 sets

Available colors: blue; green; red; purple; white.

Packing: To be packed in cartons of one set each, 120 cartons to a 40' container.

Shipment: Shipment is effected during May 2001 on the condition that the relevant L/C arrives by the end of 25th April 2001.

Payment: Payment shall be made by an irrevocable Sight Letter of Credit for full contract value through a bank acceptable to the seller.

Insurance: For 110% invoice value covering All Risks & War Risk as per PICC dated 1/1/1981.

The above quotation is valid within 7 days.

You will find that the prices quoted are very reasonable and in case you need more information, we shall be only too glad to answer you at any time.

We are looking forward to receiving an order from you.

Yours faithfully

Exercises

I. Choose the right answer.

1. If your prices are competitive, we are confident _____ the goods in great quantities in this market.

    a) to sell   b) to be selling   c) in being sold   d) in selling

2. Our quotation _____ Tiantan Brand Shirts is valid for 10 days.

    a) to   b) after   c) in   d) for

3. We confirm our fax just sent _____ these goods.

    a) offering you firm   b) firm offering you

    c) to be offered to you firm   d) to firm offer you

4. We offer you the following items _____ your reply reaching here by 4 p.m. today our time.

    a) subjecting to   b) to subject to   c) subjects to   d) subject to

5. We offer you our lowest price, _____ we have done a lot of business with other customers.

a) which b) that c) with which d) at which

6. We trust that we may be _____ with a continuance of your valued orders.

a) favor b) favoring c) favored d) do a favor

7. We hope that you will see your way to _____ us your order, and assure you in advance of its most careful execution.

a) supply b) grant c) leave d) place

8. Not having heard from you since, we should be glad to know whether there is any disadvantage in our terms which we could _____.

a) engage b) remove c) give d) move

9. You are _____ that we will quote our best prices as soon as we are told what products of ours you need.

a) sure b) ensured c) assured d) entrusted

10. In all probability this offer will not be _____ for some time, and we accordingly look forward to receiving an early reply from you.

a) repeated b) made c) given d) supplied

II. Put in each blank the right word or phrase picked from the following list.

| prevailing | engagement | open | decline | in reply to | further |
| confirmation | otherwise | so long as | repeated | line | secure |

1. We are prepared to give you a quotation which is based on the _____ market price.

2. Our quotation always comes in _____ with the world market.

3. Unless _____ stated or agreed upon, all prices are without any discount.

4. We trust that you will be able to accept our offer, which shall be kept _____ subject to reply before 12:00 a.m. of March 2.

5. We now offer you, without _____, our various items as follows.

6. The above offer is subject to our final _____.

7. Unless you make a 5% reduction, we will have to _____ your offer.

8. This offer cannot be _____. There is every indication that the prices will rise soon.

9. _____ you can maintain moderate prices, your products should have a ready sale here.

10. _____ your letter, we enclose our latest illustrated catalogue for your reference.

11. We ask you to make every effort to quote at competitive prices in order to _____ our business.

12. We received your promotional letter and brochure today. Kindly send us _____ details of your prices and terms of sale.

III. Fill in the blanks with proper prepositions.

Dear sir

Thank you for your interest _____ our ladies' tights.

_____ your request, we are now faxing you our latest price list _____ your reference. Please see the attachment _____ details.

Our usual terms of payment are _____ 90% irrevocable L/C at sight with 10% of the invoice value _____ down payment by T/T when placing your order, and shipment can be made 30 days _____ receipt of the L/C. As for the discount _____ regular purchases, we may give you a 2% discount, but not for this order.

Awaiting your early order.

Yours faithfully

● **Skills Practice**

Write a letter for a curtain material manufacturer, with a quotation enclosed therein, giving favorable comments on the goods offered and recommending their client's acceptance.

Unit 5 Counter Offers

Learning Objectives

After studying this unit, you should:

✍ Know what is counter offer(了解还盘的概念)

✍ Know the essential components of a counter offer letter(了解还盘函的内容组成)

✍ Master useful expressions in writing such letters(掌握还盘函的常用句型)

5.1 Introduction

When an offeree receives the offer, he may have disagreement to some terms such as price or payment terms in the offer and may make a counter-offer, i.e. a partial rejection of the original offer stating his own terms instead. Thus the original offer becomes invalid and unbinding and a new offer comes into being. Then the original offerer now becomes the offeree and he is entitled to acceptance or refusal.

当受盘人收到发盘后,可能对发盘中的某些交易条件,如价格或支付方式等,有不同意见,他就会进行还盘,也就是对原发盘的部分拒绝并说明自己的条件。此时,原来的发盘就失去效力,新的报盘产生了。那么,原来的报盘人现在就成了受盘人,有权接受或拒绝新的报盘。

The letter of rejection should cover the following points: thank the seller for his offer; express regret at inability to accept; make a counter-offer if, in the circumstances, it is appropriate; express hope for prompt reply and business success or suggest other opportunities to do business together.

拒绝报盘人的还盘函应该包括下列内容:感谢卖方的报盘;对不能接受卖方的报盘表示遗憾;如果可以的话,提出自己的还盘;表示希望得到卖方的早日答复和交易成功或者提出其他业务机会。

5.2 Model Letters Comments

5.2.1 Make a Counter Offer

> The United Import Co. Ltd.
> 21 Fenton Street
> Singapore
> Tel: 4353459
> Fax: 4353897

> 24 June 2007

China National Import& Export Co.
12 Hedong Road
Shanghai, China

Dear sirs

We are in receipt of your letter of June 12 offering us 300 metric tons of polished rice at US $300 per metric ton on the usual terms.

We regret to inform you that our buyers find your price much too high. We are informed that some lots of Thai's Origin have been sold here at a level about 20% lower than yours.

We do not deny that the quality of Chinese rice is slightly better but the difference in price should, in no case, be as large as 10%. To facilitate the transaction, we counter offer as follows, subject to your reply being received by us before July 10.

300 metric tons of polished rice, at US $280 per metric ton CIF Singapore, other terms as per your letter of June 12.

As the market price is falling, we recommend your immediate acceptance.

Yours sincerely

Comments

Paragraph 1: identify the reference and state the details of the offer

Paragraph 2: state the objection to the offer and the reasons for it

Paragraph 3: state the counter offer

Paragraph 4: urge the seller to accept the counter offer

A counter offer is an attempt to bargain for a lower price. Here the prospective buyer is clearly stating his objections to the price offered and giving reasons why the seller should accept.

Notes

1. find your price much too high 发现你方价格实在太高了

类似的用于还价的句型：

Your price is a bit high.

你方价格有点高。

Your price is on the high side.

你方价格偏高。

Your price leaves us little profit on our sales.

你方的价格使我方销售无利可图。

Your price is excessive.

你方价格过高。

Your price is rather high.

你方价格相当高。

Your price is too high.

你方价格太高。

Your price is prohibitive.

你方价格高得令人望而却步。

Your price is unreasonable.

你方价格不合理。

Your price is unworkable.

你方价格做不开。

Your price is impracticable.

你方价格不可行。

Your price is infeasible.

你方价格行不通。

Your price is unrealistic.

你方价格不现实。

2. in no case 绝对不可能

We are making this offer as a special inducement to take up this line. It is a proven seller and your customers can in no case get better value anywhere else.

为了鼓励你们进入这个产品市场,我们才做了这样特别优惠的发盘。这种货物已经被证明非常畅销,你们的客户绝对不可能在别处得到比我们的价格更优惠的报价了。

In local commercial circles, he is regarded as a substantial trader with a clean record and shall in no case make default in payment.

在当地的商界中,他被认为是一个实力雄厚、声誉良好的商人,所以绝不可能拖欠货款。

3. facilitate (v.) 推动、促进、使容易

Rope or metal handles should be fixed to the boxes to facilitate carrying.

请在箱子上固定上绳索或金属扶手以便搬运。

We have quoted you the lowest possible price to facilitate your sales.

为利于你方推销,我们已报出最低价格。

Please open your L/C immediately to facilitate our shipping arrangements.

请立即开出信用证,以便我们安排装船。

4. counter offer (n. v.) 还盘

We appreciate your counter offer but find it too low to accept.

谢谢你方还盘,但我方觉得太低了无法接受。

We have received a lot of inquiries from your neighboring countries, hoping to close business at something near to our prices. It is, therefore, impossible to entertain your counter offer at the moment.

我们已经从你们邻国收到许多询盘,他们都希望以接近我方报价的价格成交。因此,目前我们不可能接受你们的还盘。

While we appreciate the quality of your products, we have to point out that your price is not workable at this stage. We have to counter offer as follows:

尽管我们喜欢你们产品的品质,但我们不得不指出你方的价格目前是行不通的。我们还盘如下:

5. as per (*prep.*) 依据,按照

If you cannot supply goods as per the enclosed specifications, please send us alternates.

如不能按照所附规格供货,请寄代用品。

Please proceed with manufacturing as per the instructions we sent you.

请按照我们发给你方的指示继续生产。

6. Price is falling 价格正在下跌,同样可以用于表示价格下跌的词汇有:

go down (*v*), The $US went down 3 cents against the Yen yesterday.

fall (*v*), Unemployment fell last month from 1.7 million to just below 1.6 million.

fall (*n*), International Paper Mills reported a fall in profits from $235 million to $188 million.

drop (*v*), Consumer spending drops dramatically as interest rates go up.

drop (*n*), Arcon Inc. reports a severe drop in profits.

decline (*v*), Traditional industries such as coal and textiles have declined in Europe.

decline (*n*), Oil prices have seen a decline in recent weeks due to overproduction.

reduce (*v*), The company is planning to reduce the size of the workforce.

reduction (*n*), A reduction in the staffing budget has led to redundancies.

decrease (*v*), The price of computers is expected to decrease further as semiconductors become cheaper. Insurance companies hope to decrease the number of pay-outs.

decrease (*n*), Angry workers are protesting against a decrease in working hours.

worsen (*v*), The state of the environment is expected to worsen in the next century.

downturn (*n*), Asian economies have experienced a significant downturn in recent years.

5.2.2 Decline a Counter Offer

China National Import& Export Co.
12 Hedong Road
Shanghai
China
Tel: 2178490
Fax: 324575

30 June 2007

The United Import Co. Ltd.
21 Fenton Street
Singapore

Dear sirs

Thank you for your letter dated June 24. We very much regret that we are unable to entertain your counter offer of US $280 per metric ton of polished rice, CIF Singapore.

We must point out that your bid is out of line with the current market level. Other companies in your region are buying freely at our quoted price.

For your information, the market is firm and tending upward. There is very little likelihood of any significant change in the foreseeable future.

In view of the above, we suggest that it is in your interest to accept our price of US $300 per metric ton without delay.

Yours sincerely

Comments

Paragraph 1: identify the reference and reply to the counter offer
Paragraph 2: give the reasons for refusing the counter offer
Paragraph 3: add relevant reasons for holding to the original offer

Paragraph 4: urge the prospective buyer to accept the offer

The seller states briefly, but clearly, that she cannot accept the counter offer and gives the reasons why. The final paragraphs politely make it clear that the bargaining process is at an end. The buyer must now accept the offer or withdraw from the transaction.

Notes

1. entertain 接受,愿意考虑

We cannot entertain your proposal even if we meet you half way.

即使咱们双方都各让一步,我方也不能考虑你们这个建议。

Because of the exceptional demand for our electric blankets, we cannot entertain your order for the time being.

因为对我方电热毯的需求异常活跃,我们暂不能接受你方的订单。

Buyers entertain the idea that these two types should be similarly priced.

买方认为这两种型号的价格应该差不多。

2. point out 指出,指明,说明

We have also to point out that the men's shirts are available in our market from several European manufacturers, all of them are at prices from 10% to 15% below the price you quoted.

我们不得不指出,在我地市场也可以采购到一些欧洲生产商供应的男式衬衫,他们的价格比你们的报价要低10%到15%。

We have pointed out to you on a previous occasion the competition from Japanese manufactures, whose low prices and quick deliveries are having a striking effect on local buyers.

此前,我们曾向贵公司指出来自日本厂商的竞争,它们的产品价格低廉、交货迅速,对本地买主影响巨大。

This is not the first time a delay in delivery has occurred, and the increasing frequency of the trouble compels us to point out that business on these conditions cannot be continued for long.

这已经不是第一次交货延迟了,延迟次数越来越多迫使我们得指出在这种情况下的交易不可能维持很久。

3. bid (n. v.) 表示买方的报盘；offer 表示卖方的报盘

Will no one make a higher bid?

没有人出更高的价吗？

Will anyone bid USD50 for this painting?

有人出 50 美元买这幅画吗？

The goods were bid up far beyond their real value.

这些货物的价格被哄抬得远超出它们的真实价值。

4. out of line with 与……不相符合

Your price is out of line with the prevailing market level.

你方的价格与现行行市不相符合。

We are sorry to say your prices seem to be on the high side and out of line with the current market level.

很遗憾，你方价格似乎偏高，与行市不符。

in line with... 与……相符合

While our price is in line with the prevailing international market rate, we are not in a position to consider any concession in our price, much to our regret.

我们所报的价格完全符合当前国际市场行情，歉难在价格上作任何折让。

5. level 的本义是水平，这里被引申为价格水平

Business is hopeful if you reduce your level.

如果你方能够降低价格，成交有望。

We are prepared to sell the goods at your level.

我们愿意按你方价格出售货物。

Will you please contact your manufacturer again to see if he can come down to this price level?

请您与你们的制造商联系一下，看看他们是否还能降到这个价格水平？

To be frank, our prices could be abated somewhat, yet we could hardly bring them down to anywhere near the level your letter indicated.

坦率地说，我们的价格还可以降一点，但不太可能降到你们信中所提出的价格水平。

6. tending upward(s) 上涨，名词性短语是 upward tendency

You would benefit by ordering now, as the market is firm (strong) with an upward tendency.

现在订货对你是有利的,因为现在市场行情坚挺并且有上涨趋势。

The market is tending upward, so we cannot keep this offer open too long.

市场行情看涨,我们的报盘不可能长期不变。

We are very much concerned that your sales in recent months have fallen considerably. At first, we thought it might be due to the economical fluctuations in your country, but on looking into the matter more closely, we find that the general trend of trade during this period has been upwards.

对贵公司近月来销售大幅度下跌的情况我们很担心。起初,我们认为这是由于贵国经济波动造成的,但经深入调查,我们发现在此期间,总体的贸易趋势是上涨的。

7. likelihood 可能性

There is little likelihood of the goods remaining unsold once this particular offer has lapsed.

一旦此发盘到期失效,货物很可能已经售完。

Such a low price is exceptional indeed, so there is little likelihood of further reduction in price.

这样低的价格绝对是特别优惠,不太可能再降价了。

8. in view of 鉴于

In view of our long business relations, we have made up our mind to concede a further 1% discount. However, we will be unable to repeat this again as we are planning to advance our prices in the future.

鉴于我们之间的长期业务关系,我们决定再给你们让利1%。但是,这种情况以后不会再有了,我们正打算将来提高价格呢。

In view of the recent increases in the price of raw material, we reluctantly have to adjust some of our prices.

鉴于原材料价格近来有所上涨,我们迫不得已只好调整部分价格。

5.2.3 Partly Accept A Counter Offer

China National Import& Export Co.
12 Hedong Road
Shanghai
China
Tel: 021-21784900
Fax: 021-32457500

30 June 2007

The United Import Co. Ltd.
21 Fenton Street
Singapore

Dear sirs

Thank you for your letter dated June 2. Considering our long business relations, we agree to the payment to be made by T/T. However, you are requested to prepay 30% amount as down payment before production, with the remaining 70% to be remitted through bank within 14 days after receipt of documents.

As the price of the material are rising and the quantities you ordered are less than a 20 foot container, we may only allow you a discount of 2%. Our lowest price is USD17 per piece FOB Shanghai with the other terms as per your letter of June 2. Please note this counter offer remains open until July 1.

Please confirm your acceptance by return.

Faithfully yours

Comments

Paragraph 1: identify the reference and reply to the counter offer on payment terms

Paragraph 2: give the reasons for refusing the price reduction and suggest a

2% discount

Paragraph 3: urge the prospective buyer to accept the counter offer

The seller states briefly, but clearly, that she can accept payment by T/T with 30% amount prepaid, but cannot accept the counter offer on price and gives the reasons why. The final paragraph politely makes it clear that the bargaining process is at an end.

Notes

1. T/T (telegraphic transfer) 电汇

When the goods are ready for shipment and the freight space booked, you will fax us and we will remit the full amount by T/T.

当货物备好待运并且舱位预订好时,你方传真通知我们,我们电汇全款给你方。

All items included in your order can be supplied from stock and will be packed and shipped immediately upon receipt of your remittance by T/T.

你方订单中的货品均有存货,一收到电汇款项便可包装运输。

2. down payment 首付款、预付款

Please remit the 15% down payment to us by T/T. Payment of the balance is to be made in three installments.

请将15%的首付款电汇给我们。余款分三次付清。

In order to execute your order smoothly, please T/T your down payment as stipulated in the S/C.

为顺利执行你方订单,请按合同规定电汇预付款。

3. document (n.) 单据

Documents against acceptance deviates from our usual terms of payment.

承兑交单不是我们通常接受的付款方式。

Please be sure to attach a full set of shipping documents to your draft.

一定要在你的汇票上随附全套运输单据。

The seller needs the L/C and other documents, such as insurance policy, packing list, invoice, bill of lading, for negotiation.

议付时,卖方需要提交信用证和保险单、装箱单、发票、提单等单据。

You may consider this air waybill as negotiable document, but it is non-negotiable document and cannot be transferred.

你可能认为空运单是可以议付的单据,但它并不是可以议付的单据,不可以转让。

documentary (*adj.*) 跟单的

The buyer shall duly accept the documentary draft drawn by the seller at 30 days' sight.

买方应按时承兑卖方开立的30天远期跟单汇票。

Documentary collection has the relevant shipping documents attached to the draft, while in clean collection only draft is used.

跟单托收就是汇票上随付有关的运输单据,而光票托收则只有汇票。

If the L/C requires the seller to draw documentary draft upon the buyer, then it is a documentary L/C.

如果信用证中要求卖方以买方为受票人开立跟单汇票,则此信用证就是跟单信用证。

4. note (*v.*) 注意

Kindly note that the goods are to be delivered in exact accordance with the samples.

请注意,货物必须与样品完全相符。

Please note that, since you are one of the important importers of silk in Japan, the prices we offered you are the lowest obtainable anywhere.

请注意,贵公司在日本是重要的丝绸进口商之一,所以我们向贵公司所报价格是所能得到的最低价格了。

We regret to note that you have not entrusted us with your orders for some time, and we hope that you have no reason to be dissatisfied with the execution of your past orders.

我们非常遗憾地知悉贵公司已有很长时间未曾定货。但愿不是因为贵公司对以往订单的执行有所不满。

5. by return 立刻回复,也可以表达为 by return of mail

Moreover, to enable us to apply for the import license required, we should like you to airmail your pro forma invoice in triplicate by return.

此外,为方便本公司申请进口许可证,请贵公司即刻以航空邮件寄来形式发票一式三份。

Please send us your quotations by return mail of the items listed below, together with terms of payment and largest discount.

请速回复,报出下列货物的价格,以及付款方式和最高折扣。

If you are interested in this lot, please let us have a cable reply by return, as the lot will in all possibility be sold quickly.

如果你方对此批货物感兴趣,请速电复我方,因为这批货很可能很快就会售完。

5.3　Specimen Letters

5.3.1　Make a Counter Offer

Dear sirs

We wish to thank you for your letter of May 20 offering us 200 tons tin foiled sheets for shipment in July/August at US$150 per ton CFR Seattle.

In reply, we very much regret to state that our clients here find your price too high and out of line with the prevailing market level. Information indicates that some goods made in Japanese has been sold at level of US$138 per ton.

In such case, it is impossible for us to persuade our clients to accept your price, as materials of similar quality is easily obtainable at a much lower price. Should you be prepared to reduce your limit by, say 6%, we might come to terms.

It is in view of our long-standing relationship that we make you such a counter-offer. We hope you will consider our counter-offer most favorable and fax us acceptance as soon as possible.

We are anticipating your early reply.

Yours truly

● Activities for comprehension

1. In a letter rejecting an offer, what are the main points to be expressed?

5.3.2 Decline a Counter Offer

Dear sirs

Thank you for your letter of May 30. We are surprised to learn that you consider our price for tin foiled sheets too high.

Much as we would like to do business with you, we regret to say that we cannot entertain your counter offer. The price we have quoted is quite realistic. We would point out that we have received substantial orders from other sources at our level.

If you would improve your offer, please let us know. Since supplies of this product are limited at the moment, we would ask you to act quickly.

We assure you that any further enquiries from you will receive our prompt attention.

Yours truly

● **Activities for comprehension**

1. How to decline a counter offer without lack of courtesy?

5.3.3 Make a Concession on Price

Dear sirs

Thank you for your letter of May 30. We are disappointed to hear that our price for tin foiled plates is too high for you to work on. You mentioned that Japanese goods were being offered at a price approximately 10% lower than that quoted by us.

We accept what you say, but we are of the opinion that the quality of the other makes does not measure up to that of ours.

Although we are keen to do business with you, we regret that we cannot accept your counter offer or even meet you half way.

The best we can do is to reduce our previous quotation by 2%. We trust that this will meet with your approval.

We look forward to hearing from you.

Yours truly

● Activities for comprehension

1. How to keep the balance between price flexibility and profit objective?

5.4 Summary

If one party does not agree with the counter party's offer, he may make a counter offer. A counter offer is virtually a partial rejection of the original offer and also a counter proposal initiated by the buyer. The buyer may show disagreement to the price, or packing, or shipment and state his own terms instead. Such alterations signify that business has to be negotiated on the renewed basis. The buyer's conditional acceptance of seller's offer also amounts to a counter offer. This process can go on for many rounds till business is finalized or called off. Sometimes the two parties may come to terms without any counter offer, but sometimes several rounds of counter offers.

一方报盘后,另一方如对其内容不同意,可以进行还盘。还盘实际上是对对方发盘的部分条件的拒绝,也可以说是买方发出的一个新的发盘。买方可能对价格、包装、装运等条件有不同意见,并说明自己的条件要求。这种条件的改变表明要在新的基础上再行磋商。如果买方有条件地接受卖方的发盘,也相当于还盘。还盘的过程可能持续几个回合直到达成交易或终止谈判。一笔交易有时不经过还盘即可达成,但有时要经过往返多次的还盘才能确认。

5.5 Useful Expressions

1. Please note that we have quoted our most favorable price and are unable to entertain any counter offer.
请注意,我们已经报出了最优惠的价格,所以不能接受任何还盘。

2. There is no room for any reduction in price.
没有降价的余地了。

3. We've already cut down our prices to cost level.
我们已经将价格降到成本费的水平了。

4. Your competitors are offering considerably lower prices and unless you can

reduce your quotations, we shall have to buy elsewhere.

你们的竞争对手报出了低得多的价格,除非你方降低报价,否则我们将向别处购买。

5. We do not see any advantage in your quotations, and would like to know whether you have any better value to offer.

你们的报价没有任何优势。我们想知道你们是否还能报出更合理的价格。

6. However you will agree that the prices offered are slightly higher if you consider the large amount of our order. Therefore we would like to ask you if you can make a further discount of 2%.

但是,如果你方考虑到我们订购量之大,你们应该知道你们的价格还是有点高。所以我们希望你方再给我们2%的折扣。

7. We regret that it is impossible to accept your counter-offer, even to meet you half-way; the price of raw material has advanced 20% and we shall shortly be issuing an advanced price list.

很遗憾,我们不能接受你方的还盘,即使你我各让一步,我们都不能接受。原材料的价格已经上涨了20%,我们很快就公布上调价格后的价目表了。

8. Although we are anxious to open up business with you, we regret that it is impossible for us to allow the reduction asked for, because we have already cut our prices to the lowest point after closely examining our cost calculations.

尽管我们非常渴望与你方启动业务往来,但很遗憾我们不可能接受你方的降价要求。因为我们在进行了认真的成本核算后已经将价格压到了最低。

9. Much as we would like to do business with you, we regret to say that we cannot entertain your counter offer.

尽管我们非常希望与你方做成交易,但歉难接受你方的还盘。

10. Considering our long-standing friendly business relationship, we can allow you reduction of 4% in our price.

考虑到我们之间的长期友好贸易关系,我们同意在原价格基础上让利4%。

11. Owing to the small amount of this transaction, we'd like to ask for payment by T/T, which would certainly help us save much time and a huge

amount of cost on opening L/C.

鉴于交易金额不大,我们请求以电汇方式支付货款。这会节省我们开信用证所需的大量时间和费用。

12. As our customers are in urgent need of the goods, may we suggest that you advance shipment to May? We shall appreciate your kindness to accommodate us.

因为我们的客户急需此货,所以能否请你方将装船期提前到5月?如果你们能够答应我们的请求,不胜感激。

13. It is true that competitive prices will often result in a high market share with great profit in the future. We wish you to consider this fact.

事实上,有竞争力的价格往往带来较大的市场份额,未来的利润更丰厚。希望你们考虑这一事实。

14. For your information, the market is weak with a downward tendency. We suggest your acceptance of our counter offer.

奉告,市场疲软并有下降趋势。建议你方接受我们的还盘。

5.6 Reading Materials

5.6.1

Dear Sirs

We are glad to receive your letter, together with your quotation.

After studying your quotation, we have to say that your prices are unacceptable. The market prices for bicycles are falling here, meanwhile, we have received many quotations recently and some of which are about 10% lower than yours. May we suggest that you find a better supplier and lower your cost. To speed up our business, we can tell you that the highest prices we can accept are as follows:

  YE803 26′ USD62.00 per set CIFC5 Copenhagen
  TE600 24′ USD68.00 per set CIFC5 Copenhagen

By the way, we can accept your trade terms listed in your letter except the terms of payment. We can only accept payment by L/C at 30 days sight.

Please take these matters into serious consideration and give us your favorable reply with the least possible delay.

                    Yours faithfully

5.6.2

Dear Sirs

We have carefully considered the opinion you expressed in your mail of counter offer. We are doing the best to set our price as low as possible without a sacrifice of quality in searching the suitable suppliers. Though we may possibly accept your payment term, i. e. by L/C at 30 days sight, we have regretfully pointed out that the prices mentioned in your mail are unacceptable.

Considering the excellent quality submitted and the continual rise in export cost, it is almost impossible for us to make any further reduction. However, in view of the initial transaction between us and the special character of your market, we have decided to give you the following favorable quotation, which is the utmost we can do:

FOREVER BRAND BICYCLE:

YE803 26'   USD66.00   per set   CIFC5 Copenhagen
TE600 24'   USD71.00   per set   CIFC5 Copenhagen

Since this offer is valid only for 3 days, please take this advantage and give us your acceptance by e-mail as soon as possible.

Yours faithfully

5.6.3

Dear sirs

We have received your offer of March 24 and regret that you have turned down our counter offer.

As we are in urgent need of the goods and anxious to conclude the business with you, we have made every effort to persuade our client to accept your offer of US$13 per piece. Fortunately, our customer in Karachi has changed his mind and approached us again with an order for 100 dozen of handmade cotton embroidered tablecloths on your terms.

We are very pleased to have been able to finalized this initial business with you after protracted exchange of correspondence, and look forward to your sales contract, upon receipt of which, we will open the relative L/C without delay.

Yours sincerely

5.6.4

Dear Mr. Partnell

We have acknowledged receipt of both your offer of May 6 and the samples of men's shirts, and thank you for these.

While appreciating the good quality of your shirts, we find your price is rather too high for the market we wish to supply.

We have also to point out that the men's shirts are available in our market from several European manufacturers, all of them are at prices from 10% to 15% below the price you quoted.

Such being the case, we have to ask you to consider if you can make reduction in your price, say 10%. As our order would be worth around US $50 000, you may think it worthwhile to make a concession.

We are looking forward to your reply.

Yours sincerely

Exercises

I. Choose the right answer.

1. A comparison of your offer _____ our regular suppliers shows that their figures are more favorable.

    a) with that of   b) with what of

    c) with which of   d) with this of

2. Although we appreciate good quality of your goods, we are sorry to say that your prices appear to be _____.

    a) of the high standard   b) in the high level

    c) on the high side   d) at the high end

3. We cannot see any possibility of business _____ your price is on the high side.

 a) which   b) since   c) that   d) though

4. Generally speaking, a growing demand can _____ increased price.

 a) result   b) result from   c) result for   d) result in

5. If you cannot make reduction in your price, we will regretfully decline your offer _____.

 a) as it stand   b) as it stands   c) so it stand   d) as standing

6. No discount will be granted _____ you could place an order of more than 10 000 dozen.

 a) until   b) unless   c) otherwise   d) except

7. Because of their superior quality, our silk coats always _____ in Europe.

 a) are sold fast   b) sell fast
 c) have been sold fast   d) be sold fast

8. We are sorry to say that your prices seem to be _____ with the market level.

 a) in line   b) out line   c) out of line   d) beyond

9. Since our own overheads have increased in the last few months, this offer on our part is _____ only for this month.

 a) good   b) well   c) fine   d) low

10. We offer you our lowest price, _____ we have done a lot of business with other customers.

 a) which   b) that   c) with which   d) at which

II. Put the following sentences into English.

1. 很遗憾,我们的价格与你方还盘之间的差距太大。
2. 你方必须降价2%左右,否则没有成交的可能。
3. 我们的报价相当合理,已为你地其他客户所接受。
4. 你方报盘与现行市场价不符。
5. 因我方的价格已降到极限,所以无法满足你方进一步降价的要求。
6. 谢谢你方还盘但我方觉得太低了无法接受。

III. Translate the following letter into English in a proper form.

敬启者：

你方3月21日来函收到，从中我们遗憾地得悉你方认为我124号货定价偏高。你们也许知道，我们的商品在许多国家都深受欢迎。尽管目前供应有限，需求却在增加。如果将我们的商品与其他商品加以比较，相信你方会同意我们的价格是可行的。实际上，我们已将价格降至最低，并按此与其他买方大量成交。

如果你们同意将订货数量增至5 000箱，我们愿意将原报价再削减2%。这是我们能接受的最大限度，希望你们能接受。如蒙早复，不胜感激。

此致

敬礼

Jill

● Skills Practice

澳大利亚Bell公司收到北京雅馨益智玩具有限公司的电控玩具报盘后，认为虽然质量不错但价格偏高，于是进行还盘。

请以Bell公司Tony先生的身份拟写还盘函。

Unit 6　Order

Learning Objectives

After learning this unit, you should:

✍ Know the main points in an order(了解订单的主要内容)

✍ Know the essential components of an order letter(了解订购函的基本组成部分)

✍ Know how to confirm and decline a buyer's order(了解确认买方订单和拒绝订单的方法)

✍ Master typical sentences and expressions in writing such letters(掌握信函写作中的典型句型和短语)

6.1　Introduction

An order is a request to supply a specified quantity of goods. Very often, it is only after the exchange of a number of letters, faxes or e-mails that the two parties come entirely to terms and the buyer finally places a formal order by letter or fax. Sometimes a buyer may take the initiative by placing a firm order with the seller, which is a firm bid to buy something and contains all necessary terms and conditions. Many companies prefer official printed order forms, which save time and ensure that no information may be ignored. Still there are companies who place orders in the form of letters.

订单是购买一定数量货物的请求。通常，买卖双方之间通过若干次信函、传真或电子邮件联系才能达成一致意见，买方才最终通过信函或传真向卖方发出订单。有时，买方可能会主动向卖方订货，这种订单中包括了所有交易条件，实际上就是递盘。许多公司喜欢用印制好的订货单，因为这样可以节省时间并保证不会有信息遗漏。但还是有一些公司使用订货信的形式订货。

The essential qualities of an order are accuracy and clarity. The buyer should try to present the details clearly, definitely and concisely. An order or an order-letter should:

Include full details of description, quantities and prices and quote article numbers, if any;

State mode of packing, port of destination and time of shipment;

Confirm the terms of payment as agreed upon in preliminary negotiations.

订单务必准确、清楚。买方应该清楚、确定、简洁地说明所有交易条件的细节。一个订单或订货信应该:

包括对货物的详细描述、订购的数量、价格,如果有货号,还要说明货号;

说明包装方式、目的港以及装船时间;

确认通过交易磋商双方约定的支付方式。

Orders placed always deserve gratitude. "First orders", that is, from new customers, should most certainly be acknowledged by letter, because there remains much to be done to promote the business relationship and convert the customer into a loyal one. The best tip for such a "thank you" letter is to be "selfless": write more about the customer than your own company. The letter should:

(1) express pleasure at receiving the order;

(2) add a favorable comment on the goods ordered;

(3) include an assurance of prompt and careful attention;

(4) draw attention to other products likely to be of interest;

(5) hope for further orders.

对于买方的订单,卖方应该表示感谢。特别是对于新客户的第一份订单,绝对应该回信致谢,因为双方之间的业务关系还有待进一步提升以便将此客户发展成为忠实客户。写作这种感谢函的技巧就是多谈论客户,少谈论自己的公司。这类信函的内容包括:

(1) 对买方的订单表示感谢;

(2) 对买方所订购的货物给予积极的评价;

(3) 保证及时、认真地处理买方的订单;

(4) 向买方介绍一些其可能感兴趣的其他商品;

(5) 希望买方继续订购。

However, there are times when sellers cannot accept buyer's orders because the goods required are not available or prices and specifications have been changed. In such circumstances, letters rejecting orders must be written with the utmost care and with an eye to goodwill and future business. It is advisable to recommend suitable substitutes, make counter-offers and persuade buyers to accept them.

但是，有时会由于买方所需的货物卖方没有现货供应或者是卖方的价格或商品规格已经进行了调整等，卖方不能接受买方的订单。在这种情况下，卖方一定要非常谨慎地回复买方拒绝买方的订单，同时还要着眼于维持正常的关系以及未来的业务发展。卖方可以在信中推荐替代品，或进行还盘并说服买方接受。

6.2　Model Letters Comments

6.2.1　Place a First Order

The United Import & Export Co. Ltd.
21 Fenton Street
Seattle, Australia
Tel: 2198797
Fax: 2167905

19 June 2007

Xinxin Import & Export Co. Ltd.
12 Chifeng Road
Shanghai, China

Dear sirs

Thank you for your letter of 12 June sending us sample tins of canned mushroom. We find both quality and prices satisfactory and are pleased to give you an order for the following items on the understanding that they will be supplied from current stock at the prices named:

Description: A1 Grade Canned Mushroom
A. 6 × 68 oz. Stem & Piece
B. 24 × 16 oz. Button Slice
C. 42 × 16 oz. Whole Slice

Quantity: (case)
A. 1000
B. 1500
C. 2000

Packing: by standard export case of 120 cans each

Unit price: CIF Seattle per case in US $
A. 180
B. 195
C. 210

Payment: 100% by irrevocable letter of credit issued through the HSBC, Seattle Branch and drawn at sight

Delivery: 1 month after receipt of the L/C

  We expect to find a good market for these canned mushroom and hope to place further and larger orders with you in the near future. Since this transaction is very important to both of us, we would like you to give it your best attention to satisfy us in every aspect.

  Please send us your confirmation of sales in duplicate.

Yours truly

Comments

  Paragraph 1: identify the order

  Paragraph 2: give all the relevant details

  Paragraph 3: express hope for future business

  Paragraph 4: ask for sales confirmation

  The letter is brief and to the point. Tabulation of the essential details relating to the order clarify the terms agreed to by both parties.

Notes

1. on the understanding that 以……为条件，如果

We place this order with you on the understanding that you will do everything possible to ensure punctual shipment.

如果你们尽一切可能确保按期装运，我们就向你们订货。

We are sending you a special offer for the following goods on the understanding that you will purchase from us not less than 5 000 pieces.

对于下述商品我们向贵公司报出了优惠的价格，但你们的订购量必须不少于 5000 件。

2. stock 库存，现货

supply from stock 现货供应，in stock 有现货，out of stock 断货

The exact size you want is out of stock at present.

你想要的那个型号目前断货了。

We are sorry to tell you that Quality No. 123 has run out of stock and will not be available until after the end of October. But we can offer Quality No. 124 as an alternative now in stock, which you will find slightly better and even more suitable for your market.

很遗憾，123 号货已经断货了，直到 10 月份才能有货。但我们可以供应 124 号货物，这种货有现货，而且你会发现该货质量更好，甚至更适合你地市场。

3. irrevocable letter of credit 不可撤消信用证

As for payment of this order, we will open an irrevocable letter of credit in your favor right away to cover the total CIF value of this order.

关于此次订单的付款，本公司将即刻开一张以你方为受益人的不可撤消信用证支付全部 CIF 价格。

4. issue 开立

issuing bank 开证行

Please see to it that the letter of credit is issued 30 days before the date of shipment.

请确保装船期前 30 天开出信用证。

We have received your letter of credit No. 243 issued by Bank of China,

Beijing.

兹收到你方由中国银行北京分行开立的 243 号信用证。

Please advise your issuing bank to amend the letter of credit and increase the amount by USD120.

请通知你方开证行修改信用证,将金额增加 120 美元。

5. at sight 即期

Inasmuch the amount involved is rather small, we agree to draw on you by our documentary draft at sight on collection basis, but this should not be regarded as a precedent.

由于金额很小,我们同意按托收办法向贵方开具即期跟单汇票,但只此一次,下不为例。

sight 见票即付的

sight bill (draft) 即期汇票

We'll draw a sight bill in favour of the Export Bank Singapore.

我们要开立一张以新加坡出口银行为收款人的即期汇票。

6. attention 执行,处理

Your early (careful) attention to this order will be appreciated.

如能尽快(认真)执行我方订单不胜感激。

Thank you for this order, which shall have our best attention.

感谢你方的订单,我们将非常认真地执行。

We expect your utmost attention to this transaction, which is very important to us, so that you will satisfy us in every way possible.

这笔交易对我们意义重大,我们希望你方能非常认真地执行这笔交易,各个方面都能让我们满意。

7. confirmation of sales 或 sales confirmation 销售确认书,是销售合同的简化形式,与销售合同具有同样的法律效力。通常,确认书是一式两份,由双方代表分别签字后各执一份。

For the above order, we enclose our Sales Confirmation No. 123 in duplicate. Please sign and return one copy for our file at your earliest convenience.

对于上述订单,我们现随函附上 123 号销售确认书一式两份。请尽快会签并退回我方一份以便我方存档。

8. in duplicate 一式两份

类似的表达方式还有：in triplicate 一式三份

       in quadruplicate 一式四份

       in quintuplicate 一式五份

       in sextuplicate 一式六份

6.2.2 Request an Increase in Order Quantity

            Phoenix Electronics Inc.
            12 Jianxiang Road
            Shenzhen, Guangdong
            China
            Tel: 2390443
            Fax: 2398502

            4 July 2007

J. B. Simpson Co. Ltd.
192 South Street
Sydney, Australia

Dear sirs

  Thank you for your order No. 761 for 600 units of DVD players of special specifications.

  Much as we should like to accept your order, we cannot see our way to do this. You will understand that the alteration of one of our standard sizes to your specifications means a substantial adjustment of our production methods which are entirely based on the automatic production line.

  It is obvious that this entails a considerable increase in labor cost and material. Our compromise proposal was based on a minimum order of 2 000 units, and it would raise the cost of production if we had to make all the complicated arrangements to manufacture 600 units to a different specification.

We hope that you will find it possible to increase your order to 2 000 units, otherwise we shall be compelled reluctantly to turn down the order.

We trust you will understand that it is not lack of cooperation and goodwill on our part but sheer necessity which makes it impossible for us to meet your wishes in this case.

Yours sincerely

Comments

 Paragraph 1: identify the reference

 Paragraph 2: refuse the order and give reasons

 Paragraph 3: propose the buyer to increase the quantity

 Paragraph 4: urge the buyer to make a decision

 Paragraph 5: regret being unable to meet the buyer's special requirements

The letter politely explains why the order cannot be fulfilled. It goes on to persuade the customer to increase the order quantity.

Notes

 1. much as we should like to accept your order

这是一个倒装的让步状语从句,意思是尽管我们愿意接受你方的订单。

 2. see one's way (clear) to do (或 to doing) 设法做某事

I hope you can see your way to settle the matter.

我希望你能设法解决这件事。

We cannot see our way to grant your request.

我们恐怕不能满足你的要求。

 3. substantial 大量的,充足的,足够的

We are afraid there is little prospect of doing business with you unless some substantial discount is allowed.

恐怕我们与你们做成生意的可能性不大,除非你们给我们足够大的折扣。

We believe you can afford us a substantial discount off your list prices, which we see are quoted net cash.

价目单上的价格是以现金支付的净价,我们相信你方还能在此基础上给我们很大的折扣。

4. entail 必需,需要

The work entails precision.

这工作需要精确性。

The alteration of delivery point entailed great increase in cost on the seller.

交货地点的变动使卖方承担的费用增加了。

5. be compelled to do 不得不做某事,被迫做某事

Upon unpacking this shipment, we found the goods were much inferior in quality to your counter sample and slightly different in shade also. We are compelled to write to you for compensation.

打开货物包装后,我们发现货物品质不如你方的对等样品,而且色泽也略有不同。我们不得不写信给你方要求赔偿。

Should you fail in your obligations, we shall be compelled to cancel the order.

如果你方不能履行合同义务,我们不得不撤消订单。

With reference to our order No. 35 executed by you, we have to inform you that owing to negligent packing, several bales were damaged to such an extent that we were compelled to dispose of them at a greatly reduced price.

关于你方执行的我们的 35 号订单,我们必须告诉你方,由于包装疏忽,几包货损坏如此严重以至我们必须大减价处理货物。

6. turn down 拒绝

The council turned down our suggestion.

委员会拒绝考虑我们的建议。

We are compelled to turn down any new fresh orders because we are heavily committed now.

因为承约过多,我们不得不拒绝任何新订单。

We have to turn down his proposal to act as our agent because we find through investigation that he is not reliable and his business status not good.

我们拒绝了他的代理申请,因为经过调查我们发现他不可靠而且生意状

况不好。

7. meet 满足(要求)等

Did our price meet your approval?

你接受我们的价格吗?

The successful companies must be those that readily meet the requirements of the clients.

成功的企业一定是很好地满足客户需求的企业。

Your performance in the competition did not meet our expectation.

你在竞赛中的表现没有达到我们的预期水平。

We enclose with pleasure a cheque for our payment of USD100 to meet your claim in full for the damage done to your Order No. 111.

我们随函寄去 100 美元的支票以全额偿付你方因 111 号订单的货物受损而提出的索赔。

6.2.3 Accept an Order

Phoenix Electronics Inc.
12 Jianxiang Road
Shenzhen, Guangdong
China
Tel: 2390443
Fax: 2398502

4 July 2007

J. B. Simpson Co. Ltd.
192 South Street
Sydney, Australia

Dear sir

It is a pleasure to receive your trial order No. LNG231 for 600 units of DVD players. And we are happy that you are one of our customers now.

For the above order, we are enclosing our Sales Confirmation No. 0012 in duplicate. Please sign and return one copy for our file at your earliest convenience.

We are expecting a letter of credit in our favor to be established immediately, upon receipt of which, we shall dispatch the shipment. Please be assured that we shall spare no effort to satisfy your wishes.

We hope this order will be just the first of many and that we may have many years of pleasant business relations together.

Yours faithfully

Comments

Paragraph 1: "thank you" line

Paragraph 2: enclose the Sales Confirmation and give the necessary instructions

Paragraph 3: confirm the payment method

Paragraph 4: end with a friendly message

The letter makes it clear that it refers to a trial order. It politely requests the buyer to sign the sales confirmation and open the relative letter of credit immediately.

Notes

1. trial order 试订购,试订购订单

If this trial order turns out satisfactory, we may consider stocking your brand.
如果试订购订单执行令我方满意,我们可能考虑购存你方品牌的货物。

If the present trial order is satisfactory (gives us satisfaction), we shall repeat it on a larger scale.
如果试订购订单执行令我方满意,我们将重复、大量订购。

2. sign and return one copy for our file 会签并退回我方一份以便我方存档

3. at your earliest convenience 在你们方便的时候尽快做

We now submit the above-mentioned claim amounting to US $250 as per Debit Note No. 222 attached, and shall be glad to receive settlement at your earliest convenience.

按照随函附上的 222 号借记通知，我们提出上述 250 美元的索赔，希望你们在方便的时候尽快支付给我们。

4. spare no effort 尽全力，同义的短语有 make every effort

We are extremely sorry this mistake occurred. You may be sure that we will make every effort to see that it does not happen again.

对发生这样的错误我们深表歉意，您放心我们会尽一切努力防止这样的事情再次发生。

5. We hope this order will be just the first of many. 就是表示希望双方之间的业务长期发展

类似的表达方式有：

We hope our products will satisfy you and you will let us have the chance of serving you again.

And it is our hope that this first business will be the beginning of a long and happy association.

We hope our goods prove satisfactory to you and ask you to allow us to serve you again.

We also hope that this first transaction will lead to happy, lasting business relations between you and us.

6.2.4　Decline an Order

Oriental Computer Inc.
90 West Road
Balham
London, UK
Tel: 349876
Fax: 342904

2 September 2003

Lee Electronics Co.
21 Top Road
Singapore

Dear sirs

    Thank you very much for your order for our computers.

    We sincerely appreciate your interest and wish that we could fill your order. However, as a manufacturer, we sell through our agents, and not directly.

    We regret, therefore, that we must return your check with the request that you either visit or telephone our agent in your area, who will be glad to deliver your computers at the fixed price.

    The name, address, and telephone number of our agent in your area is Rooter Inc., 55 Main Street, Manchester, telephone: 507-643-2112.

                                            Yours sincerely

Comments

    Paragraph 1: "thank you" line
    Paragraph 2: express regret and give a brief explanation for declining the order
    Paragraph 3 and 4: provide useful information

    This letter gives a clear and adequate explanation for the inability to fill the customer's order and manifests the manufacturer's sincere desire to help users of its products.

Notes

    1. fill (the order) 执行(订单), 同义词有 execute, carry out

    Owing to the energy shortage, we fear we may be unable to fill your order before January 10.

    由于能源缺乏,本公司恐怕不能在1月10日以前执行贵公司的订单。

    We were unable to fill the order for immediate delivery due to short supply of raw materials.

由于原材料短缺,我们不能执行立即交货的订单。

We can fill your order for 300 pieces of bicycles immediately.

我们马上就可以执行你方 300 辆自行车的订货单。

We thank you for your order for 5 000 yards cotton piece goods but regret that we are unable to execute the order from stock.

感谢贵公司向我方订购 5 000 码棉布,但是我们不能以现货交付。

2. directly 与 direct 都做副词时,意思都是"直接地",但含义有区别。

direct 表示位置直接移动,中间不停留。

He flew direct to Shanghai. 他直接飞往上海。

directly 是表示事物之间的直接关系。

The production schedule is not directly affected by lack of working staff.

工人数量不足并没有直接影响生产进度。

3. deliver ($v.$) 交付

As you have failed to deliver these goods on the date asked, we are obliged, very regretfully, to cancel this order.

因为贵公司未能于要求的日期交货,我们不得不取消订单。

Under CIF term, the seller has the obligation to deliver the goods to the named port of destination in specified time.

在 CIF 术语下,卖方有义务在规定时间在指定的目的港交付货物。

A postman is a man employed to deliver letters and parcels.

邮差就是雇来投递信件及包裹的人。

delivery ($n.$) 交货,交货期

You will understand that we would lose much of our chance of selling them if their delivery were put off any further.

你应该清楚,如果再推迟交货我们将这些货物销售出去的机会就很小了。

Owing to the rush of orders from your country, all the mills will be fully engaged for some time to come. In these circumstances, the price we have offered is the very best and the delivery is the nearest possible.

由于来自贵国的订单激增,所有的工厂未来一段时间都是满负荷运转。这种情况下,我们报出的价格已经是最好的了,交货期也是最近的。

6.3 Specimen Letters

6.3.1 Place an Order

Dear sirs

As a result of our recent exchange of faxes, we wish to confirm our purchase from you of 500 metric tons of Trust brand white cement. The following terms and conditions will apply.

Price: US800 per metric ton net shipping weight CIF Liverpool

Packing: in paper bags of 25 kg net each

Quality: against the seller's own guarantee that the goods conform to the relevant British Standard

Payment: by confirmed and irrevocable letter of credit in your favor, payable by draft at sight

We are pleased that this first transaction with your company has come to a successful conclusion. We look forward to a continuing and mutually beneficial trade between our companies.

Yours truly

● **Activities for comprehension**

1. How does the buyer usually give an order to the seller?
2. In a letter confirming an order, what particulars are to be repeated?

6.3.2 Acknowledge the first order

Dear sirs

We are pleased to receive your order of June 24 for black silk and welcome you as one of our customers.

For goods ordered we require payment to be made by a confirmed and irrevocable letter of credit payable at sight upon presentation of shipping documents. Please let us know immediately whether you agree to our terms. As soon as we receive your reply in the affirmative, we shall confirm supply of the silk at the prices stated in your letter and arrange for dispatch by the first available steamer upon receipt of your L/C.

When the goods reach you, we feel confident you will be completely satisfied with them—at the prices offered they represent exceptional value.

As you may not be aware of the wide range of goods we deal in, we are enclosing a copy of our catalogue and hope that our handling of the first order of yours will lead to further business between us and mark the beginning of a happy working relationship.

Yours sincerely

● **Activities for comprehension**

1. Why should a first order be acknowledged by letter?

2. In reply to a first order, what information may the seller convey besides acknowledgement?

6.3.3 Confirm a Repeat Order

Dear sirs

Thank you for your fax duplicating your order for 500 dozen bed sheets.

Although prevailing prices are somewhat higher, in view of our long-standing relationship we are prepared to accept the order on the same terms as before and are sending you herewith our Sales Confirmation No. LG-239 in duplicate. Please sign and return one copy to us for our file.

We are pleased to learn that a letter of credit in our favor will be established immediately. We wish to point out that the stipulations in the relevant credit should strictly conform to the terms stated in our sales confirmation in order to avoid possible delay upon receipt of the credit.

We appreciate your cooperation and look forward to receiving your further orders.

Yours truly

● **Activities for comprehension**

1. What are the necessities of writing a letter to confirm a buyer's order?
2. In a letter confirming an order, what particulars are to be repeated?

6.3.4   Decline an Order

Dear sirs

Thank you for your order No. GL-197 for black silk which we received today.

We regret that, owing to a shortage of stocks, we are unable to fill your order.

Moreover, our manufacturers cannot undertake to entertain your order for future delivery owing to the uncertain availability of raw materials. We will, however, contact you by e-mail once supply improves.

In the meantime, please feel free to send us your specific enquiries for other types of textiles. You can be assured of our best attention at all times.

Yours sincerely

● **Activities for comprehension**

1. What may be the causes for a seller to decline the buyer's order?
2. How to write a letter rejecting the buyer's order?

6.3.5   Request for Order Amendment

Dear sirs

Your purchase order dated May 29, 2007 has been received by our firm, but cannot be filled without the inclusion of a purchase order number.

We are requesting that you either provide us with a number for your order or issue a new purchase order for the items you have requested.

To insure our quick delivery, please comply with this request as soon as possible.

Yours faithfully

● **Activities for comprehension**

1. What are the basic requirements on content of the purchase order?

6.4　Summary

The buyer and seller may come to terms after discussion and negotiation, after which the buyer may send an order to the seller to signify his purchasing intention. An order in essence is a formal request from a buyer for a certain quantity of specific goods at a certain price to be fulfilled within a certain period of time. An order should include details of trade terms about description of the goods, specification, quantity, unit price, total amount, packing, terms of payment and shipment date. To avoid misunderstandings and troubles in future, you should keep the principles of clarity and accuracy in your letter. Upon receipt of an order, you should write a letter of acknowledgement. If you accept the order, you should reiterate the main terms in your letter. If you are unable to accept the order, you should reply in time. In such a letter, you could propose some substitutes or offer other help to protect future business.

买卖双方经过磋商、谈判，就交易条件达成一致后，买方向卖方寄出订单，表示购买意愿。订单实际上就是买方请求卖方在规定的时间内按约定的价格提供约定数量的某种货物。订单上面详细列出品名、规格、数量、单价、总值、包装、支付条件、装运期等主要交易条件。为了避免日后出现误解和麻烦，订购函的内容必须清楚、准确。卖方收到订单后应及时回复。卖方接受订单，最好在回复时重申订单条款。如果卖方拒绝买方的订单，及时写回绝订单的信，并且可以在信中推荐替代品或提供其他帮助以维护日后的业务关系。

6.5　Useful Expressions

1. We are pleased to place our order for 2 metric tons of corn oil with you if you can guarantee shipment from Seattle to Keelung by May 10.

如果你方能够保证在5月10日前将货物从西雅图运到基隆，我们将很高兴向你方订购2公吨玉米油。

2. We are pleased to make a trial order for 1 000 units of your laser printers. If these printers prove satisfactory, we shall send you regular orders.

我们愿意试订购1 000台激光打印机。如果这些打印机令我们满意的话,我们将长期订购。

3. The materials supplied must be absolutely waterproof, and we place our order subject to this guarantee.

所供应的材料必须绝对防水。我们订货的前提就是你们保证这一点。

4. Your prompt attention to this order will be appreciated.

如果你方能够立即处理此订单,我们不胜感激。

5. Your order is booked and will be handled with great care. Please open the relevant L/C, which must reach here one month before the date of shipment.

我们接受你方订单,并将认真处理。请开立相关信用证,信用证必须在装船期之前1个月开到。

6. With reference to your letter of October 14, we have pleasure in informing you that we have booked your order for 500 units of DVD players. We are sending you our Sales Confirmation No. 4S56 in duplicate, one copy of which please sign and return for our file.

关于你方10月14日来函,我们很高兴通知你方我们已经接受了你方订购500台DVD机的订单。现正寄给你方4S56号销售确认书一式两份,其中一份签字后请退回,以便我方存档。

7. Thank you for your order No. THG342. We have accepted the terms you proposed. However, this concession is exceptional and future orders can be executed only on our normal trade terms.

感谢你方THG342号订单。我们接受你方所提出的条件。但这次让步是特例,以后的订单还要按我们正常的贸易条件执行。

8. While thanking you for your order, we have to explain that supplies of raw materials are becoming difficult to obtain and we have no alternative but to decline your order.

非常感谢你方的订单,但我们要向你方说明,由于原材料紧张,我们现在别无选择只能拒绝你方订单。

9. The chief difficulty in accepting your orders now is the heavy backlog of

commitments. But you may rest assured that as soon as we are able to accept new orders, we shall give priority to yours.

现在接受你方订单最大的困难是我们承约过多,订单大量积压。但是,你们放心,我们一旦可以接受新订单了,将优先考虑你方订单。

10. Thank you for your order No. TGH 346. However, wages and prices of materials have risen considerably in addition to the increase of taxes and we are reluctantly compelled to adjust our prices in order to cover these increases. We regret our inability to accept the order at the prices we quoted before.

感谢你方 TGH 346 号订单。但是,由于工资和原材料价格大幅度上涨、税收增加,我们为了支付更高的成本不得不提高价格。很遗憾,我们不能按照过去的报价接受你方的订单。

6.6 Reading Materials

6.6.1

Dear sirs

We appreciate your immediate response dated June 20 to our request for a 5% reduction in price and through your full cooperation we have been able to confirm the following order with you at your revised price:

"Thirty metric tons of Bitter Apricot Kernels at US $1 750 per metric ton CFR Qingdao for shipment in August."

Enclosed please find our Purchase Confirmation No. 231 in duplicate. Please sign and return one copy for our records as soon as possible.

We are arranging for the establishment of the relative letter of credit with the Bank of China, Sweden, and shall let you know by fax as soon as it is opened.

As we are in urgent need of the goods, we find it necessary to stress the importance of making punctual shipment within the validity of the L/C; any delay in shipment would be harmful to our future business.

Yours sincerely

6.6.2

Dear sirs

In reply to your letter dated March 3, we have pleasure in confirming your order for 1 000 sets of transistor radios. Enclosed you will find Sales Confirmation No. 2001 in duplicate, a copy of which is to be signed and returned to us for our file.

It is understood that the letter of credit covering the above goods will be opened immediately. Please make sure that the stipulations in the relative credit are in exact conformity with the terms set forth in our sales confirmation so as to avoid subsequent amendments. Upon receipt of your L/C, we will effect shipment of your order without delay.

We appreciate your cooperation and hope that this transaction will pave the way to future dealings between us.

Yours truly

6.6.3

Dear Mr. Chapman

We thank you for your order of October 5.

However, we have to inform you that we cannot grant you the discount of 15%. As we stated in our letter of September 20, we can not possibly make a discount exceeding 10%. Our computer is so fine and our profit margin is so small that it is impossible for us to make any further concession.

If you really take into consideration our serious situation, you will agree, we wish, to the 10% discount we have offered. We would ask you, therefore, to confirm this as soon as possible because we can guarantee prompt shipment if we can start on your immediate order. We promise you that we will give your order our best attention.

Yours sincerely

6.6.4

Dear Mr. Partmell

We have received your letter of October 14 and regret that our counteroffer was refused.

As your products are very much appreciated by our local customers and there is a high demand at our market, we are very desirous of concluding this transaction with you. For the purpose of strengthening our friendship and cooperation, we agree to accept your offer:

DVD players US $200 per unit CIF Karachi with an order of 5 000 units.

We are very much pleased to have been able to transact this order with you after exchange letters in the past two months and we are now looking forward to your sales confirmation for this order so as to enable us to open the L/C duly.

As your make is comparatively famous here, the sales will be somewhat quicker. If this first order is executed satisfactorily, we shall be able to place repeat orders with you soon.

Yours sincerely

6.6.5

Dear sirs

We take pleasure in acknowledging your letter of May 14, informing us that you intend to place a duplicate order with us for 100 metric tons of polished rice.

While we appreciate your intention, we are regretful that we cannot entertain any fresh orders for the goods mentioned above at present, due to heavy demand for the goods both domestically and abroad.

However, we will keep your inquiry before us and, as soon as we are in a position to accept new orders, we will contact you with the least possible delay.

Yours sincerely

6.6.6

Dear Sirs

Thank you for your sample of bicycles. As we find the quality and the price satisfactory, we are pleased to enclose our trial order No. JI246.

Please kindly send us your sales confirmation by return mail, so that we can issue the L/C in your favor for a prompt shipment accordingly.

Look forward to hearing from you soon.

Yours truly

6.6.7

Dear Sirs

Your quotation has been accepted and we are glad to place our order No. 9711 as follows:

FOREVER BRAND BICYCLE:

YE803 26'	USD66.00	per set	CIFC5 Copenhagen	600 sets
TE600 24'	USD71.00	per set	CIFC5 Copenhagen	600 sets

Total Amount: US $82,200.00

Assortment of colors: Blue、green、red、purple and white
　　　　　　　　　　equally assorted with single color in one container

Shipment: To be effected before the end of May 2001

Other terms and conditions remain the same as we agreed in our previous mails.

As this is the first transaction between us, we will be pleased if you make the inspection and ship the goods on time for the urgent need. When the goods are ready for shipment, please send us shipping advice by e-mail to facilitate making the necessary arrangement.

We are looking forward to your sales confirmation and thank you in advance.

Yours faithfully

Exercises

I. Fill in the blanks with your choices.

1. This order _____ the sample you sent us on March 24.

   a) is placed on   b) places on   c) is placed at   d) places at

2. We hope you will give your usual best attention _____ this order.

   a) for carrying out   b) to the execution of

   c) by filling out   d) in the performance of

3. We have decided to place a trial order for the following, _____ stated in your letter.

   a) with the terms   b) on the terms

   c) by the terms   d) at the terms

4. _____ we would like to supply you with the product, we are unable to fill you order owing to the heavy backlog of commitments.

   a) As much as   b) Much as   c) Very much   d) As

5. We must apologize _____ you _____ being unable to fill your present order.

   a) to...on   b) to...as   c) to...about   d) to...for

6. We have accepted your order No. 234. Please open the relevant L/C, _____ here two weeks prior to the date of shipment.

   a) which must reach   b) when must reach

   c) it reaches   d) that reaches

7. We are enclosing our latest catalogue _____ some of the items may be of interest to you.

   a) at the hope that   b) by the hope that

   c) in the hope that   d) for the hope that

8. The _____ order is given strictly on the condition that shipment must be made not later than the first day of May.

   a) enclosing   b) enclosed   c) enclosure   d) enclose

9. We have received orders _____ US $1,000,000 since the new prod-

uct was introduced to the market.

    a) amount for   b) amount to   c) account for   d) amounting to

    10. That trading company in Tokyo did consider _____ the transaction with you.

    a) concluding   b) to conclude   c) conclude   d) conclusion

    II. Fill in each blank space with the word that fits naturally.

Dear sirs

    For your first-time order, I want to thank you on _____ of the company. This is your initial order and I know of no greater kick a sales manager can get _____ the beginning of business with a _____ customer.

    The signing of an order is an expression of confidence, and I want you to know that we are fully aware of the _____ we have for maintaining that _____.

    The most important thing _____ the buyer of any product is the character of the supplying organization, its resources, its facilities, its reputation, and its standards of service.

    You have _____ your disposal every facility of our company. We would like to be useful to you _____ the mere necessities of business transaction.

    We appreciate your business. We want to continue to deserve it.

                                                                 Yours sincerely

    III. Fill in the blanks with proper preposition words.

    1. We thank you for your sales confirmation No. C0014 _____ response to our order No. 2411 for 400 sets of bicycle.

    2. Please make sure that there is no difference _____ quality between the samples and the actual goods.

    3. And the color and package should be identical _____ the sample.

    4. Our L/C will be issued _____ receiving your confirmation.

    5. Reference is made _____ your offer dated March 12, and we are pleased to advise you that we shall be in the position to place an order for 50 000

pieces of pipe fittings for a rush shipment.

6. We wish to place with you a repeat order _____ 500 dozens of the same style and sizes.

7. If the goods are not available _____ stock, we would be grateful if you could advise us of replacement goods.

8. This does not include a postal charge of US $20 _____ overseas subscribers.

9. They may be able to give you the quality you desire _____ a fair price.

10. We regret very much that we are unable to supply the desired goods due _____ excessive demand.

IV. Put the following into an English business letter in a proper form.

敬启者：

你公司十一月五日的报价单和真丝女成衣样品都已收到，谢谢。我公司对品质和价格均感满意，并乐意按你方报价单所提条件订购下列货物：

每打 80 美元的小号真丝女成衣 5 打；

每打 120 美元的中号真丝女成衣 7 打；

每打 160 美元的大号真丝女成衣 4 打。

以上价格均为成本加保险费加运费到伦敦价。只有在十二月十五日前将货运到的条件下，我公司才订购上述真丝女成衣。逾期不到货，我公司保留取消订单拒收货物的权利。

我公司通常的付款条件是 60 天付款交单。请告你公司是否同意这一条件。

此致

敬礼

Jill

● Skills Practice

A. Write a letter for Marks & Spencer Co. 14 Maple Street, London to Chinese supplier, China Light Industrial Products Import & Export Corp., Beijing Branch, confirming an order for 1 000 DVD players. The letter should be written according to the instructions mentioned below:

1. 谢谢对方 4 月 4 日报价和寄来的样品;
2. 认为对方的 DVD 机品质优良,价格合理;
3. 随信附寄 1 000 台 DVD 机的定单一份,定单号为 LK150;
4. 要求 6 月底前交货,不可转船;
5. 由于客户急需该货,希望尽快交货。

B. Write a letter to your customer, acknowledging receipt of his order, but regret being unable to accept it at the prices quoted previously. Quote your current prices and ask for your customer's opinion.

C. Write a letter for Galaxy Electronics Co. Ltd. whose digital camera division has received a big order from an Indian company, which the division is unable to supply because of insufficient production capacity.

Unit 7　Foreign Sales Contracts

Learning Objectives

After learning this unit, you should:

✍ Know the structure of foreign sales contracts(了解商务合同的结构)

✍ Know the main clauses in a foreign sales contract(了解外销合同的主要条款)

✍ Know the stylistic features of foreign sales contracts(了解商务合同的语言风格)

7.1　Introduction

Once the exporter and his client have agreed to the deal, they will need to draw up a contract to cover the transaction. In essence, this means that one party makes an offer and the other accepts it. The arrangements governing this exchange constitute the contract and can be legally enforced.

一旦出口商与客户达成了交易,他们就需要起草交易合同。实际上,也就是一方做出报盘,另一方接受。与交易有关的安排构成合同内容并具有法律效力。

In international trade, however, contractual arrangements can be much more prone to complications than domestic ones. Exporters and their customers are usually from different countries. Language barriers may cause misunderstandings. Cultural and geographical impediments may crop up. Words may have different meanings in different places. Most important, they both may be used to different laws and business practices. This is why international business contracts must be precise, specific and all-encompassing. This will go a long way toward reducing misunderstandings, misconceptions and disputes.

但是,国际贸易合同要比国内贸易合同复杂得多。出口商和客户常常是来自不同的国家。语言障碍可能会引起一些误解。文化和地理障碍也可能带来问题。在不同的地方,同样的词语可能代表不同的含义。更关键的是,他们可能运用于不同的法律和商业惯例。这就是为什么国际商务合同必须要准确、具体和周全。而要减少误解、错误的概念和纠纷还需要做很多工作。

Trade contracts therefore should be prepared or at least reviewed by a lawyer specializing in International Trade. It will cost you some money; sometimes it may cost a lot of money depending on the complicity of the contract. However, it still would be a fraction of the amount of the goods you are selling and can save you a fortune in the case of a dispute and legal action.

所以,应该请国际贸易方面的律师准备合同,或者至少应该让他们审查一下合同。虽然,这可能会造成一定的花费,甚至有时由于合同内容复杂而造成很大的花费。但是,与货价相比,那只是一小部分,而且万一发生纠纷和法律诉讼,却能节省一笔开支。

7.2 Components of a Foreign Sales Contract

No one contract serves as a model for all export situations. You'll find that sometimes the export contract may be just a one-page document and sometimes-a very complicated more than 10 pages' booklet including several appendices, additional conditions, etc. There are, however, minimum general requirements for an export contract. A contract should contain the following items in the order mentioned: the title, contract proper, the signature and attached schedules, if any.

不存在一种适用于所有出口业务的合同范本。可能你会发现,有的出口合同只有一页,但有的出口合同非常复杂,有10多页,而且还有附录、补充条件等。但是,出口合同有其基本要求。按先后顺序,合同应该包括下列几个部分:首部、正文、签名,如果有附件,最后是附件。

1. The title

The type of the contract is indicated here, like Sales Contract, or Leasing Contract, all typed in capital letters. Under the title the number of the contract is typed.

SALES CONTRACT
No. CHF-324

1. 首部

在此说明合同的类型,如销售合同、租赁合同等,所有字母必须大写。合同类型名称下面是合同编号。

2. The contract proper

2.1 Opening paragraph

The opening paragraph includes the complete corporate or personal names of the parties in the contract, followed by their nationalities, full addresses, date of the contract, as well as indications of whether they are the buyer or the seller. The legal addresses of the parties serve three purposes: they help to identify the parties concerned; they can be used as the basis for determining the litigation body in case of litigation; they facilitate exchange of correspondence between the parties. But note that the addresses refer to the principal places of business rather than those of their branches or affiliates, the permanent addresses rather than temporary addresses. The nationalities of the legal representatives indicate the countries to which the representatives belong, and to whose laws their actions are subject. Examples of the opening paragraph are provided as follows:

2. 正文

2.1 开头

开头应该说明合同当事人的完整的法人名称或个人名字,还要说明国籍、详细地址、签约日期以及各个当事人的身份。写明当事人的法定地址有三个意义:可以帮助识别当事人,在发生诉讼时可以作为确定裁决机构的依据,便于当事人之间进行联络。但要注意,所写的地址应该是当事人的主要地址,而不是它的分支机构或加盟商的地址,应该是永久地址而不是临时地址。法人代表的国籍表明了该法人代表是哪个国家的,以及他们的行为是受哪国法律约束的。开头段落的范例如下:

> This contract is made this 23rd of June, 2003 by and between Hansen Ltd. (hereinafter called the Buyer) with its registered office at 23 Jefferson Street, New York, USA and Johns Industrial Corporation (hereinafter called the Seller) with its office at 12 Auzhou Street, Shanghai, China. Through friendly discussion, both parties have hereby agreed on the terms and conditions stipulated hereunder...

Hansen Ltd. (hereinafter referred to as the Buyer) as one party and Johns Industrial Corporation (hereinafter referred to as the Seller) as the other party agree to sign by their authorized representatives, as a result of friendly negotiation, the present Contract under the following terms and conditions.

THIS CONTRACT, made and entered into in (place of signature) on this _____ day of _____, 20 _____, by and between (name of one party) a corporation duly organized and existing under the laws of (name of country) with its domicile at (address) (hereinafter referred to as party A), and (name of the other party), a company incorporated and existing under the laws of (name of country) with its domicile at (address) (hereinafter referred to as party B).

WITNESS THAT:

WHEREAS Party A has been a leading trading company in the field of the said products and is willing to arrange the manufacture, assembly and marketing of the said Products, and

WHEREAS both parties are desirous to establish a joint venture company to manufacture, assemble and market the said products.

NOW, THEREFORE, in consideration of the premises and mutual covenants herein contained, the parties hereto agrees as follows:

2.2　Terms and conditions

2.2　正文条款

In a legal contract, all the terms and conditions agreed upon by the two parties are logically arranged in different articles. These articles may include:

在法律合同当中,双方达成的所有条件都必须按照一定的逻辑写在不同的条款中,这些条款包括:

The name, category and scope of the object of the contract, state the product technical name, if any.

合同标的物的名称、种类和范围等,如果有专业名称,还要说明专业名称。

The technical conditions, quality, applicable national or international standards, specifications, specific buyer requirements; and quantities of the object of the contract; sizes in which the product is to be supplied (if relevant).

产品的技术要求、品质、适用的国家或国际标准、规格、买方具体的要求以及数量,如果有必要,说明产品的型号。

Packaging, labeling and marking. Note all packaging, labeling and marking requirements in the contract.

包装、标签和标志。合同中要写明所有的包装、标签和标志要求。

The time limit, place, and ways of delivery, also state whether the period of delivery will run from the date of the contract, from the date of notification of the issue of an irrevocable letter of credit, or from the date of receipt of the notice of issuance of the import licence by the seller, state whether the parties to the contract have agreed on partial shipment or transshipment. Indicate the port of transshipment and the number, if any, of partial shipments agreed.

交货的时间、地点和方式,还要说明交货期是从合同签订之日起计算,还是从不可撤消信用证的开立通知日起计算,亦或是从卖方收到进口许可证开立通知之日起计算;说明双方是否同意分批装运和转船运输。说明转运港和分批装运的批次。

The price terms, amount to be paid; state the trade terms, based on one of the Incoterms 2000. State the total contract value in words and figures, and specify the currency.

贸易术语和合同金额,选择《国际贸易术语解释通则2000》中的一种贸易术语,以文字和数字两种方式说明合同总金额,并规定币种。

Discounts and commissions. Specify the amount of discount or commission to be paid and by whom (by the exporter or by the importer). Stipulate the basis of calculation of commission and rate to be applied. Discount or commission rates may or may not be included in the export price agreed upon by the exporter and importer.

佣金和折扣。规定应付的佣金或折扣的金额,以及由谁支付(进口商还是出口商)。规定计算佣金的价格基础和佣金率。进出口商约定的价格中可能含佣金或折扣,也可能不含。

Ways of payment, and various types of additional duties and charges. Clarify responsibility for all taxes. The prices quoted by the seller may be inclusive of taxes, duties, and charges. Levies in the country of importation (if any) may be the buyer's responsibility. Address payment terms for exchange rate fluctuations as well.

支付方式以及各种税、费支付,规定所有税费的分担问题。卖方的报价中可能包含了所有税费。进口国的税费可能由买方负担。还要考虑到汇率波动的处理。

Inspection. State the nature, manner and focus of the envisaged inspection, as well as the inspection agency. A number of goods are now subject to pre-shipment inspection by designated agencies, and foreign buyers may stipulate their own inspection agencies and conditions for inspection. Example:

> Before delivery the manufacturer should make a precise and overall inspection of the goods regarding quality, quantity, specification and performance and issue the certificate indicating the goods in conformity with the stipulation of the contract. The certificates are one part of the documents presented to the bank for negotiation of the payment and should not be considered as final regarding quality, quantity, specification and performance. The manufacturer should include the inspection written report in the Inspection Certificate of Quality, stating the inspection particulars.

商品检验。规定检验的性质、方式、重点内容以及检验机构。现在有许多货物是由指定机构做装船前检验,国外的买主可以自己指定检验机构和检验条件。

Insurance. A contract should provide for the insurance of goods against loss, damage, or destruction during transportation. Specify the type of risk covered and the extent of coverage.

保险。合同中应当规定对货物运输过程中可能发生的破损、灭失进行投保。规定投保的险种和金额。

Claim. A contract should include provisions defining the circumstances which would entitle either party to the contract to claim against the other party. And also the time limit and basis for claim right, even methods for settlement, should be provided.

> Any discrepancy about quality should be presented within 30 days after the arrival of the goods at the port of destination; any discrepancy about quantity should be presented within 15 days after the arrival of the goods at the port of destination, both of which cases should be on the strength of the certificates issued by the related surveyor. If the Seller is liable he should send the reply together with the proposal for settlement within 20 days after receiving the said discrepancy.
>
> Any discrepancy on the shipped goods should be put forward within 30 days after the arrival of the vessel carrying the goods at the port of destination and the Buyer should present the Survey Report issued by the Surveyor agreed by the Seller. If the goods have been processed the Buyer will loss the right to claim. The Seller shall not settle the claim within the responsibility of the Insurance Company or Ship Company.

索赔。合同中应该规定合同任何一方在哪些情况下对对方有索赔的权利。并要规定索赔的时限和依据,以及赔偿的方式。

Force majeure or excuse for non-performance of contract. Include provisions in the contract defining the circumstances which would relieve partners of their liability for non-performance of the contract. Such provisions are called force majeure and are intended to identify the relief which may be available to either party to the contract should supervening circumstances occur during the period of validity of the contract. Example:

> Any event or circumstance beyond control shall be regarded as Force Majeure but not restricted to fire, wind, flood, earthquake, explosion, rebellion, epidemic, quarantine and segregation. In case either party that encounters Force Majeure fails to fulfill the obligation under the contract, the other party should extend the performance time by period equal to the time that Fore Majeure will last.
>
> If the Force Majeure last over 6 months, the two parties of the contract should settle the case of continuing the contract by friendly negotiation as soon as possible. Should the two parties fail to reach an agreement will be settled by arbitration according to Clause 12 of the contract thereof.

不可抗力。合同中界定了当事人可以免除履行合同义务的情况。对这种情况加以规定的条款被称为不可抗力条款,是用以明确在合同执行过程中特殊事件的发生可以使任何一方当事人免除合同义务。

Arbitration. Include an arbitration clause to facilitate amicable and quick settlement of disputes or differences that may arise between the parties. Example:

> All disputes arising out of the performance of, or relating to this Contract, shall be settled amicably through negotiation. In case no settlement can be reached through negotiation, the case shall then be submitted to the China International Economic and Trade Arbitration Commission for arbitration in accordance with its arbitration rules. The arbitral award is final and binding upon both parties.

仲裁。为了迅速、友好地解决合同当事人之间的纠纷和分歧,在合同中可以规定仲裁条款。

Remedial action. As defaults in contractual obligations by any of the parties can occur, it is always advisable to include in the sale or purchase contract certain specific remedial actions. These remedial actions should reflect the mandatory provisions of the law applicable to the contract.

救济措施。合同的任何一方可能会不履约,所以,应该在买卖合同中规定具体的救济措施。所规定的救济措施应该反映合同所适用的法律的强制规定。

Applicable law. State the law of the country which is to govern the contract.

适用的法律。说明合同适用哪个国家的法律。

Sample

Article 1 COMMODITY

At the request of the Buyer, the Seller agrees to supply the Buyer with the "Sunshine" Brand Umbrellas.

Article 2 QUANTITY AND PRICE

The total number of "Sunshine" umbrellas is 50 000 with each at the price of 4 dollars CIF New York. Therefore the total amount is US $200 000 (say two hundred thousand US dollars).

Article 3 PACKING

All umbrellas shall be packed as per manufacturer's standard.

Article 4 SHIPMENT

All goods shall be shipped on or before July 23, 2003 subject to receipt of L/

C by the end of May. Immediately after loading is completed, the Seller shall notify by fax the number of contract, quantity and name of vessel to the Buyer.

Article 5   TERMS OF PAYMENT

The Buyer shall open a confirmed, irrevocable, payable at sight letter of credit through a bank to the Bank of China in favor of the Seller within 20 days after signing the contract. The Bank of China shall claim the reimbursement by T/T on behalf of the Seller within 3 days when the following shipping documents submitted by the Seller are found in order.

1. Clean bill of lading: non-negotiable duplicate.
2. Commercial invoice: duplicate.
3. Packing list: triplicate.
4. Quality guarantee: duplicate.

Article 6   INSURANCE

Insurance of the goods covering FPA shall be effected by the buyer at 110% of the invoice value.

Article 7   TAXES AND DUTIES

All taxes and duties due inside the Seller's country to which the Seller is liable in connection with this contract shall be borne by the Seller. All taxes and duties due after the goods on board of the carrying vessel and to which the buyer is liable in connection with the contract, shall be borne by the Buyer.

All banking charges shall be borne by the applicant respectively.

Article 8   INSPECTION AND CLAIMS

It is mutually agreed that the Inspection Certificate of quality and quantity issued by the China Import and Export Commodity Inspection Bureau at the port of shipment shall be part of the documents to be presented for negotiation under the relevant L/C.

The seller guarantees that the goods supplied under the present contract are currently manufactured in the Seller's country, the quality and performances of the contracted goods are in conformity with the current technical specifications laid down by the Johns Industrial Corporation.

The Buyer shall have the right to inspect the quality and quantity of the goods. The inspection fee shall be borne by the Buyer. Should the quality and/or quantity be found not in conformity with that of the contract, the Buyer shall put forward claims on shortage within 3 months after the goods arrived at the port of destination, and claims on quality within 12 months with certificate issued by the commodity inspection department or inspection record relating the quality being presented to the Seller. The Seller is entitled to reinspect the goods. The Seller shall only take the responsibility for replacing the items due to faulty material or bad workmanship without any extra charges to the Buyer. Other than this, no matter what reason is given for the quality claims, the Seller shall not take the responsibility.

Article 9　SHIPPING MARK AND PORT OF DESTINATION

　　Shipping mark：ZheGan 78

　　Port of destination：New York

Article 10　FORCE MAJEURE

　　Should the Seller fail to deliver the contracted goods or effect shipment in time by reason of war, flood, fire, storm, or any other causes beyond their control, the time of shipment might be duly extended or a part or whole of the contract be cancelled without any liability attached to the Seller, but the Seller has to furnish the Buyer with a certificate attesting such event or events.

Article 11　ARBITRATION

　　Any dispute arising from or relating to this contract shall be settled amicably through negotiation. In case no settlement can be reached through negotiation, the case shall be submitted to China International Economic and Trade Arbitration Association, Beijing, for arbitration in accordance with its rules of procedures. The arbitral award is final and binding upon both parties. The fees for arbitration shall be borne by the losing party unless otherwise specified.

　　2.3　Last paragraph

　　The last paragraph stipulates the number of original copies, the language used in the contract, the term of validity and possible extension of the contract.

　　最后一段说明合同正本的份数,合同所使用的语言,合同的有效期以及可能进行合同展期的情况。

> Any and all notices and communications in connection with the Contract shall be written in the English Language.
>
> The present contract is drawn in duplicate in the Chinese and English languages, both two texts being equally authentic. In case of any divergence of interpretation, the Chinese text shall prevail.
>
> This contract is executed in two counterparts each in Chinese and English, each of which shall deemed equally authentic. This Contract is in _____ copies, effective since being signed/sealed by both parties.

3. The signature

The signing of the contract indicates the agreement of both parties to the terms and conditions of the contract. Above or below the signatures, type "The Buyer" and "The Seller". The example is offered below:

The Buyer	The Seller
Hansen Ltd, USA	Johns Industrial Corporation, China
Manager	Manager
John Harbor	张岚

3. 签名

签署了合同意味着双方同意了合同中的所有条款。在签名的上方或下方需要打印"买方"和"卖方"字样。

7.3 Stylistic Features of Foreign Sales Contracts

1. precision

The writer of the contract must say precisely what he means, no more and no less. Saying precisely what one means is not easy. You may see it from the following two examples.

合同的写作者必须做到表达准确,文字恰当。要准确地表达意思并不是一件易事。从下面两个例子中你会有所体会。

"This contract is signed by the authorized representatives of both parties on Dec. 9, 2007. After signing the contract, both parties shall apply to their respective Government Authorities for ratification. The date of ratification last obtained shall be taken as the effective date of the Contract. Both parties shall exert their utmost efforts to obtain the ratification within 60 days and shall advise the other party by telex and thereafter send a registered letter for confirmation."

"Know-how refers to any valuable technical knowledge, data, indices, drawings, designs and other technical information, concerning the design, manufacture, assembly, inspection of Contract Products, developed and owned or legally acquired and possessed by Licensor and disclosed to Licensee by Licensor, which is unknown to either public or Licensee before the Date of Effectiveness of the Contract, and for which due protection measures have been taken by Licensor for keeping Know-how in secrecy. The specific description of know-how is set forth in Appendix 2."

And if the contract stipulation is not precise, the contractor may suffer a great loss. For example, a careless contract writer wrote "not before April" while he means to say "in April", as a result, the goods came only in June and the writer's company suffered a great loss.

如果合同中的规定不准确,当事人就会遭受巨大的损失。例如,一位粗心的合同撰写人想要表达的意思是"在四月份",却写成了"不在四月以前",结果货物在六月份才到,公司遭受了很大的损失。

Precision often demands repeating the same term to express the same idea. Never be afraid of using the same word over and over again. Elegant variation has no place in strict legal writing. For instance, throughout a trade agreement, it is referred to as "agreement". Any attempt to shift "agreement" to "document" or "arrangement" will only cause confusion. To achieve accuracy, one must guard against obscurity and ambiguity. Obscurity means unclear and ambiguity refers to something which can be understood in more than one way. Therefore, in order to avoid ambiguity and obscurity, repetition of the same word or synonym use is necessary and pronoun is not preferred. For example:

为了表达准确,可能经常需要我们在表达同一概念时重复使用同一个词汇。所以,在反复使用同一个词汇时不要担心。在严肃的法律文书写作中,巧妙的文字变化是没有任何意义的。例如,在一份贸易协议中,我们通篇只使用"agreement"一词,如果想更换使用"document"或"arrangement",只会造成理解困难。为了表达准确,还要避免言辞含糊和语义有歧义。言辞含糊就是表达得不清楚,语义有歧义就是可以有多种不同的解释。所以,为了避免言辞含糊和语义有歧义,有必要重复同一个词或者使用类义词汇,而最好不要用代词。例如:

The sellers shall not be held responsible for the delay in shipment or non-delivery of the goods due to Force Majeure, which might occur during the process of manufacturing or in the course of loading or transit. The sellers shall advise the Buyers immediately of the occurrence mentioned above the within 14 days thereafter. The Sellers shall send by airmail to the Buyers for their acceptance a certificate of the accident. Under such circumstances the Sellers, however, are still under the obligation to take all necessary measures to hasten the delivery of the goods.

In the above example, you may see that the writer does not use "they" to replace "the sellers, the buyers", but just repeat using the two words to avoid obscurity.

在上面的例子中,我们可以看到,合同中并没有用"they"代替"the sellers, the buyers",而是反复使用这两个词以避免含糊。

Other examples:

"Party A wishes to be released and discharged from agreement as from the effective date."

In this sentence, "release" has the same meaning with "discharge".

这一句中的"release"和"discharge"意思几乎相同。

"The parties have agreed to vary the Management on the terms and subject to the conditions contained herein."

In this sentence, "on the terms" and "subject to the conditions" both mean "pursuant to the stipulations of the contract".

这里的"on the terms"和"subject to the conditions"是一个意思都表示"依照本协议的条款规定"。

"This agreement is made and entered into by and between Party A and Party B."

In this sentence, there are two groups of words with the same meaning, "made and entered into" and "by and between".

句中"made and entered into"和"by and between"两组属于同义词和相关词。

2. conciseness

This is particularly important for contractors, for any additional word might be a source of ambiguity. To be concise, a sentence should contain no unnecessary words. This, of course, does not mean that particulars may be omitted, but rather that every word must be to the point.

To achieve the effect of conciseness, the contract is generally expressed in a straightforward way with the frequent use of active voice as:

"Workers shall observe the rules and regulations of the work-site."

We would not express the same meaning in this way: "The rules and regulations of the work-site shall be observed by workers."

合同订立者必须保证合同内容简洁,这非常重要,因为额外增加的一些词就有可能造成歧义。为了保证合同简洁,就不要使用一些不必要的单词。当然,这并不是说就可以省略细节内容了,而是说每一个词必须精当。

为了确保合同内容简洁,合同一般都是使用主动语态进行直接的表述,如:

"工人应遵守工地的规章。"

我们不会将这个意思这样表达"工地的规章应该被工人遵守。"

3. impersonal tone

A written contract should be constructed in the official language, which is stylistically labeled as formal. The solemnity in the language of contracts is attributable to the tradition that formality conveys importance, and that formal and legal terms eliminate ambiguity and vagueness in the meaning of words. This formal style in contract writing is usually demonstrated in diction and structure.

书面合同的语言必须正式,之所以要求合同语言要严肃正式是因为正式性能够体现重要性,而且正式的法律用语可以减少词汇含义的模糊性和歧义的发生。合同的"正式性"文体特点通常体现在用词和篇章结构上。

A formal contract should be written without any personal intention. To avoid prejudice and bias, it should also be written fair and square. In this way, such expressions as "we" or "you" should be replaced by Party A/Party B, or the

Seller/the Buyer. For example:

The Buyer should pay 100% of the sale amount to the Seller in advance by telegraphic transfer not later than Dec. 15th.

写作正式的合同应该是没有任何个人意图在其中的。为了避免成见和倾向性,合同的写作应该是公平、公正。所以,我们在合同中都是使用"甲方"、"乙方"或者"买方"、"卖方",而不是用"我方"、"你方"。

"shall" is one of the most frequently used words in formal legal documents with the third person singular as its subject. It implies a type of legal right or duty rather than the future tense or the modal meaning of volition. For example:

在正式的法律文书中"shall"一词是最常使用的,并以第三人称单数做主语。"shall"所表达的不是将来发生的事情或者个人意志,而是表示一种法律意义的权利或义务。

"The Employer shall make a prepayment of 20% of the contract value to the Contractor within 10 days after signing the Contract."

雇主应于签约后十天内向承包人支付相当于承包合同价值20%的预付款。

"In order to guarantee the performance of the contract and its appendices, both Party A and Party B shall provide each other the bank guarantees for the performance of the contract."

为保证本合同及其附件的履行,甲、乙各方应相互提供履约的银行担保书。

"The purchaser shall not make available or otherwise disclose to any third party the core technology or any part thereof or any information relating thereto without the prior written consent of CAE."

事先未经CAE书面同意,买方不得将核心技术或其中的任何部分或与其相关的任何资料向第三方公开或供其使用。

"The quality and prices of the commodities to be exchanged between the ex-importers in the two countries shall be acceptable to both sides."

货物的质量和价格必须使进出口双方都能接受。

"In case one party desires to sell or assign all or part of his investment subscribed, the other party shall have the preemptive right."

如一方想出售或转让其所投资的全部或一部分，另一方应有优先购买权。

A contract may consist of many formal expressions like "whereas"(鉴于，就……而论)"pursuant to"(根据，按照)"provided that"(但规定，规定，但是)，"in witness whereof"(以此立(证)据)，"now therefore"(特此，因此)，know all men by these presents (根据本文件,特此宣布).

Whereas the first party is willing to employ the second Party and the second Party agrees to act as the first party's engineer in Bamako, it is hereby mutually agreed as follows:

鉴于甲方愿意聘请乙方，乙方同意应聘为甲方在巴马科(工程)的工程师,合同双方特此达成协议如下:

"Retention Money" means the aggregate of all monies retained by the Employer pursuant to Sub-Clause 60.2(a).

"保留金"是指业主根据第60.2(a)款规定留存的所有款项的总额。

Instructions given by the Engineer shall be in writing, provided that if for any reason the Engineer considers it necessary to give any such instruction orally, the contractor shall comply with such instruction.

由工程师发出的指令应为书面形式。但规定,如果由于某种原因,工程师认为有必要以口头形式发出指令,承包人应遵照执行。

In witness whereof the Parties hereto have caused this Agreement to be executed on the day and year first before written in accordance with their respective laws.

本协议书于上面所签订的日期,由双方根据各自的法律签订,开始执行,特立此据。

And whereas we have agreed to give the Contractor such Bank Guarantee; Now therefore we hereby affirm that we are the Guarantor and responsible to you, on behalf of the Contractor, up to a total of _____ (amount of guarantee) _____ (in words) _____, such sum being payable in types and proportions of currencies in which the Contract is payable.

本银行(或金融机构)已同意为承包人出具保证函,我们因此同意作为保证人,并代表承包人以支付合同价款所规定的货币种类和比例,向你方担保总金额为_（大写）_____的保证金。

In a written contract, we may also find such formal expressions as "here", "there" and "where" frequently combined with some particles. They basically mean "this", "that" and "which" respectively, and can be used to avoid repetition or redundancy and achieve conciseness and accuracy. For example：

书面合同中，我们还会经常发现这样的正式词汇，就是由"here""there""where"与一些介词搭配而成的词汇。这三个词分别表示"this""that""which"，使用这样的词汇可以避免重复或句子罗嗦，达到简洁、准确的效果。

（1）hereby：by reason of this

特此、因此、兹等意，常用于法律文件、合同、协议书等正式文件的开头语；在条款中需要强调时也可用。

This Contract is hereby made and concluded by and between _____ Co. (hereinafter referred to as Party A) and _____ Co. (hereinafter referred to as Party B) on _____ (Date), in _____ (Place), China, on the principle of equality and mutual benefit and through amicable consultation.

本合同双方，_____公司（以下称甲方）与_____公司（以下称乙方），在平等互利基础上，通过友好协商，于_____年_____月_____日在中国_____（地点），特签订本合同。

The Parties to this Contract, in the spirit of friendly cooperation, hereby signed and concluded this Contract in accordance with the following terms and conditions：

双方本着友好合作的精神，特签订本合同，其条件如下。

（2）hereof：of this 关于此点，在本文件中

Foreign trade dealers as mentioned in this Law shall, in accordance with the provisions hereof, cover such legal entities and other organizations as are engaged in foreign trade dealings.

本法所称对外贸易经营者，是指依照本法规定从事对外贸易经营活动的法人和其他组织。

If, as a result of withdrawal or any other reasons, an arbitrator fails to perform his duties as an arbitrator, another arbitrator shall, in accordance with the provisions hereof, be selected or appointed.

仲裁员因回避或者其他原因不能履行职责的,应当依照本法规定重新选定或指定仲裁员。

(3) hereto: to this 至此,对此

This Contract shall be in duplicate, to be held by each of the Parties hereto and shall have two copies kept by each of the Parties hereto for the record.

本合同一式两份,合同双方各执一份,并各保留两份复印件,供双方存档。

The scope of Works of this Contract shall be specified in such Drawings and bills of Quantities as are attached hereto.

本合同工程范围应按所附的图纸及工程量表中规定的范围。

(4) herein: in this 此中,于此

The term "company" mentioned herein refers to a limited liability company or a company limited by shares established within the territory of China in accordance with this Law.

本法所称公司是指依照本法在中国境内设立的有限责任公司和股份有限公司。

The procedures contained herein shall be followed by the concerned agencies of the People's Republic of China (PRC), responsible for the implementation of the World Bank supported projects.

执行世界银行贷款项目的中华人民共和国各有关机构,均遵循本文所规定的程序。

(5) hereinafter: later in this same paper 以下,在下文

In accordance with the Law of the People's Republic of China on Chinese-Foreign Equity Joint Ventures and the Contract signed by and between _____ Co. (hereinafter referred to as Party A) and _____ Co. (hereinafter referred to as Party B), the articles of association hereby is formulated and prepared.

根据《中华人民共和国中外合资经营企业法》以及由_____公司(以下称甲方)与_____公司(以下称乙方)所订的合资经营的合同,特制订本公司章程。

When existing Chinese-foreign equity joint ventures, Chinese-foreign cooperative joint ventures and wholly foreign-owned enterprises (hereinafter referred to as "enterprises with foreign investment") apply to reorganize themselves into a company, the enterprises with foreign investment shall have a record of making profits for the recent three consecutive years.

已设立的中外合资经营企业、中外合作经营企业、外资企业(以下简称外商投资企业),如申请转变为公司的,应有最近连续3年的盈利记录。

(6) therein: in that; in that particular context; 在其中

The Contractor shall, with due care and diligence, design (to the extent provided for by the Contract), execute and complete the Works and remedy any defects therein under the provisions of the Contract.

承包人应根据合同的各项规定,以应有的细心和勤勉,设计(在合同规定的范围内)、施工和完成工程,并修补工程中缺陷。

A certificate of the Borrower shall, substantially, comply with the form set forth in Appendix 4, and the attachments specified therein.

借款人证明书,其格式基本上应遵照附录4规定的格式及其规定的附件。

(7) thereof: of that, of it 它的,其

Arbitration: All disputes in connection with the Contract or arising in the execution thereof shall first be settled amicably by negotiation. In case no settlement can be reached, the case under dispute may then be submitted for arbitration.

凡有关该合同或因执行该合同而发生的一切争执,双方应以友好的方式协商解决,如协商不能解决,可提交仲裁。

"Time for Completion" means the time for completing the execution of and passing the Test on Completion of the Works or any section or part thereof as stated in the Contract (or as extended under Clause 44) calculated from the Commencement Date.

"竣工时间"指合同规定从工程开工日期算起(或按第44条延长工期)到工程或其任何部分或区段施工结束并且通过竣工检验的时间。

(8) Thereafter: after that 其后

The Contractor shall, during the execution of the Works and thereafter, provide all necessary superintendence as long as the Engineer may consider necessary for the proper fulfilling of the Contractor's obligations under the Contract.

只要工程师认为是为正确履行合同规定的承包人义务所必需时,承包人应在工程施工期间及其后,提供一切必要的监督。

There are more such expressions as:
hereafter: after this 此后
heretofore: until now 在此之前
hereunder: following this 在下文中
hereupon: at this time 随即
herewith: with this 随函附上
thereby: by saying or doing that 由此,因而
thereinafter: later in the same paper 在下文中
thereon: on that 就此
thereto: to that 加于……之上
whereby: by which 以……方式
wherein: in which 在……方面
whereof: of which 关于
whereupon: upon which 于是,不久以后
whereto: to which 对于……

7.4 Summary

All international transactions are conducted according to the terms and conditions negotiated between you and your buyer. By negotiating terms you secure the deal, minimize risks and protect your company in case of possible trade disputes, claims and/or legal actions. Usually terms of trade are stipulated in the trade contract and clearly indicate your and the buyer's responsibilities. In this unit, we learn that a foreign sales contract contain the title, contract proper and the signature. And the stylistic features of contracts are precise, concise and formal.

所有的国际贸易活动都是在你和买方磋商达成的条件基础上进行的。通过条件磋商,你得到了生意,减少了风险,也在发生贸易纠纷、索赔或诉讼时可以保护本公司的利益。通常,交易条件都写在合同中,明确规定买卖双方的责任。在这一单元,我们了解了外销合同是由首部、正文和签名三部分

组成。合同的文体特点是准确、简洁和正式。

7.5　Useful Expressions

1. Any disputes arising from the execution of, or in connection with, the contract shall be settled through friendly consultations between both parties.

凡因执行本合同所发生的或与本合同有关的一切争议,双方应通过友好协商解决。

2. The Buyer should make immediate payment against the presentation of the draft issued by the Seller.

买方应凭卖方开具的即期汇票于见票时立即付款。

3. Should such negotiations fail, such dispute may be referred to the People's Court having jurisdiction on such dispute for settlement in the absence of any arbitration clause in the disputed contract or in default of agreement reached after such dispute occurs.

如果协商未果,合同中又无仲裁条款约定或争议发生后未就仲裁达成协方的,可将争议提交有管辖权的人民法院解决。

4. All the activities of both parties shall comply with the contractual stipulations.

双方的一切活动都应遵守合同规定。

5. Before delivery the manufacturer should make a precise and overall inspection of the goods regarding quality, quantity, specification and performance and issue the certificate indicating the goods in conformity with the stipulation of the contract. The certificates are one part of the documents presented to the bank for negotiation of the payment and should not be considered as final regarding quality, quantity, specification and performance. The manufacturer should include the inspection written report in the Inspection Certificate of Quality, stating the inspection particulars.

在交货前制造商应就订货的质量、规格、数量、性能做出准确全面的检验,并出具货物与本合同相符的检验证书。该证书为议付货款时向银行提交单据的一部分,但不得作为货物质量、规格、数量、性能的最后依据,制造商应将记载检验细节的书面报告附在品质检验书内。

6. The formation of this contract, its validity, interpretation, execution and settlement of the disputes shall be governed by related laws of the People's Republic of China.

本合同的订立、效力、解释、履行和争议的解决均受中华人民共和国法律的管辖。

7. The Attachments to this Contract shall be deemed a part hereof and shall be effective as any other provision hereof.

本合同的附件应被视为本合同的一部分,与其他条款有同样效力。

8. The undersigned Seller and Buyer have agreed to close the following transaction in accordance with the terms and conditions stipulated as follows.

兹经签约的买卖双方同意,按下列条款,达成这笔交易。

9. Either Party hereto may terminate this Agreement in the event of the bankruptcy or insolvency of the other party.

本协议任何一方可以在对方破产或资不抵债的情况下终止本协议。

10. All prices to be paid by the Buyer under its obligations of the buyback/counter-purchase Contract shall be the world market prices taking into account the other delivery terms for the goods in question.

买方根据返销或回购货物合同的义务所支付的价格应为世界市场价格,结合考虑该货物的其他交货条件。

11. In the case of carriage by sea or by more than one mode of transport including carriage by sea, banks will refuse a transport document stating that the goods are or will be loaded on deck, unless specially authorized in the credit.

如属海运或多种类型运输中包括海运,除非信用证特别授权,银行将拒受注明货装舱面或将装舱面的运输单据。

12. The contract is made out in English and Chinese languages in quadruplicate, both texts being equally authentic, and each Party shall hold two copies of each text.

本合同用英文和中文两种文字写成,一式四份。双方执英文文本和中文文本各一式两份,两种文字具有同等效力。

13. The contract shall be valid for 10 years from the effective date of the contract, on the expiry of the validity term of contract, the contract shall automatical-

ly become null and void.

本合同有效期从合同生效之日算起共 10 年,有效期满后,本合同自动失效。

14. In witness whereof the Parties hereto have caused this Agreement to be executed on the day and year first before written in accordance with their respective laws.

本协议书于上面所签订的日期,由双方根据各自的法律签订,开始执行,特立此据。

7.6 Reading Materials

SALES CONTRACT(ORIGINAL)

Contract No.: CE102　　　　　　　　　　　　　　Date: Jun. 2, 20—

Signed at: Qingdao

Sellers: Sinochem Shandong Import & Export Group Corporation

　　　　 20, Hong Kong Middle Road, Qingdao, China

Buyers: Pacific Trading Co., Ltd.

　　　　 1118 Green Road, New York, U.S.A.

This Sales Contract is made by and between the Sellers and the Buyers whereby the Sellers agree to sell and the Buyers agree to buy the under-mentioned goods according to the terms and conditions stipulated below:

1.

Name of Commodity Specifications & Packing	Quantity	Unit Price	Total Amount
Lithopone ZnS content 28% min. Paper-lined glass-fibre bags	100 M/Ts	USD360.00 per M/T CIFC3% New York	USD36 000.00

(The Sellers are allowed to load **5% more or less** and the price shall be calculated according to the unit price.)

2. Shipping Marks:

PTC
New York
No. 1—1000

3. Insurance: To be covered by the Sellers for 110% of the invoice value against All Risks and War Risk as per the relevant Ocean Marine Cargo Clauses of the People's Insurance Company of China. If other coverage or an additional insurance amount is required, the Buyers must have the consent of the Sellers before shipment, and the additional premium is to be borne by the buyers.

4. Port of Shipment: Qingdao, China.

5. Port of Destination: New York, U.S.A..

6. Time of Shipment: During August, 20—, allowing partial shipments and transshipment.

7. Terms of Payment: The Buyers shall open with a bank acceptable to the Sellers an Irrevocable Letter of Credit at sight to reach the Sellers 30 days before the time of shipment specified, valid for negotiation in China until the 15th day after the aforesaid time of shipment.

8. Commodity Inspection: It is mutually agreed that the **Certificate of Quality and Weight** issued by the **State General Administration for Quality Supervision and Inspection and Quarantine** of P. R. China at the port of shipment shall be taken as the basis of delivery.

9. Discrepancy and Claim: Any claim by the Buyers on the goods shipped shall be filed within 30 days after the arrival of the goods at the port of destination and supported by a survey report issued by a surveyor approved by the Sellers. Claims in respect to matters within the responsibility of the insurance company or of the shipping company will not be considered or entertained by the Sellers.

10. **Force Majeure**: If shipment of the contracted goods is prevented or delayed in whole or in part due to Force Majeure, the Sellers shall not be liable for non-shipment or late shipment of the goods under this Contract. However, the Sellers shall notify the Buyers by fax or e-mail and furnish the latter within 15 days by registered airmail with a certificate issued by the China Council for the

Promotion of International Trade attesting such event or events.

11. **Arbitration**: All disputes arising out of the performance of or relating to this Contract shall be settled amicably through negotiation. In case no settlement can be reached through negotiation, the case shall then be submitted to the **Foreign Economic and Trade Arbitration Commission** of the **China Council for the Promotion of International Trade**, Beijing, China, for arbitration in accordance with its Provisional Rules of Procedure. The award of the arbitration is final and binding upon both parties.

12. Other Terms:

THE SELLERS   THE BUYERS
(Signature)   (Signature)

Exercises

I. You are required to find the Chinese/English equivalents in the tables below. Then you should put the corresponding letters in the brackets.

A—hereby B—hereof C—hereto D—herein E—hereinafter
F—therein G—thereof H—thereafter I—thereto J—therewith
K—whereas L—whereby M—notwithstanding N—undersigned
O—unless otherwise P—in accordance with Q—in respect of
R—in the event of S—provided that T—be deemed U—in question
V—in case W—be liable for X—in witness whereof
Y—know all men by these presents Z—now therefore

1. (　) 以下,在下文   2. (　) 鉴于,就……而论
3. (　) 凭此条款,凭此协议   4. (　) 尽管
5. (　) 除非   6. (　) 根据,依照
7. (　) 被认为   8. (　) "这"或"该"问题
9. (　) 应负有责任   10. (　) 根据本文件,特此宣布

II. Choose the best answer.

1. The buyer lodged a claim _____ the shipping company _____ the loss sustained in transit.

a) to... to   b) before... on   c) of... with   d) against... for

2. The Sellers shall effect insurance for 110% of the invoice value against All Risks and War Risk _____ the relevant Ocean Marine Cargo Clauses of the People's Insurance Company of China.

a) with   b) of   c) as per   d) as of

3. The Sellers are allowed to _____ 5% more or less and the price shall be calculated according to the unit price.

a) make   b) load   c) add up to   d) unload

4. We shall _____ if you will do your best to promote this new product of ours.

a) enjoy   b) please it   c) appreciate   d) appreciate it

5. During the period of this Agreement, both Parties should strictly _____ the terms and conditions of this Agreement.

a) abide by   b) abide with   c) abide of   d) abide in

6. In the event of any breach of the terms by one party, the other party _____ to claim the termination of this Agreement.

a) are entitled   b) be entitled   c) is entitled   d) entitles

7. You must be responsible for all the loss _____ from your delay in shipment.

a) arising   b) rising   c) arousing   d) have arisen

8. This contract enters into force upon _____ for a period of one whole year.

a) recognition   b) consent   c) signature   d) acceptance

9. This Agreement is _____ in quadruplicate, each party holding two copies.

a) made out   b) made on   c) made into   d) made off

10. This contract is _____ concluded through consultation between the Service Co., Guangzhou and WXY Co., Hong Kong in respect of engagement of Chinese employees.

a) hereby   b) whereby   c) thereof   d) thereon

III. Prepare a sales contract for the transaction stated in the following letter.

敬启者：

很高兴从您 7 月 21 日来信得悉您已接受我 7 月 8 日的报盘。作为答复，我们确认向贵公司出售 3000 打型号 PMC 9-71323 天坛牌男衬衫，颜色蓝、黄、白平均搭配，每打尺码搭配为 S/3、M/6、L/3，价格每打 47.50 英镑 CIF 汉堡，半打装一纸盒，十打装一大纸箱，由卖方按发票金额 110% 投保一切险和战争险，2007 年 9 月由中国港口运往汉堡，允许转船和分批装运，唛头由我方选定，以不可撤销的即期信用证付款，信用证必须在装运前 30 天到达我方。按照惯例，信用证议付有效期为最后装运期后第 15 天在中国到期。

兹随函将我方 2007 年 8 月 3 日在北京所签第 07/546 号售货合同一式两份寄去，请会签并退回我方一份。

此致

敬礼

汉堡服装公司
中国服装出口公司经理 谨上
2007 年 8 月 4 日

CONTRACT

No.

Sellers：

Buyers：

This Contract is made by and between the Buyers and the Sellers, where by the Buyers agree to buy and the Sellers agree to sell the under-mentioned commodity according to the terms and conditions stipulated the below：

Commodity：

Specifications：

Quantity：

Unit Price：

Total Value：

Packing：

Insurance:
Time of Shipment:
Port of Shipment:
Port of Destination:
Shipping Marks:
Terms of Payment:

Done and signed in _____ on this _____ day of _____, 200 _____.

Unit 8　Terms of Payment

Learning Objectives

After learning this unit, you should:

✍ Know the three major modes of payment in international trade(了解国际贸易中三种主要付款方式)

✍ Get familiar with the major instruments for payment settlement(熟悉结算票据)

✍ Know how to request for easier payment terms and how to respond to such requests(知道如何要求用更方便的结算方式以及如何答复这种要求)

✍ Master some specific terms and expressions concerning payment(掌握有关支付的特定短语和句型)

8.1　Introduction

As we know, payment plays a decisive role in the course of business. In international trade, instruments, which are commonly used for the payment or transfer of money, include draft, promissory note and check. Among them, the most often used is draft. And there are also many ways to make payment.

如我们所知,支付在交易过程中起着非常重要的作用,国际货款结算中,基本上都采用票据作为结算工具,票据可分为汇票、本票和支票三种,其中以汇票使用为多。而具体的付款方式也有很多。

The basic methods of payment are:

1. Remittance

Remittance includes Telegraphic Transfer (T/T), Mail Transfer (M/T) and Demand Draft (D/D). when remittance is adopted in international trade, the buyer will on his own initiative remit money to the seller through a bank according to the terms and time stipulated in the contract.

Remittance is often used in payment in advance, cash with order and open account. Therefore, either the exporter or the importer takes risk in remittance. Usually, it is used between companies that are trustworthy to each other.

汇付包括电汇、信汇和票汇。在国际贸易中,如果采用汇付,买方应该按照合同规定的条款和时间,将货款通过银行主动汇寄给卖方。

汇付常用于预付、订货付现和记账贸易。所以,采用汇付对出口商可能有风险,也可能对进口商有风险。通常,只有交易双方相互信任时才采用汇付。

2. Documentary collection or draft

Payment is sometimes made by collection through banks under the terms of Documents against Payment (D/P) or Documents against Acceptance (D/A). Under collection, the exporter takes the initiative to collect the payment from the buyer. Upon the delivery of the goods, the exporter draws a bill of exchange on the importer for the sum due, with or without relevant shipping documents attached, and authorizes his bank to effect the collection of the payment through his branch bank or correspondent bank in the country of the importer. In this case, the banks will only do the service of collecting and remitting and will not be liable for non-payment of the importer.

Payment by collection spares the expenses and the complicated procedures of using a letter of credit. However, there is obviously a risk involved in collection since payment is made after shipping. So before adopting this mode, the exporter should be sure that the buyer is reliable and able to make the payment.

有时,也可以通过银行按付款交单或承兑交单的方式收款。托收方式下,出口商是主动向买方收款。出口商一发货就按应付款金额开立给买方一张汇票,相关运输单据可以随附也可不随附,然后委托银行通过其在进口国的分支行或业务往来行办理向买方收款事宜。此时,银行只是负责收款和汇寄,对进口商不付款不承担责任。

托收方式可以省去开立信用证的许多费用与烦琐手续。但是,因为付款是在发货之后进行,所以托收明显是具有风险性的。因此,采用托收方式之前,出口商应该确认买方是信誉可靠、有支付能力的。

3. Documentary letter of credit

The most generally used method is the letter of credit which is a reliable and safe method of payment, facilitating trade with unknown buyers and giving protection to both sellers and buyers.

A letter of credit adds a bank's promise to pay the exporter to that of the foreign buyer provided that the exporter has complied with all the terms and conditions of the letter of credit. The foreign buyer applies for issuance of a letter of credit from the buyer's bank to the exporter's bank and therefore is called the applicant; the exporter is called the beneficiary.

Payment under a documentary letter of credit is based on documents, not on the terms of sale or the physical condition of the goods. The letter of credit specifies the documents that are required to be presented by the exporter, such as an ocean bill of lading (original and several copies), consular invoice, draft, and an insurance policy. The letter of credit also contains an expiration date. Before payment, the bank responsible for making payment, verifies that all documents conform to the letter of credit requirements. If not, the discrepancy must be resolved before payment can be made and before the expiration date.

Exporters may wish to confirm letters of credit issued by foreign banks if they are unfamiliar with the foreign banks or concerned about the political or economic risk associated with the country in which the bank is located. This confirmation means that a domestic bank (the confirming bank), adds its promise to pay to that of the foreign bank (the issuing bank). A letter of credit may either be irrevocable and thus, unable to be changed unless both parties agree; or revocable where either party may unilaterally make changes. A revocable letter of credit is inadvisable as it carries many risks for the exporter.

信用证是可靠安全的结算方式,推动了彼此不了解的买卖双方之间的交易,为双方都提供了利益保护,因而得到广泛采用。

信用证是银行为买方向出口商做出的付款承诺,承诺只要出口商按照信用证的条款规定行事银行便付款。国外的买方向其银行申请开立信用证,被称为申请人,出口商被称为受益人。

跟单信用证支付方式的基础既不是合同条款,也不是货物本身,而是单据。信用证中会规定出口商应该提交的单据,如海运提单(正本和若干副本),领事发票,汇票和保险单等。信用证中规定有到期日。付款前,付款银行要确认所有的单据与信用证相符。如果有不符之处,必须在支付前以及信用证到期日之前解决不符点。

如果出口商不熟悉国外的开证行或者担心开证行所在国的政治经济风险,他可以要求做信用证保兑。信用证保兑也就是出口商国内的银行(保兑行)为国外的开证行向出口商承诺支付。信用证可以是不可撤消的,即除非当事人同意否则不能修改,也可以是可撤消的,即任何当事人可以单方面修改信用证。可撤消信用证对出口商来说风险太大,不宜采用。

8.2　Model Letters Comments

8.2.1　Requesting Easier Payment Terms

Elite Industrial Inc.
12 Sunset Road
Liverpool, U.K.
Tel: 423209
Fax: 423098

June 2, 2003

Brown & Smith plc.
21 Downcaster Road
Dallas, Texas, U.S.A.

Dear sirs

　　In the past, our purchases of steel pipes from you have normally been paid by confirmed, irrevocable letter of credit.

　　This arrangement has cost us a great deal of money. From the moment we open the credit until our buyers pay us normally ties up funds for about four months. This is currently a particularly serious problem for us in view of the difficult economic climate and the prevailing high interest rates.

If you could offer us easier payment terms, it would probably lead to an increase in business between our companies. We propose either cash against documents on arrival of goods, or drawing on us at three months' sight.

We hope our request will meet with your agreement and look forward to your early reply.

Yours sincerely

Comments

Paragraph 1: state the current payment arrangements

Paragraph 2: outline the financial problems affecting the company

Paragraph 3: make the request for easier payment terms

Paragraph 4: urge acceptance of the proposal

The letter lays out the company's financial problem with the current payment terms. It then makes a request for easier payment terms. It supports the request by holding out the prospect of a possible increase in business.

Notes

1. confirmed L/C 保兑信用证, irrevocable L/C 不可撤消信用证

其他还有 documentary L/C 跟单信用证、transferable and divisible L/C 可转让与可分割信用证、revolving L/C 循环信用证、back to back L/C 背对背信用证、reciprocal L/C 对开信用证。

2. open 开立(信用证, 账户等), 还可以用 establish

We would like you to open an irrevocable L/C for the approximate invoice amount with a British bank.

我们希望你方请一家英国银行开立相当于发票金额的不可撤消信用证。

We have so far not received your L/C though you promised to establish it immediately after the signing of the Sales Contract.

尽管你方承诺签完合同后立即开立信用证但我们至今尚未收到。

3. tie up 占压资金, 冻结资金

When we open a letter of credit with a bank, we have to pay a deposit. That will tie up part of our fund.

在银行开立信用证,我们必须先付一笔押金,这样便占压了我们的部分资金。

The tie-up of our fund for 3 months in the bank is particularly taxing, owing to the tight money conditions.

由于银根很紧,资金冻结在银行 3 个月的负担确实过重。

4. in view of 鉴于

In view of your special market condition, we accept your suggestion of 3% discount.

鉴于你方市场的特殊性,我们接受你们提出的 3% 的折扣。

The material does not seem to be the same as that of the sample. Such goods are really of no use to us, and you will recognize that we ought to reship them to you, but in view of our long connections such a drastic step would be most unpleasant to both of us.

所用材料与样品所用的材料似乎不一样。这样的货物对我们没有任何用处。你应明白我们是可以把货退回给你方的,但鉴于我们之间长期的业务关系,这种过激的做法会令我们双方都不愉快。

5. draw on sb. 向某人开具汇票,也可以表示为 draw a draft on sb.

We've drawn on you for payment of the invoice amounting to \$20 000.

我们已经按照发票金额 20 000 美元向你方开出了汇票。

As arranged, we have drawn on you against the documents for the amount of invoice through the Bank of Asia.

按照安排,我们已经凭货物单据通过亚洲银行向你公司开出了发票面额的汇票。

We regret to note that our draft drawn on you on the terms of D/P 30 days after sight was dishonored.

我们很遗憾得知我们开给你方的 30 天远期付款交单汇票没有被承兑。

6. request 要求,请求

Considering the good relationship between us, we will entertain your request for payment by D/P this time.

鉴于我们之间的友好关系,我们考虑接受你方这次按付款交单方式付款

At your request, we are sending you our latest catalogue.

应你方要求,现寄去我方最新的产品目录。

8.2.2 Request Modified Payment Terms

United Furnishing Inc.
45 Aston Road
Birmingham, U. K.
Tel: 0044-121-85436100
Fax: 0044-121-87688000

16 June 2003

Granger Tiles Inc.
16 Main Street
Dallas, Texas, U. S. A.

Dear sirs

We have examined the specifications and price list for your range of ceramic tiles and now wish to place an order with you. Enclosed please find our Order No. FC-674.

As we are in urgent need of new stock, we would be grateful if you would make up the order and ship it as soon as possible.

In the past we have traded with you on a sight credit basis. We would now like to propose a different arrangement. When the goods are ready for shipment and the freight space booked, you phone us and we then remit the full amount by telegraphic transfer.

We are asking for this concession so that we can give our customers a specific delivery date and also save the expense of opening a letter of credit. As we believe that this arrangement should make little difference to you, but should help our sales, we trust that you will agree to our request.

We look forward to receiving confirmation of our order and your agreement to the new arrangements for payment.

                     Yours truly

Comments

 Paragraph 1: identify the reference
 Paragraph 2: urge quick delivery, giving the reasons
 Paragraph 3: state the modified payment terms requested
 Paragraph 4: give the reasons for requesting the modified payment terms
 Paragraph 5: urge acceptance of the proposal

The letter politely requests modified payment terms. The reasons given for the request are logical. Since the seller will not be at risk, it is very likely that the proposal will be accepted. Telegraphic transfer is a completely secure method of payment.

Notes

 1. range 产品系列

 As soon as we are in the procession of details and samples of your range, we shall be in a position to advise you on their suitability for this particular market.

 一旦我们收到你方产品的详细资料和样品，我们便可告知你方这些产品是否适合此地市场。

 This year a large number of purchase contracts have been signed covering a wide range of technology and equipment.

 今年已经签订了大量的购货合同，包括品种繁多的技术项目和设备。

 2. sight credit 即期信用证（在商业书信中常用）

 还可以表示为 letter of credit available by draft at sight, letter of credit payable against draft at sight, letter of credit available by sight draft, letter of credit payable against sight draft, sight L/C.

 3. be ready for shipment 备好待运

 The shipment covered by your order No. 231 has been ready for shipment for quite some time, but we have not received your L/C and we must point out that unless your L/C reaches us by the end of this month, we shall not be able to effect shipment within the stipulated time.

你方231号订单下的货物备妥待运已经多时了,但我们尚未收到你方的信用证,我们必须说明,除非本月底我们收到信用证,否则我们不可能在规定的时间内装运货物。

4. freight space,或 shipping space 舱位

The deadline for booking freight space is long past.

订舱位的时间早过了。

The shipping space for sailing to New York up to the end of this month has been fully booked up.

本月底开往纽约的船舱位早已经订完了。

5. remit (*vt. vi.*) 汇寄,汇款

I hope you will remit me the money in time.

我希望你能及时把钱汇给我。

They request us to remit USD150 for the samples.

他们要求我们为样品汇付150美元。

Kindly remit by cheque.

请汇支票付款。

6. telegraphic transfer 电汇,缩写为 T/T

7. concession (*n.*) 让步,妥协

As a concession, we are ready to make a quantity discount of 2% on the order of five hundred pieces and upwards.

作为让步,我们对订购量在500件以上(含500件)的订单给予2%的折扣。

There is so great difference between your offer and our expectation. We will be pleased to know about the concession you agree to make for the case.

你方的发盘与我们的预期水平差距太大。我们想知道你方为此能做出的让步。

We are, however, willing to make a concession by replacing the goods at a reduced price of $1.20 each.

但我们愿意让步,同意按每件 1.2 美元的低价格更换产品。

8. make difference 带来影响

We have not decided whether to accept their proposal to act as our agent. It is a decision of utmost importance since that will make great difference to our future business mode.

我们还没有决定是否接受他们提出的代理申请。这是个至关重要的决定,因为它将对我们未来的业务模式产生深刻影响。

Whether to pay in cash or by cheque will make little difference to us since the amount is relatively small.

因为金额相对较少,所以是用现金支付还是用支票对我们影响不大。

8.2.3 Accept Modified Payment Terms

Granger Tiles Inc.
16 Main Street
Dallas, Texas, U.S.A.
Tel: 001-214-8905498
Fax: 001-214-8906548

24 June 2003

United Furnishing Inc.
45 Aston Road
Birmingham, U.K.

Dear sirs

Thank you for your letter of 16 June. We are pleased to acknowledge your order No. FC-674 of the same date for ceramic tiles.

The modified terms of payment you propose are quite acceptable. A fax has been dispatched to you to this effect.

All the terms in your order can be supplied from stock and will be packed and shipped immediately your remittance by telegraphic transfer is received.

The following documents will be airmailed to you immediately after shipment is made:

Bill of lading in duplicate;

Invoice in triplicate;

Insurance policy for 110% of invoice value;

Guarantee of quality.

We will notify you by fax as soon as your order is shipped.

You can rely on us to give prompt attention to this and any future orders you may place with us.

Yours truly

Comments

Paragraph 1: identify the reference

Paragraph 2: accept the proposal and give written confirmation

Paragraph 3: detail the availability of goods and the conditions for shipment

Paragraph 4: list the documents which will be forwarded later. Assure that further notification on shipment will be given

Paragraph 5: end with a friendly message to the customer

The letter accepts the proposal and, in a thoroughly businesslike manner, includes all the necessary information for the transaction to proceed.

Notes

1. terms of payment 也可以表述为 payment terms, 支付条件,付款方式

This is the normal terms of payment in international business.

这是国际贸易中惯用的付款方式。

We can't accept any other terms of payment.

我们不能接受其他的付款条件。

If you can't be more flexible, we won't accept your terms of payment.

如果你们不能灵活些,我们将不接受此种付款方式。

2. to this (that) effect 意思为"有这样或那样的内容、意思"

In our telephone conversation, we have settled on the main terms of the transaction and we are now faxing you to this effect.

我们在电话中已经商定了主要交易条件,现在将这些内容传真给你们。

Prices on your side are showing signs of recovery and we received information to that effect.

我们得到消息,大意是你地价格正在显出恢复的迹象。

We have decided to meet you halfway by offering a discount of 10%, and cabled you today to that effect. We hope you will approve this solution.

我们决定与你方各让一步,给予你方10%的折扣,今天给你方发去电报表达了此意思。希望你方能够同意这个解决办法。

3. ship (v.) 装船,装运

We expect to ship the goods next week.

我们预期下周把货装出。

We accept your offer provided you ship the goods so as to arrive here not later than August 20 as called for by the time limit of our import licence.

由于进口许可证的期限关系,如果你们将货物在8月20日以前装运到这里,我们就接受你们的报盘。

Please advise name of the steamer on which you will be shipping the goods.

请告知我们你们装货的那条船名。

shipping 运输的

Please let us have your shipping instructions immediately so that we can arrange to make shipment.

请立即发出装船指示以便我们安排装运。

The shipping date is coming near and please open your L/C urgently.

装船期临近了,请立即开立信用证。

In order to book shipping space, we have to take a shipping order from the shipping company.

为了预订舱位,我们需要拿到船公司的下货单。

On finishing shipment, we will fax you the shipping advice.

装运完毕,我们就将装船通知给你方传真过去。

A full set of shipping documents are required for negotiation.

议付需要全套运输单据。

4. remittance 汇款

It is very important that all remittances be received at our office on the dates specified in the contract.

重要的是,要保证我公司在合同规定的日期收到各笔汇款。

Please return the enclosed order form with remittance to the address given.

请将所附订单及汇款按指定的地址退回。

5. document 单据

Documents against acceptance deviates from our usual terms of payment.

承兑交单并不是我们惯常的结算方式。

Please be sure to attach a full set of shipping documents to your draft.

请务必保证汇票要随附全套货运单据。

The seller needs the L/C and other documents, such as insurance policy, packing list, invoice, bill of exchange, for negotiation.

卖方议付时要提交信用证以及保险单、装箱单、发票和汇票等单据。

You may consider this air waybill as negotiable document, but it is non-negotiable document and cannot be transferred.

你可能认为航空运单是可转让单据,但它实际上是不可转让的。

documentary (adj.) 跟单的

The buyer shall duly accept the documentary draft drawn by the seller at 30 days' sight.

买方应该按时承兑卖方开立的 30 天远期跟单汇票。

Documentary collection has the relevant shipping documents attached to the draft, while in clean collection only draft is used.

跟单托收就是汇票随附了有关货运单据,而光票托收则只有汇票。

If the L/C requires the seller to draw documentary draft upon the buyer, then it is a documentary L/C.

如果信用证要求卖方向买方开立跟单汇票,这个信用证就被称做跟单信用证。

6. bill of lading（B/L）提单

提单的类型可以分为：

On board B/L 或 Shipped B/L 已装船提单，received for Shipment B/L 备运提单；

Direct B/L 直达提单，Transhipment B/L 转船提单，Through B/L 联运提单；

Clean B/L 清洁提单，Unclean B/L 或 Foul B/L 不清洁提单；

Straight B/L 记名提单，Open B/L 或 Bearer B/L 不记名提单，Order B/L 指示提单；

Long Form B/L 全式提单，Short Form B/L 简式提单，On Deck B/L 舱面提单；

Stale B/L 过期提单，Ante Dated B/L 倒签提单，Advanced B/L 预借提单。

7. invoice（n.）发票（vt.）开发票

Please send us four additional copies of invoice.

请多寄给我们发票副本 4 份。

You may invoice the goods at contract price less commission.

这批货物你可以按合同价格扣减佣金开发票。

The shipment was over-invoiced by USD500.

这批货物发票金额多开了 500 美元。

8. rely on 信任，相信

We rely on your careful execution of this order.

我们相信你方会认真执行我们的订单。

If it is found that some mistakes have been made in our selection of the materials, then you can most certainly rely on us to replace the materials.

如果发现我们在选料时出现了差错，你方一定放心，我们会更换材料的。

8.3　Specimen Letters

8.3.1　Request Payment by D/A

Dear sirs

　　We are a chain of department stores in Manchester and have recently decided to stock a range of silver cutlery.

　　We believe that there is a possibility of reasonable sales but we cannot count on this. Prices for the range will be considerably higher than for our present lines and, in the circumstances, we do not feel able to make purchases on our own account.

We would like to ask, therefore, whether you would be willing to send us a trial delivery for sale on D/A terms. We would hope to place firm orders once the demand for this cutlery has been ascertained.

We believe our proposal is a logical way to test the market and hope that you will be willing to cooperate with us.

As to our financial standing, you can check this with our bankers, the Scotland Bank, Manchester.

Yours sincerely

8.3.2 Decline Payment by D/A
Dear sirs

We have received your letter of May 4th and noted your kind intention of pushing the sale of our silver cutlery.

Although we are appreciative of your trial order, we regret that we are unable to consider your request for payment under D/A terms, the reason being that we generally ask for payment by Letter of Credit.

But, as an exceptional case, we are prepared to accept payment for your trial order on D/P basis. In other words, we will draw on you a documentary draft at sight through our bank on collection basis.

We hope that the above payment terms will be acceptable to you and look forward to hearing from you soon.

Yours sincerely

● **Activities for comprehension**

    1. Which method is safer and better for the seller, D/P or D/A? Why?

    2. Under what circumstances shall a seller agree to payment by D/A?

8.3.3 Propose to Pay by an L/C

Dear sirs

We would like to place an order for 1 000 dozen of tablecloth at your price of US$15 each, CIF Singapore, for shipment during October/ November.

We would like to pay for this order by a 30-day L/C. This is a big order involving US$180 000 and, since we have only moderate cash reserves, tying up funds for three or four months would cause problems for us.

We much appreciate the support you have given us in the past and would be most grateful if you could extend this favor to us. If you agree, please send us your contract. On receipt, we will establish the relevant L/C immediately.

Yours sincerely

- **Activities for comprehension**

    1. What is the advantage of payment by L/C?
    2. Tell the whole process of how an L/C is issued.

8.3.4 Request for Sight Payment

Dear sirs

Your purchase order has been referred to me. I note that the third item on the order is 50 000 of our Model 310 T-shirt at a price of $13.10 each. While we appreciate an order of this size, the terms and conditions on page 23 of our catalog clearly specify that overseas orders are accepted with full payment in advance, and with an amount sufficient to cover shipping.

We are therefore returning your purchase order. Please resubmit your order with either a sight draft, or an irrevocable letter of credit. We anticipate shipping charges to be in the neighborhood of $1.00 U.S. per T-shirt ordered.

Thank you for your order. We look forward to serving you in the near future.

Yours faithfully

● **Activities for comprehension**

1. What is the payment term for overseas orders?

8.3.5 Request for Full Payment

Dear Sir

Your check in the amount of us $20 000 is being returned to you because it has been made out for the wrong amount.

As we have explained previously, the 2% discount we offer can only be applied when your payment is mailed within 10 days of delivery. By waiting beyond that period, you forego the opportunity to deduct the discount from the amount of your invoice.

Since your payment of the above referenced invoice was not made within the specified time period, you are not entitled to a discount on this order.

We are appreciative of your business and are most willing to accommodate you in any way possible. Our policy, however, in regard to open account terms, is strict, and in fairness to all of our customers, must be even handed.

Please remit your check for the full amount of the invoice.

Your cooperation in this matter is appreciated.

Thank you for your understanding.

Yours faithfully

● **Activities for comprehension**

1. Why has the seller returned the buyer's check?
2. What is open account terms?

8.4 Summary

Paying for goods supplied in foreign trade is very complicated. The most generally used method of payment in the financing of international trade is the letter of credit, which is a reliable and safe method of payment, facilitating trade with unknown buyers and giving protection to both sellers and buyers. Sometimes, payment is made by collection through banks under the terms of Documents against Payment or Documents against Acceptance. In this case, the banks will only do the service of collecting and remitting and will not be liable for non-payment of the importer, while in the case of an L/C the opening bank offers its own credit to finance the transaction.

对外贸易中,付款方式是非常复杂的。最普遍采用的支付方式是信用证。信用证方式推动了彼此不了解的买卖双方之间的交易,为双方都提供了利益保护。有时,可以通过付款交单或承兑交单的方式由银行办理托收。但托收方式下,银行只是负责收款和汇寄,对进口商不付款不承担责任。而信用证方式下,交易中利用了开证行自身的信用。

8.5　Useful Expressions

1. Our terms of payment are by confirmed, irrevocable letter of credit in our favor, available by draft at sight, reaching us one month ahead of shipment, remaining valid for negotiation in China for a further 21 days after the prescribed time of shipment, and allowing transshipment and partial shipment.

我们的付款条件是以我方为受益人的、保兑的、不可撤消的即期信用证,信用证应该在装船前一个月开到我处,在规定的装船期后 21 天内在中国议付有效,信用证中允许转船和分批装运。

2. In view of the small amount of this transaction, we are prepared to accept payment by D/P at sight (or at 30 days' sight) for the value of the goods shipped.

鉴于此次交易金额较小,对于已装运货物的价款我们愿意接受即期付款交单的支付方式。

3. In compliance with your request, we will make an exception to our rules and accept delivery against D/P at sight, but this should not be regarded as a precedent.

按照你方的要求,我们破例接受即期付款交单,但下不为例。

4. We regret having to inform you that although it is our desire to pave the way for a smooth development of business between us, we cannot accept payment by D/A.

很遗憾,尽管我们愿意为我们之间贸易往来的顺利开展做出贡献,但我们不能接受承兑交单的支付方式。

5. As a special accommodation, we will accept document against payment for this trial order.

作为特殊照顾,对于你方的试订购订单我们接受付款交单方式支付。

6. As arranged, we are handing you our bill of exchange for USD2 000 and ask you to protect it upon presentation.

按约定,我们寄去2 000美元汇票一张,请见票即付。

7. Having some difficulties in opening a letter of credit, we have to request you to book our order on D/P basis.

我方现在开立信用证方面有些困难,请你方同意按付款交单支付方式接受我方订单。

8. If you would kindly grant easier payment terms, we are sure that such an accommodation would be conducive to the development of business between us.

如果你方同意采用更简单的支付方式,我们相信这一定会有利于我们之间的业务发展。

9. These payment terms are exceptional for such an order in small quantity.

对于这种小额订单,这样的付款条件是特别优惠。

10. We enclose a statement of account, made up to and including June 1, 2007, from which you will observe that there is a balance in our favor of USD2 000. An early settlement would be appreciated.

现随附账目明细表一份,账款日期是到2007年6月1日。贵公司会看到你方尚欠本公司2 000美元。若早日结付,不胜感激。

11. Reluctantly compelled to say that, failing receipt of your cheque by next Friday, we must have recourse to legal proceedings for its recovery.

如果在下星期五以前不能收到你方支票,为收回款项,我们将不得不通过法律途径,实属遗憾,特此奉告。

12. We regret very much that it is not in our power to satisfy your claim upon us immediately. We will, however, make every effort to send you either the whole or part of the amount on or before 10 July.

很遗憾,我们不能立即满足你们的支付要求。但我们会尽力最迟于7月10日前结清全部或部分款项。

8.6 Reading Materials

8.6.1

Dear sirs

We have received your letter dated 18 November. As already pointed out in our previous letter, we had made arrangements with our manufacturers to make delivery as punctually as possible in future. We shall see to it that your interest is well taken care of at all times.

Regarding the terms of payment, while we have every confidence in your integrity and ability, we wish to reiterate that our usual terms of payment by confirmed and irrevocable letter of credit remain unchanged in all ordinary cases. For the time being, therefore, we regret our inability to accept D/A terms in all transactions with our buyers abroad.

For further shipments, however, we shall do our best to fulfil your orders within the time stipulated. If, by any chance, it is impossible for us to do so, we will effect shipment on a D/P basis in order to avoid putting you to so much trouble in the extension of letter of credit. We trust you will appreciate our cooperation.

Yours sincerely

8.6.2

Dear sirs

We have received your letter of June 21 and noted your kind intention of pushing sales of our handmade embroidery tablecloth in your district.

Although we are appreciative of your trial order for 100 pieces of tablecloth, we regret that we are unable to consider your request for payment under D/A term, the reason being that we generally ask for payment by letter of credit.

In consideration of the friendly relations between us, we are, as an exceptional case, prepared to accept payment for your trial order on D/P basis. In other words, we will draw on you a documentary draft at sight through our bank on collection basis.

We hope that the above payment terms will be acceptable to you and look forward to hearing from you soon.

Yours sincerely

8.6.3

Dear sirs

We have received your letter of 15th March in which you ask for an extension of our terms.

In consideration of the very pleasant business relationship we have had with your firm for more than 15 years, we have decided to agree to your suggestion. We shall, therefore, in future draw on you at 60 d/s, documents against acceptance (D/A), and trust that these terms will suit your requirements.

We hope that our concession will result in a considerable increase of your orders and assure you that we shall always endeavour to execute them to your complete satisfaction.

Yours sincerely

8.6.4

Dear Sirs

We have just received your letter dated April 2 concerning our delayed payment (Order No. 391mrg). It had been our intention to clear this now, but the declined sales figure here has resulted in an extremely slow payment from some of our clients.

It has caused us a temporary inconvenience. However, you can be assured that the amount of the settlement will be paid in full to you shortly. Your understanding on this matter is highly appreciated.

Sincerely yours

Exercises

I. Fill in the blanks with your choices.

1. We enclose our cheque for US $200 _____ your invoice No. D-124.
   a) in payment of   b) by payment at
   c) to payment on   d) for payment in

2. We have _____ at 30 days' sight for the amount of the invoice.
   a) written to you   b) called on you
   c) sent to you by air mail   d) drawn on you

3. We regret having to remind you that 30% of the freight is still _____.
   a) owned   b) owning   c) outstanding   d) understanding

4. Our usual terms of payment are _____ L/C and we hope they will be satisfactory _____ you.
   a) by, for   b) by, to   c) for, to   d) for, with

5. _____ you fulfill the terms of the L/C, we will accept the drafts drawn under this credit.
   a) Provided   b) To provide   c) In the case   d) Only if

6. We regret _____ to accept your terms of payment and therefore have to return the order to you.
   a) cannot   b) being unable   c) not able   d) not be able

7. Payment should be made _____ sight draft.
   a) by   b) on   c) at   d) after

8. In compliance with your request, we exceptionally accept delivery _____ D/P at sight.
   a) with   b) to   c) against   d) as

9. We have to make a request for an easier payment term, for our funds are being _____ in numerous commitments.
   a) tied   b) tied up   c) tied to   d) tied for

10. All items included in your order can be supplied from stock and will be packed and shipped immediately upon _____.

a) receiving remitting   b) receipt of remit
c) receipt of remittance   d) remittance

II. Put in each blank the right word or phrase picked from the following list.

| insufficient | drawing on | establish | terms | overdue | at sight |
| available | drawn under | balance | extension | cashed | |

1. Most of our suppliers are _____ us at 60 days sight D/A, and we should be grateful if you could grant us the same terms.

2. After long years of satisfactory trading we feel that we are entitled to easier _____.

3. We will make our first payment by the end of this month and pay the _____ in the coming two months.

4. As the amount is now more than a month _____, we hope you will settle it within the next few days.

5. If it is impossible for us to effect shipment within the stipulated time, we will do it on a D/P basis in order to avoid putting you to so much trouble in the _____ of letter of credit.

6. On examination, we find that the amount of your L/C is _____. Please increase the total amount to US $20 000.

7. We have so far not received your L/C though you promised to _____ it immediately after the signing of the S/C.

8. Payment is to be made against sight draft _____ a confirmed, irrevocable letter of credit.

9. We will draw on you a documentary draft _____ through our bank on collection basis.

10. Our usual payment term is by irrevocable letter of credit, _____ by draft at sight for the full amount of the invoice value.

11. This is a confirmation regarding your payment of US $10 000. It has been _____ to our account.

III. Translate the following sentences into Chinese.

1. It has been our usual practice to do business with payment by D/P at sight instead of by L/C. We should, therefore, like you to accept D/P terms for this

transaction and for future ones.

2. We suggest payment by bill of exchange drawn on us at 60 days' sight. Please let us know whether this is agreeable to you.

3. Your proposal for payment by time draft for Order No. 1156 is acceptable to us, and we shall draw on you at 60 days' sight after the goods have been shipped. Please honor our draft when it falls due.

4. We are both surprised and disappointed not to have heard from you in answer to our two letters of 10th and 23rd March reminding you of the balance of US $1 256 still owing on our statement of 28 February. This failure either to clear your account or even to offer an explanation is all the more disappointing because of our past satisfactory dealings over many years.

5. Reluctantly compelled to say that, failing receipt of your cheque by next Friday, we must have recourse to legal proceedings for its recovery.

6. As you have failed to establish in time the L/C covering our sales confirmation No. 1022, we have to rescind this sales confirmation and hold you responsible for all the losses arising therefrom.

7. Thank you again for your cooperation on this transaction and we assure you always of our best and immediate service.

IV. Fill in each blank space in the letter below with a word that fits naturally.

Dear Sirs

We are pleased to inform you that your order (No 3388) _____ 3 200 pieces of pipe fitting is now _____ for shipment. We kindly ask you to send us US $8 000 _____ per the attached invoice. We will arrange shipment to you upon _____ of your payment.

Thank you and we look forward to _____ from you soon.

Sincerely yours

Unit 9 Establishment, Extension and Amendment of L/C

Learning Objectives

After studying this unit, you should:

✎ Understand the main procedures a letter of credit goes through(了解信用证的结算流程)

✎ Know how to urge the establishment of an L/C(知道如何催开信用证)

✎ Know how to write the advice of the establishment of L/C(知道如何写信用证开证通知函)

✎ Know how to make a request for extending an L/C(知道如何请求信用证展期)

✎ Know how to request the amendment of an L/C(知道如何提出信用证修改请求)

9.1 Introduction

In international trade practice, a letter of credit can be seen as a document by which a bank, upon the request of an importer, promises to effect the payment of the goods to the exporter. The letter of credit solves the possible problem arising from the distrust between the seller and the buyer. Under L/C, the seller can feel assured that so long as he has made the delivery of the goods and got the required documents he can get the payment of the goods in time and the buyer can also feel at ease that he can get the shipping documents at the same time when he effects the payment of the goods.

国际贸易实务中,信用证是银行在进口商的请求下向出口商做出的付款承诺。信用证解决了买卖双方之间缺乏信任而可能引起的问题。信用证方式下,卖方可以放心,只要他交货并提交必要的单据,他就可以及时得到付款;而买方也可以放心,他只要付款就可以得到运输单据。

It is the usual practice that the L/C is to be established and to reach the seller one month prior to the date of shipment so as to give the seller ample time to make preparations for shipment. However, there may be circumstances where the buyer fails to establish the letter of credit, or the letter of credit does not reach the seller in time; then a letter has to be sent to the buyer to urge him to expedite the L/C.

信用证通常是在装船期之前一个月左右开到卖方,以便卖方有足够的时间做装运准备。但是,有时可能买方不能开立信用证或信用证不能按时开到卖方,那么就需要写信给买方督促买方加快开立信用证。

Errors in the terms and conditions of a letter of credit may occur as a result of the applicant's error in preparing the L/C application and/or the issuing bank's error in preparing the L/C. The exporter must check the L/C immediately and thoroughly upon receipt from the bank, to ensure that the terms and conditions stipulated in the L/C are correct and conform to the sales contract, and that he/she can comply exactly to the L/C requirements. Otherwise, the exporter must immediately ask the importer to amend the L/C. A change made to a letter of credit after it has been issued is called an amendment. Banks also charge fees for this service. Every effort should be made to get the letter of credit right the first time since these changes can be time-consuming and expensive.

由于信用证申请人在填写信用证申请表时可能出现错误,或开证行在准备信用证时出现错误,所以信用证的条款中有可能有错误。出口商必须在收到银行送过来的信用证之后立即审核信用证,以确保信用证的条款正确无误,与合同相符,以及自己能够完全履行信用证的要求。否则,出口商必须立即要求进口商修改信用证。信用证开立之后发生内容变动被称为修改。银行是要对此收取服务费的。所以,修改信用证内容费时、费钱,一定在开立信用证时就要尽力保证一次做对。

The exporter should check the details of letter of credit, including the following:

The names and addresses are complete and spelled correctly;

The L/C is irrevocable and confirmed by the advising bank, conforming to sales contract;

The amount is sufficient to cover the consignment;

The description of goods is correct;

The quantity is correct;

The unit price of goods, if stated in the L/C, conforms to the contract price;

The latest date for shipment or the shipping date is sufficient to dispatch the consignment;

The latest date for negotiation or the expiry date is sufficient to present the documents and draft(s) to the bank;

The port (or point) of shipment and the port (or point) of destination are correct;

The partial shipment/drawing is permitted or prohibited;

The transhipment is permitted or prohibited;

The L/C is transferable or non-transferable;

The type of risk and the amount of insurance coverage, if required;

The documents required are obtainable.

出口商应该审核信用证的所有细节,具体包括:

名称、地址完整、拼写正确;

信用证是不可撤消的,按合同规定经过通知行保兑的;

信用证金额足以支付货款;

品名正确;

数量正确;

如果信用证中写明了货物单价,单价应该与合同价格一致;

规定的最迟装运期给卖方足够时间完成装运;

规定的最迟议付期或信用证到期日能给卖方足够的时间向银行提交单据和汇票;

装运港和目的港正确;

是否允许分批装运、分批付款;

是否允许转运;

信用证是否可以转让;

如果要求卖方投保,投保的险种和金额是否正确;

要求交付的单据是否可以提供。

The following words, or similar, are present in the L/C: "Unless otherwise expressly stated, this Credit is subject to the Uniform Customs and Practice for Documentary Credits, 1993 Revision, International Chamber of Commerce Publication No. 500."

下面这样的语句,或类似内容的语句应该在信用证中出现:"除非另有明确说明,否则该信用证适用跟单信用证统一惯例,1993 年修订版,国际商会第 500 号出版物。"

Every L/C has its expiry date. Sometimes the seller may fail to get the goods ready for shipment in time or the buyer may request that the shipment be postponed for one reason or another; then the seller will have to ask for extension of the expiry date as well as the date of shipment of the L/C.

每个信用证都有到期日。有时,卖方可能不能按时备好货物或者买方可能因某种原因要求推迟装运,那么卖方就要要求延长信用证的到期日以及装运期。

9.2　Model Letters Comments

9.2.1　Urge Establishment of L/C

China National Import & Export Corporation
12 Chifeng Road
Shanghai, China
Tel: 021-89045600
Fax: 021-89043200

30 June 2003

Messers. Wright & Co.
1902 Thames House
London, U.K.

Dear sirs

We refer you to your order for 1 000 dozen of tablecloth and our sales confirmation No. 219.

We wish to draw your attention to the fact that the delivery date is approaching and we have not yet received the covering letter of credit.

We would be grateful if you would expedite establishment of the L/C so that we can ship the order on time.

In order to avoid any further delay, please make sure that the L/C instructions are in precise accordance with the terms of the contract.

We look forward to receiving your response at an early date.

Yours sincerely

Comments

Paragraph 1: identify the reference

Paragraph 2: state the problem

Paragraph 3: ask for action

Paragraph 4: foresee any further problems and give instructions so that they will be avoided

Paragraph 5: urge a prompt answer

The customer is causing a delay by not issuing the requisite letter of credit. The letter is polite but conveys the correct note of urgency. There can be no progress until the L/C is delivered.

Notes

1. draw one's attention to 引起某人对某事的注意

The large trade deficit draws our attention to foreign exchange rate.

巨额的贸易逆差引起我们对汇率的关注。

We wish to draw your attention to the necessity of prompt delivery.

我们希望你方注意到立即交货的重要性。

2. delivery (n.) 交货

Could you manage to hasten the delivery?

你们能否加快装运?

There's still another possibility to ensure a prompt delivery of the goods.

还有另一种可能可以确保即期交货。

I'm sorry to say that we can't advance the time of delivery.

非常抱歉我们不能把交货期提前。

The buyer has the obligation to take delivery within the stipulated time.

买方有义务在规定的时间内提货。

deliver *vt.* 交货

I want the goods to be delivered in June.

我希望你们能在6月份交货

3. expedite 加快

But our customers say that they would oblige us by accepting the defective goods at a reduction of 20% on the invoice amount. We consider it quite a reasonable proposal and ask you to expedite settlement by placing the same amount to our credit.

我方的客户说,如果价款在发票金额基础上给个20%的折扣,他们愿意接受质量有瑕疵的货物。我们觉得这个建议非常合理,所以请你方尽快处理,将相应的款项划入我方账户。

As we are in urgent need of the goods, could you manage to expedite the shipment?

由于我方急需该货,你方能否加快装运?

4. make sure 确保,保证

Please make sure that the shipment will be effected within two weeks.

请保证在两周内装运货物。

In order to avoid any amendment, please make sure that the L/C instructions are in precise accordance with the contract terms.

为了避免对信用证做任何修改,请确保信用证条款与合同内容完全相符。

5. in accordance with 与……一致、相符,依照

After unpacking the case we found the goods were not in accordance with the original sample.

打开货箱后,我们发现货物与原样不符。

We are glad to supply you with the machines in accordance with your requirements.

我们很高兴按照你方的要求供应机器。

In accordance with your letter of yesterday, I am sending tonight 5 cases of whisky.

依照昨日来函,今晚已发出威士忌5箱。

9.2.2 Explain the Necessity of L/C Extension

China National Import & Export Corporation
12 Chifeng Road
Shanghai, China
Tel: 021-89045600
Fax: 021-89043200

5 July 2007

Messers. Wright & Co.
1902 Thames House
London, U.K.

Dear sirs

We have received your letter of June 30th and regret to learn that you are unable to extend the L/C No. NEW 2980.

As is known to you, there is only one vessel sailing for your port each month and it usually leaves here in the first half of a month. So far as we know, the only vessel available in this month will leave here in a day or two and the deadline for booking shipping space is long past. Therefore it is impossible to ship the goods this month, and we would ask you to do your best to extend the L/C as requested in our letter of June 20th.

Please act promptly and let us have your reply by return airmail.

Yours sincerely

Comments

Paragraph 1: identify the reference and express regret at the buyer's inability to extend the L/C

Paragraph 2: outline the reasons for the new delivery date arrangement

Paragraph 3: urge confirmation of the extension to the L/C

When there is a delay in shipment, the relevant letter of credit may need to be extended. The letter explains the reason for the request and outlines the new arrangements.

Notes

1. extend (*vt.*) 延长期限,展期

Please extend the shipment date and the validity of your L/C No. 343 to the end of March and April 15 respectively.

请将你方343号信用证的装船期和有效期分别延长至3月底和4月15日。

We hope you will extend your offer for two weeks.

希望你方能将报盘延长两个星期。

2. port 港口

It makes no difference to us to change the loading port from Shantou to Zhuhai.

将装运港由汕头改为珠海对我们来说问题不大。

He exchanged views on the choice of the unloading port with Mr. Smith.

他和史密斯先生就选择卸货港问题交换了意见。

Shall we have a talk on the port of discharge this afternoon?

咱们今天下午是不是谈谈卸货港的问题?

3. so (as) far as... 就……而言

There is little doubt that he is acting in the utmost good faith, but we ourselves should hesitate to accept the conditions they suggest. As far as we can see, payment of half this sum in cash would be advisable.

毫无疑问,该公司的表现极为诚恳。但我们仍不能毫不犹豫地接受他们的建议。因此,以我方之见,应该以现金形式先付一半货款。

So far as we know, they are sound enough, but we have no certain knowledge of their true financial position.

就我方所知,该公司名声不错,但关于它们的财务状况,我们就不得而知了。

9.2.3 Amend a Letter of Credit

China National Import & Export Corporation
12 Chifeng Road
Shanghai, China
Tel: 021-89045600
Fax: 021-89043200

15 June 2007

Messers. Wright & Co.
1902 Thames House
London, U.K.

Dear sirs

We are pleased to have received your L/C No. LNF231 against S/C 2998 for tablecloth.

However, we find that the L/C stipulates for the invoice to be certified by your consul, which is unacceptable to us as there is no consul of your country here.

It is our usual practice to have our invoice certified by the China Council for the Promotion of International Trade and this has universally been accepted by our clients abroad. We hope you will agree to it as well.

You are, therefore, requested to contact your bank to delete this clause immediately upon receipt of this letter, or you may replace it by inserting the clause to read " Invoice in quintuplicate to be certified by the China Council for the Promotion of International Trade".

If your amendment could reach us by the end of this month, we would effect shipment in the first half of next month.

We thank you in advance for your co-operation.

Yours sincerely

Comments

Paragraph 1: identify the reference

Paragraph 2: state the problem and give the reason for requesting amendment

Paragraph 3: make a suggestion

Paragraph 4: request the appropriate action

Paragraph 5: urge a prompt reply

The seller, quite rightly, does not wish to infringe the exact terms of the L/C. He seeks the amendment in order to protect himself.

Notes

1. usual practice 惯例

When opening new accounts it is our usual practice to ask customers for trade reference. Will you therefore please send us the name and address of two other suppliers with whom you have dealings?

接收新客户时,我方有一惯例,即要求客户提供商业资信证明人。所以,特请贵公司寄来两家曾与贵公司有业务往来的供货商的字号和地址。

It is our usual practice to insure the consignment for 110% of the invoice value. Any additional premium for insurance coverage over 110% of the invoice value, if so required, shall be borne by the buyer.

我们的惯例是按照发票金额的110%对货物投保,如果买方要求按照超过发票金额110%的金额投保,额外的保费将由买方承担。

2. （up）on 后面接名词或动名词,意思是"一……就……",与 no sooner...than...意思一样

Upon receipt of your letter, we have given this matter our immediate attention.

一收到你方来函,我们立即处理此事。

We have duly received your prompt shipment of 100 motors on June 20, but regret to find on checking that of 50 pieces do not quite correspond to the sample motor as specified in our Indent No. 1234.

我们在 6 月 20 日准时收到了你方紧急装运的 100 台发动机,但一经验货,我们遗憾地发现其中 50 台与我方 1234 号订单规定的样品不相符。

On receiving your telegram of October 3, we carried your claim to the makers, who flatly denied its acceptance, insisting that there could be no such difference between the shipping sample and the duplicate sample.

一收到你方 10 月 3 日的电报,我们就向制造商说明了你们的索赔要求,他们明确拒绝接受你方索赔要求,坚持认为在发货样品和复制样品之间不可能有这样的差异。

No sooner had we received your telegram of October 3 than we forwarded your claim to the manufacturers.

一收到你方 10 月 3 日的电报,我们就向制造商说明了你们的索赔要求。

3. amendment 修改通知书,修改

Upon receipt of your amendment to the L/C, we shall immediately make the shipment of the goods.

一收到信用证的修改书,我们就会立即装船。

Please inform us any discrepancy in the L/C so that we can make amendments accordingly.

若信用证中有任何不符请告知我们以便做相应的修改。

4. effect（vt.）完成,实现

we hope you can effect payment upon the presentation of the draft.

我们希望你方能够在汇票提示时即刻付款。

Shipment can generally be effected within 30 days after receipt of the L/C.

通常在收到信用证后 30 天内都可以装运。

The seller is required to effect insurance on the goods before loading.

卖方必须在装船前为货物投保。

5. in advance 预先

The buyer paid USD500 000 in advance for the order.

买方预付了 50 万美元的货款。

We thank you in advance for your cooperation.

对于你方的协助我们提前表示感谢。

9.3 Specimen Letters

9.3.1 Urge Establishment of L/C

Dear sirs

We wish to inform you that the goods under S/C No. 7525 have been ready for quite some time. According to the stipulations in the foregoing sales confirmation, shipment is to be made during May/June. We sent you a fax two weeks ago asking you to expedite the relevant L/C.

But much to our regret, we have not received any reply up to now. We feel it necessary to advise you to open your L/C immediately. The shipment date is approaching. Unless your L/C reaches us by the end of this month, we shall not be able to effect shipment within the stipulated time limit.

Your co-operation in this respect will be appreciated.

Yours sincerely

● **Activities for comprehension**

1. What should the seller write in his first letter to urge the buyer to expedite the L/C?

2. Why must letters urging establishment of L/C be written with tact?

9.3.2 Reply

Dear sirs

Your letter of April 21 as well as your fax of April 6 has been received. The

L/C in question has already been opened and sent. It might have crossed your letter under reply.

For your information, we are enclosing a photostatic copy of Documentary Credit No. FE213 dated April 3. Please verify this matter with your bank.

We are pleased to learn that the goods we ordered are ready for dispatch, and hope you will let us know at your earliest convenience the name of the carrying vessel and its sailing date.

Yours sincerely

9.3.3 Request for L/C Amendment

Dear sirs

Thank you for your L/C No. LNG207 in our favor to cover your contract of 10 000 gas lighters.

We find, however, that the L/C amount for US $500 does not agree with that listed in our Sales Contract No. G115. The correct amount is US $550. It must be a typographical error or an oversight on the part of your bank. We wish to request you to ask your bank to amend the credit by cable to increase an amount by US $50 to it.

The goods will be ready for shipment within 10 days as soon as we receive your cable amendment to the L/C.

We appreciate your immediate attention to this matter.

Yours truly

● **Activities for comprehension**

1. What should the seller do if any discrepancies or some unforeseen special clauses are found in the L/C?

2. What should the seller take care of when writing letters concerning L/C amendment?

9.3.4 Reply

Dear sirs

In reply to your letter of June 4, we wish to inform you that we have instructed our bank to amend the L/C No. LNG207 by increasing the amount to US $550.

As the amendment was made by cable, you must have received it. And we trust that everything is now in order and you will be able to ship the goods in the first half of next month.

Should your goods prove to be satisfactory upon arrival, we are confident that further large orders will be placed.

We are looking forward to hearing from you about the shipment of the goods.

Yours truly

9.3.5 Ask for L/C Extension

Dear sirs

We thank you for your L/C No. 2781 covering your order of 10 metric tons of Bens tomato sauce. We are sorry that owing to some delay on the part of our suppliers, we are unable to get the goods ready before the end of this month. So we faxed you yesterday requesting an extension of the L/C.

It is expected that the consignment will be ready for shipment in the early part of June and we are arranging to ship it on S.S. Liver Bird sailing from Tianjin on or about 7 June.

We trust you will extend the shipment date of your L/C to June 10 and the validity to 25 June, thus enabling us to effect shipment of the goods in question.

We thank you for your cooperation.

Yours truly

● **Activities for comprehension**

1. Under what conditions is an extension of L/C necessary?

9.3.6 Reply

Dear sirs

We have received your letter of May 15 requesting us to extend the L/C No. 2781 to June 10 and June 25 for shipment and negotiation respectively.

We are quite willing to do whatever we can to cooperate with you, but as the present import regulation do not allow any extension of licence, we regret having to say that it is beyond our ability to meet your request to extend the above L/C.

Please do your best to ship the goods in time and we thank you for your cooperation.

Yours truly

9.4 Summary

Letter of credit is a commonly used method of payment in international trade. Under L/C, an exporter will not deliver the goods without receipt of the L/C. And upon arrival of the L/C, the seller will check it to see if it corresponds with the agreement or contract. If he finds any discrepancy, he will immediately ask the importer or the advising bank to require the opening bank to make amendments. If for any reason the exporter find it impossible to make delivery as stipulated in the L/C, he may request extension to the L/C.

信用证是国际贸易中普遍使用的一种结算方式。在信用证结算方式下，出口商只有在收到信用证后才会发货。一收到信用证，出口商就检查信用证是否有与合同或协议不相符的地方。如果发现不符点，他会立即与进口商或通知行联系要求他们通知开证行修改信用证。如果因为种种原因，出口商不能在信用证规定的期限内交货，他还可以要求将信用证展期。

9.5 Useful Expressions

1. It would be advisable for you to establish the covering letter of credit as early as possible so as to enable us to arrange shipment in due time.

你方最好尽快开立相关信用证，以便我们按时安排货物装运。

2. We wish to draw your attention to the fact that the goods have been ready

for shipment for a considerable length of time and the covering letter of credit, due to arrive here before March 23, has not been received up to now. Please let us know the reason for the delay.

敬请注意,货物备妥待运已经多时了,应于3月23日前开到的相关信用证至今未到。请告知我方耽搁的具体原因。

3. To our disappointment, we have not yet received the required letter of credit up to the present. Please give this matter your immediate attention and let us have your reply soon.

我们很失望,至今未收到所需的信用证。请立即处理此事并尽快回复我方。

4. We have received your L/C No. 767, but we find it contains the following discrepancies:... We would therefore request you to instruct your bank to make the necessary amendment.

我方已收到767号信用证,但该信用证中有如下不符点:……所以,请你方指示开证行做出必要的修改。

5. On examination, we find that the amount of your L/C is insufficient. Please increase the unit price from US \$2.2 to US \$3.2 and total amount to US \$3 200.

经检查,我们发现你方信用证的金额不足。请将单价从2.2美元调整为3.2美元,总金额增加到3200美元。

6. Owing to the late arrival of the steamer on which we have booked space, we would appreciate your extending the shipment date and the validity of your L/C No. 456 to 21st January and 5th February respectively.

由于我们订舱的货船晚到了,所以请你方将456号信用证的装船期和有效期分别延长至1月21日和2月5日,谢谢。

7. The shipment covered by your L/C No. 598 has been ready for quite some time, but the amendment advice has not yet arrived, and now an extension of 15 days is required.

598号信用证项下的货物备妥多时了,但信用证的修改通知至今未到,所以现在需要将信用证展期15天。

8. We are glad to inform you that we have now opened the confirmed, irrevo-

cable letter of credit No. SC231 in your favor for USD5 000 with the National Bank, London, valid until 10 April.

很高兴通知你方我们已经通过伦敦国民银行开出了以你方为受益人的、金额为5 000美元的保兑的、不可撤消的信用证,信用证编号为SC231,有效期至4月10日。

9. If we again fail to receive your L/C in time, we shall cancel our Sales Confirmation and ask you to refund to us the storage charges we have paid on your behalf.

如果我们还不能按时收到你方信用证,我们将取消售货确认书并要求你方退还我们代你方所支付的仓储费用。

10. We hope you will understand our situation and let us have your amendment notice by return.

希望你方能理解我方的处境,并回寄修改通知书。

11. As to partial shipment, it would be to our mutual benefit because we could ship immediately whatever we have on hand instead of waiting for the whole lot to be completed.

至于分批装运,这对我们双方都有利,因为我们可以将现有货物立即装船而不用等整批货物备齐。

12. As such delay will certainly cause us a lot of unnecessary inconvenience and expenses, we would ask you to try your utmost to effect shipment according to the original schedule.

由于该延期会给我们造成许多不必要的麻烦和费用,因此请你们尽最大努力按原计划装运。

9.6 Reading Materials

9.6.1

Dear sirs

Referring to the 500 pieces of tablecloth under our sales confirmation No. 564, we wish to call your attention to the fact that the date of delivery is drawing near, but up till now, we have not received the covering L/C. Please do your utmost to expedite its establishment, so that we may execute the order within the prescribed time.

For your information, S. S. Bright is due to sail for your port around the middle of next month, according to the shipping company here. If we have your L/C before the end of this month, we might catch that steamer.

In order to avoid subsequent amendments, please see to it that the L/C stipulations are in strict conformity with the terms of the contract.

We look forward to receiving your favorable reply at an early date.

Yours sincerely

9.6.2

Dear sirs

We have received your letter of credit No. SDL 1287 with thanks, but we regret to say that there are some discrepancies between your L/C and sales contract No. 233. They are as follows:

Your L/C No. SDL 1287

(1) Transhipment not allowed;

(2) Equal part shipment in March and April;

(3) No more or less clause.

The S/C No. 233

(1) Transshipment allowed;

(2) Shipment not later than April 10;

(3) 5% more or less allowed.

In order to effect shipment smoothly, please make necessary amendment to your L/C with the least possible delay.

Yours sincerely

9.6.3

Dear Sirs

At the request of our supplier, we would appreciate your amending the Letter of Credit No. AH3638 by mail in favor of ABC Corporation San Francisco, Calif. U.S.A. Please amend the L/C as following:

(1) Extending the shipping date to before June 1.

(2) Extending the expiry date to before June 15.

As you know, this amendment is subject to an acceptance by the beneficiary. All the other conditions remain unchanged.

Sincerely yours

9.6.4

Dear Sirs

Thank you very much for your Letter of Credit No. BOC 910. However, upon checking, we have found the following discrepancies and would appreciate it very much if you will make the necessary amendments as early as possible so as to facilitate our shipping arrangement:

(1) The amount of the credit should be CAN $125 000 (Say Canadian Dollars one hundred and twenty-five thousand only) instead of CAN $120 000.

(2) The Bill of Lading should be marked "freight prepaid" instead of "freight to collect".

(3) Please delete Insurance Policies (or Certificates) from the credit.

(4) The port of destination should be Vancouver instead of Montreal.

(5) The goods are to be in tins of 340 grams instead of 430 grams.

(6) The credit should expire on Dec. 15 in 2002 for negotiation in China instead of Nov. 30 in 2002.

We await your early amendments.

Yours faithfully

Unit 9　Establishment, Extension and Amendment of L/C

Exercises

I. Fill in the blanks with your choices.

1. As requested, we have immediately arranged _____ our bankers to extend the expiry date of our L/C for two weeks _____ 10th March.
   a) with... up to
   b) with... on
   c) for... until
   d) for... to

2. As arranged, we would ask you to open an irrevocable credit in _____ favor and shall hand over shipping documents _____ acceptance of our draft.
   a) your... against
   b) your... for
   c) our... against
   d) our... for

3. We inform you that we have opened an irrevocable credit _____ the London Bank in your favor.
   a) at
   b) in
   c) by
   d) with

4. We advised the bank to amend the clause _____ "partial shipment are permitted".
   a) to reading
   b) to read
   c) to be read
   d) to be reading

5. It is important that your client _____ the relevant L/C not later than April 10.
   a) must open
   b) opens
   c) open
   d) has to open

6. The relative L/C should be issued through a third bank in Austria _____ the sellers.
   a) available by
   b) available to
   c) acceptable by
   d) acceptable to

7. _____ the terms of payment as stipulated in the contract, please establish an irrevocable letter of credit in our favor.
   a) In fact
   b) As a matter of fact
   c) In contrast with
   d) In accordance with

8. _____ shipment, please amend the L/C to allow transshipment.
   a) Regarding
   b) Covering
   c) Concerning
   d) Referring

9. As there is no direct steamer from Shanghai to your port during March, it

is imperative for you to delete the clause "by direct steamer", and _____ the wording "partial shipment and transshipment are allowed".

  a) insert   b) make   c) stipulate   d) cover

  10. Upon examination, we have found a _____ in quantity. Please amend the quantity to read "500 M/T (3% more or less)".

  a) difference   b) wrong   c) discrepancy   d) problem

II. Fill in the blanks with proper prepositions.

  1. As the goods _____ Contract No. 123 are now ready for shipment, please rush your L/C _____ the least possible delay.

  2. _____ receipt of your L/C we shall make shipment immediately.

  3. Please open as soon as possible the relevant L/C _____ our favor.

  4. We are pleased to inform you that we have established _____ the Westminster Bank the confirmed, irrevocable L/C available by demand draft.

  5. We acknowledge your L/C No. 231 _____ our S/C No. R493.

  6. As soon as the bank notifies us _____ the arrival of the L/C, we shall ship the goods.

  7. As the world market continues to boom, we are not _____ a position to fulfill the contract at the price agreed.

  8. You are kindly appreciated to see to it that punctual delivery is made _____ the validity of the L/C.

  9. We grant your request for payment by L/C with draft _____ 30 days, sight.

  10. We shall be glad if you should arrange to open an irrevocable L/C for USD20 000 _____ our account.

III. Fill in each blank space in the letter below with a word that fits naturally.

Dear Mr. Jones:

  We thank you for your L/C for the captioned goods. We are sorry that _____ to some delay _____ the part of our suppliers at the point of origin, we are not able to get the goods ready _____ the end of this month. As a result, we sent you a cable yesterday _____ : L/C1415 PLS CABLE EXTENSION SHIPMENT VALIDITY 15/31 MAY RESPECTIVELY AS FOLLOWS.

Unit 9 Establishment, Extension and Amendment of L/C **221**

It is expected that the consignment will be ready _____ shipment in the early part of May and we are arranging to ship it on S/S "Hanyan" sailing from Dalian on or about 10th May.

We are looking forward to receiving your cable extension of the above L/C thus enabling us to _____ shipment of the goods _____ question.

We thank you for your cooperation.

Yours sincerely

● **Skills Practice**

Write a letter in English asking for amendment to the following letter of credit by checking it with the given contract terms.

National Bank of Singapore
Singapore
Irrevocable Documentary Credit No. 12/2234 dated Nov. 30, 20××

Advising Bank Bank of China Head Office Beijing	**Applicant** ABC Trading Co. Singapore
Beneficiary China National Garments Imp./Exp. Corporation Beijing, China	**Amount** HKD5,600,600.00
	Expiry Date: Feb. 15, 2004 for negotiation in China

We hereby issue in your favor this documentary credit which is available by presentation of your draft drawn at 60 days after sight on us bearing the clause: Drawn under documentary credit No. 12/2234 of National Bank of Singapore accompanied by the following documents:

(1) Signed Commercial Invoice in Triplicate, indicating S/C No. PS-234 dated 11 Oct. 20××.

(2) Full set of clean on board Ocean Bills of Lading issued to order and blank endorsed showing "Freight Paid" covering 65 000 dozen men's shirts at

USD300.00 per dozen CIF Singapore

(3) Partial shipments prohibited. Transshipment allowed.

We hereby engage with drawers and/or bona-fide holders that drafts drawn and negotiated in conformity with the terms of this credit will be duly honored on presentation and that drafts accepted within the terms of this credit will be honored at maturity.

National Bank of Singapore

合同条款

卖方:北京中国服装进出口公司(China National Garments Imp./Exp. corp. Beijing)

卖方:新加坡通用贸易公司(General Trading Company, Singapore)

商品名称:雅格尔(Younger)男式衬衣

规格:每打 39/3,40/6,42/3

数量:60 000 打

单价:新加坡成本加保险加运费每打 100 美元,含佣 3%

总值:6 000 000.00 美元

装运期:2004 年 1 月 31 日前中国港口至新加坡,允许分批

付款条件:凭不可撤销即期信用证付款,于装运期前 1 个月开到卖方并在装运期后 15 天内在中国议付有效

保险:由卖方根据中国人民保险公司 1981 年 1 月 1 日中国保险条款按发票金额的 110% 投保一切险和战争险

签订合同日期和地点:20—年 10 月 11 日于北京

合同号码:PS-1234

Cable Letter of Credit

--------------------------------- Transmission ---------------------------------

Received from SWIFT

Network priority: Normal

Message output reference: 6543 010126

Message input reference: 6543 010125

-- Message Header --

SWIFT output delivery status: Open Asked
FIN 701 Issue of a documentary credit

Sender: The Sun Bank
       Sunlight City
       Import-Country

Receiver: The Moon Bank
       5 Moonlight Blvd.
       Export-City and Postal Code
       Export-Country

NUR: SB-87654   Banking priority: Normal

-- Message Text --

20 : Documentary credit number
     SB-87654
23 : Issuing bank's reference
     SBRE-777
31C : Date of Issue
     January 26, 2001
31D : Date and place of expiry
     March 26, 2001 Export-City, Export-Country
32B : Currency code amount
     Twenty Five Thousand U.S. Dollars (USD 25 000.00)
39B : Maximum credit amount
     Not exceeding Twenty Five Thousand U.S. Dollars (USD 25 000.00)
40A : Form of documentary credit
     Irrevocable
41D : Available with... by...
     Draft(s) drawn on The Moon Bank, by payment
42C : Drafts at
     At sight for full invoice value
42D : Drawee-Name and Address

The Moon Bank, 5 Moonlight Blvd., Export-City and Postal Code, Export-Country

43P: Partial shipments
Prohibited

43T: Transhipments
Permitted

44A: On board/disp/taking charge
Moonbeam Port, Export-Country

44B: For transportation to
Sunny Port, Import-Country

44C: Latest date of shipment
March 19, 2001

45A: Description of goods and services
100 Sets "ABC" Brand Pneumatic Tools, 1/2" drive,
complete with hose and quick couplings, CIF Sunny Port

46A: Documents required
1. Signed commercial invoice in five (5) copies indicating the buyer's Purchase Order No. DEF-101 dated January 10, 2001.
2. Packing list in five (5) copies.
3. Full set 3/3 clean on board ocean bill of lading, plus two (2) non-negotiable copies, issued to order of The Sun Bank, Sunlight City, Import-Country, notify the above accountee, marked "Freight Prepaid", dated latest March 19, 2001, and showing documentary credit number.
4. Insurance policy in duplicate for 110% CIF value covering Institute Cargo Clauses (A), Institute War and Strike Clauses, evidencing that claims are payable in Import-Country.

47A: Additional conditions
1. All documents indicating the Import License No. IP/123456 dated January 18, 2001.
2. Draft(s) drawn under this credit must be marked: "Drawn under documentary credit No. SB-87654 of The Sun Bank, Sunlight City, Import-Country, dated January 26, 2001."
3. This credit is subject to the Uniform Customs and Practice for Documentary Credits, 1993 Revision, International Chamber of Commerce Publication No. 500.

48 : Period of presentation
   Documents must be presented for payment within 15 days after the date of shipment.
49 : Confirmation instructions
   Add your confirmation
50 : Applicant
   DEF Imports, 7 Sunshine Street, Sunlight City, Import-Country
52A : Issuing bank
   The Sun Bank, Sunlight City, Import-Country
57D : Advise through bank
   The Moon Bank, 5 Moonlight Blvd., Export-City and Postal Code, Export-Country
59 : Beneficiary
   UVW Exports, 88 Prosperity Street East, Suite 707, Export-City and Postal Code, Export-Country
71B : Charges
   All charges outside the Import-Country are on beneficiary's account
72 : Sender to receiver information
   This is an operative instrument, no mail confirmation to follow
78 : Instruction to pay/accept/negot. bank
   Documents to be forwarded to us in one lot by courier

---Message Trailer---

MAC: ABCD1234
CHK: ABCDEFG12345

Airmail Letter of Credit

THE MOON BANK
INTERNATIONAL OPERATIONS
5 MOONLIGHT BLVD.,
EXPORT-CITY AND POSTAL CODE
EXPORT-COUNTRY

OUR ADVICE NO.	ISSUING BANK REF. NO. & DATE
MB-5432	SBRE-777 January 26, 2001

TO UVW Exports
88 Prosperity Street East, Suite 707
Export-City and Postal Code

Dear Sirs:

We have been requested by The Sun Bank, Sunlight City, Import-Country
to advise that they have opened with us their irrevocable documentary credit number SB-87654
for account of DEF Imports, 7 Sunshine Street, Sunlight City, Import-Country
in your favor for the amount of not exceeding Twenty Five Thousand U.S. Dollars (US $25 000.00)

available by your draft(s) drawn on us at sight for full invoice value
accompanied by the following documents:

1. Signed commercial invoice in five (5) copies indicating the buyer's Purchase Order No. DEF-101 dated January 10, 2001.
2. Packing list in five (5) copies.
3. Full set 3/3 clean on board ocean bill of lading, plus two (2) non-negotiable copies, issued to order of The Sun Bank, Sunlight City, Import-Country, notify the above accountee, marked "Freight Prepaid", dated latest March 19, 2001, and showing documentary credit number.
4. Insurance policy in duplicate for 110% CIF value covering Institute Cargo Clauses (A), Institute War and Strike Clauses, evidencing that claims are payable in Import-Country.

Covering: 100 Sets "ABC" Brand Pneumatic Tools, 1/2" drive,
complete with hose and quick couplings, CIF Sunny Port

Shipment from   Moonbeam Port, Export-Country to Sunny Port, Import-Country
Partial shipment   prohibited
Transhipment   permitted
Special conditions:

1. All documents indicating the Import License No. IP/123456 dated January

18, 2001.

2. All charges outside the Import-Country are on beneficiary's account.

Documents must be presented for payment within 15 days after the date of shipment. Draft(s) drawn under this credit must be marked:

Drawn under documentary credit No. SB-87654 of The Sun Bank,

Sunlight City, Import-Country, dated January 26, 2001

We confirm this credit and hereby undertake that all drafts drawn under and in conformity with the terms of this credit will be duly honored upon delivery of documents as specified, if presented at this office on or before March 26, 2001

Very truly yours,

Authorized Signature

Unless otherwise expressly stated, this Credit is subject to the Uniform Customs and Practice for Documentary Credits, 1993 Revision, International Chamber of Commerce Publication No. 500.

Unit 10 Packing

Learning Objectives

After learning this unit, you should:

✍ Know the importance and function of packing and shipping mark(了解包装和运输标志的重要性及功能)

✍ Write letters to negotiate on the packing terms(掌握包装条款磋商函的写作)

10.1 Introduction

Packing is a prerequisite condition for the protection of quality and quantity of the goods in logistics. Every buyer expects that his goods will reach him in perfect condition. Nothing is more infuriating to a buyer than to find his goods damaged or part missing on arrival. It should go without saying that the seller must try to pack the goods in such a way that they will go through the ordeal of transport unscathed. Moreover, suitable packing plays an important role in protecting and preserving as well as prettifying and advertising the goods and forms an important process in the storage, transportation, sales and usage of commodities. So packing requirement is a main term in negotiation.

商品包装是保护商品在流通过程中的品质完好和数量完整的重要条件。每个买主都期盼自己购买的货物能够完好无损地运到自己手中。对于买主来说,没有什么比在货物到达时发现货物破损或缺失更令人恼怒。所以,无须赘言,卖方必须妥善包装货物以使它们能够在运输过程中不发生破损。此外,适当的商品包装对保护、保存商品,美化、宣传商品以及方便商品的储存、运输、销售和使用都起着重要作用。因此,它是交易磋商的主要贸易条件之一。

The type and nature of the export transportation packing is influenced by factors such as:

出口货物运输包装材料和形式受以下因素影响:

Kind of product, Use crates for large and heavy objects like machines, bags for powder like cement, plastic drums or containers for liquids like acetic acids, wooden cases for small and heavy items like nails, and bales for bulky materials like cotton.

产品类型。如机器这样的大而重的货物需要用板条箱装,水泥这样的粉末状货物要用袋子装,乙酸这类液体要用塑料桶或容器装,铁钉这样小而重的货物用木箱装,玉米这样的散装货物可以打包。

Mode of transportation, generally, air freight requires less packing than ocean and land freight, and containerized shipments require less packing than non-containerized shipments due to lower risks of loss or damage.

运输方式。通常空运的货物比海运和陆运货物需要更少的包装,集装箱运输的货物比非集装箱运输的货物因为破损或灭失的风险更小,因而需要更少的包装。

Ports of destination, In areas with higher incidence of loss or damage due to mishandling, theft and pilferage, the more and stronger packing is necessary. Buyers are often familiar with the port systems overseas, so they will often specify packaging requirements.

目的港。如果在目的港,由于搬运不当、偷窃等导致货物破损或灭失发生率很高,就需要更结实、更充分的包装。因为买方对目的港的设施情况更熟悉,所以经常由买方提出包装要求。

Climatic conditions, Desiccants (drying agent) and/or special packing materials, such as waxed paper and laminated foil, may be required in areas with high moisture levels and for goods that are prone to sweating.

气候状况。如果空气湿度大、货物易受潮,则需要使用干燥剂和/或蜡纸及锡箔纸。

Customs duties and freight rates, Lighter and less packing material is preferred in cases where the specific duty or the freight rate is by weight basis.

关税和运费。如果按重量征收从量税或运费,那就要使用更少、更轻的包装材料。

Cost of packing materials. The exporter, being a manufacturer, may select the most economical materials and method of packing that can adequately protect the export goods.

包装成本。出口商如果也是生产商的话，会在保证对出口货物提供充分保护的前提下选择最经济的包装材料和包装方法。

Buyer's requirements. Buyers may specify the type of packing required, particularly in the OEM arrangements. If the buyer's demand for packing is "too much" which adds to the export cost, the manufacturer may recommend suitable packing.

买方的要求。买方可以提出对包装形式的要求，特别是在 OEM 的情况下。如果买方对包装的要求过高将导致成本增加，制造商可以就适合的包装提出建议。

Shipping marks are integral to packing. The shipping marks of a shipment are analogous to the identification (ID) card of a person. They identify the cargo the same way an ID card identifies a person. The exporter, customs, carriers, and importer rely on them to distinguish one consignment from another. The purpose of the marks is to identify the cargo, not the consignee, and they must be easily identifiable.

运输标志（唛头）是包装上必不可少的一部分。运输标志就像一个人的身份证。身份证用以识别每一个人，而运输标志用以识别货物。出口商、海关、承运人以及进口商都要靠运输标志识别货物。所以，运输标志的作用是识别货物，而不是识别收货人，它们必须特别容易辨认。

The shipping marks consist of the following four parts.

1. Abbreviations of consignees or buyers

For security reasons—to avoid being the target of pilferage—avoid using the full company name as it is too conspicuous. The mark can be enclosed in any shape (triangle, diamond, etc.) or without enclosure, unless otherwise specified by the buyer.

运输标志由四个部分构成。

1. 收货人或买方名称的缩写

为了货物的安全——避免成为偷窃的目标，标志中不使用收货人的全称,那样就太显眼了。名称的缩写可以放在一些几何图形(如三角型、钻石型)中,也可以不用几何图形,听从买方的指示。

2. Reference No.

It is one of the numbers of the shipping documents, such as the sales contract number, and should not be too long.

2. 参考号码

使用运输单据的编号即可,如销售合同的编号。编号不要太长。

3. The name of the unloading port

It should be clear and complete. In case the name refers to more than one place, it should be followed by the name of its country.

In case of transhipment to a landlocked country, put "VIA { + the named transshipping point}" below the point of final destination. For example if the cargo is destined for Zurich, Switzerland, and the transshipping point is Rotterdam, Netherlands, put "VIA ROTTERDAM, NETHERLANDS" below the point of final destination which is "ZURICH, SWITZERLAND".

For goods to be transported by OCP, both unloading ports and the destinations of the OCP should be listed. For example, Seattle OCP Boston. Optional ports should be preceded with "option", for example, Option Hamburg, Rotterdam.

3. 卸货港

内容应该清楚、完整。如果有同名港口,则在卸货港名称后面要写上国名。如果货物是转运到内陆国,则在最终目的地下面应该写上"VIA 转运地名称"。例如,货物是运往瑞士苏黎士,中途在荷兰鹿特丹转运,则正确的写法是:

ZURICH, SWITZERLAND

"VIA ROTTERDAM, NETHERLANDS"。

如果货物是进行 OCP 运输,应该列出卸货港和目的地。例如,Seattle OCP Boston。选择港前面应该加"option",如 Option Hamburg, Rotterdam。

4. Package No.

Exporters should list in the shipping mark the total number of the whole lot of cargoes and number the individual packages consecutively. The carton number can be in a running number, for example "C/NO. 1/50" or "C/NO. 1 OF 50" identifies the carton number 1 from a total of 50 cartons.

4. 包装编号

出口商应该在运输标志中写明货物包装总数量以及每个包装的编号。例如,纸箱上的编号"C/NO. 1/50" 或 "C/NO. 1 OF 50",表示这批货共 50 箱,这箱是第一箱。

Each country has regulations governing the manner in which imported goods should be marked, including the size of the letters. Sometimes, the language of the importing country must be used.

每个进口国对进口货物包装上的标志都有规定,甚至规定了字体大小。有时,可能必须使用进口国的文字。

10.2　Model Letter Comments

10.2.1　State Packing Requirements

Patel Clothing Ltd.
10 Clapham Street
London, U. K.

8 June 2003

China National Import & Export Co.
15 Chifeng Road
Shanghai, China

Dear sirs

　　We received your consignment of 20 cardboard cartons of men's shirts on June 4.

　　We regret to inform you that 2 cartons were delivered damaged and the contents had spilled, leading to some losses.

　　We accept that the damage was not your fault but feel that we must modify our packing requirements to avoid future losses. We require that future packing be in wooden boxes of 10 kilos net, each wooden box containing 2 cardboard cartons of 5 000 grams net.

Please let us know whether these specifications can be met by you and whether they will lead to an increase in your prices.

We look forward to your early confirmation.

Yours truly

Comments

Paragraph 1: identify the shipment

Paragraph 2: state the problem

Paragraph 3: make request for future packing requirements

Paragraph 4: ask for approval and information about any effect on prices

Paragraph 5: urge a prompt reply

The letter seeks to change packing requirements on the legitimate grounds that losses have occurred. It goes on to give exact details of the new requirements and anticipates that there may be additional costs incurred.

Notes

1. consignment 托运,运输,托运之物

The logistics department will take care of the consignment of the contract goods.

物流部门将负责合同货物的运输。

The consignment reached us in good order.

货物达到时完好无损。

2. carton 纸板箱,纸箱

We'll pack them two dozen to one carton, gross weight around 25 kilos a carton.

我们一纸箱装两打,每箱毛重约 25 公斤。

Ten bottles are put into a box and 100 boxes into a carton.

10 支装入一小盒,100 盒装入一个纸箱。

Such shirts packed in cardboard cartons can save freight cost.

使用硬纸箱包装这批衬衣可以节省运费。

The canned goods are to be packed in cartons with double straps.

罐装货物在纸箱里,外面加两道箍。

其他常见的包装方式有 case 箱、wooden case 木箱、crate 板条箱、chest 箱、casket 小箱、box 盒子、cask 桶、keg 小桶、wooden cask 木桶、barrel 琵琶桶、drum 圆桶、iron drum 铁桶、gunny bag 麻袋、plastic bag 塑料袋、container 集装箱、pallet 托盘。

3. fault 过错,错误

As you are in no way at fault for this overshipping, we suggest, along with our apology, that you take this overshipment at no extra cost.

溢装货物绝对不是你方的过错,所以我们向你方致歉并建议你方收下溢装的货物而不必付费。

We admit that we are at fault in so far as we should have provided for this special case.

我们承认我们错了,我们应该对这种特殊情况做出规定。

4. packing (n.) 包装

We agree to use cartons for outer packing.

我们同意用纸箱做外包装。

I think you'll find the packing beautiful and quite well-done.

您一定发现我们产品的包装美观讲究。

The packing must be strong enough to withstand rough handling.

包装必须十分坚固,以承受野蛮搬运。

Packing charge is about 3% of the total cost of the goods.

包装费用占货物总值的3%。

pack (vt.) 包装

It would cost more for you to pack the goods in wooden cases.

使用木箱包装成本会高些。

The piece goods are to be wrapped in kraft paper, then packed in wooden cases.

布匹在装入木箱以前要用牛皮纸包好。

We'll pack them two dozen to one carton, gross weight around 25 kilos a carton.

我们一纸箱装两打,每箱毛重25公斤。

The canned goods are to be packed in cartons with double straps.
罐装货物在纸箱里,外面加两道箍。

10.2.2 State Packing Requirements

ABC Containers plc.
8 Dock Road
London, U.K.

30 November 2003

Oriental Foods plc.
6 Walton Street
Southampton
U.K.
Dear sirs

 Thank you for your quotation No. 356 on Punches S40. We wish to order 500 units of them with you if our packing requirements can be met.

 Taking into account the specialty of this article, we request you to pack the goods in strong wooden cases so as to withstand the hazards of ocean transportation. To waterproof the goods, you need to cover the machines with waterproof cloth and strap them horizontally and vertically with plastic bands. For the sake of precaution, indicative mark like KEEP DRY should be shown, too.

 Should the packing requirements be acceptable to you, we would give you the order promptly.

 We look forward to hearing from you.

Yours truly

Comments

 Paragraph 1: identify the reference
 Paragraph 2: state the request for special packing

Paragraph 3: urge the seller to accept the requirement

Paragraph 4: hope for response

The letter is easy to understand. It covers all the packing requirement by the prospective client.

Notes

1. take...into account 考虑到

Taking the current market situation into account, we decide to lower our price by 10%.

考虑到目前的市场状况,我们决定降价10%。

You should take the brisk demand into account in deciding the order quantity.

你在确定订货数量时要考虑到这种旺盛的需求状况。

2. waterproof (*adj.*) 不透水的,防水的 (*vt.*) 使不透水,使防水

This object is coated with waterproof material.

这个东西的表面涂了一层防水材料。

Shirts are to be packed in plastic-lined waterproof cartons.

衬衣应放在内衬塑料防水的箱子里。

3. strap (*n.*) 铁皮条 (*vt.*) 捆扎,打箍

The canned goods are to be packed in cartons with double straps.

罐装货物在纸箱里,外面加两道箍。

You must reinforce the packing with metal straps.

你们必须用铁箍加固包装。

The goods are to be packed in strong export cases, securely strapped.

货物应该用坚固的出口木箱包装,并且牢牢加箍。

4. for the sake of 为了

He gave up smoking for the sake of health.

为了健康,他戒烟了。

For the sake of convenience, they asked the carrier to transport the goods from the rail terminal to the warehouse.

为了方便,他们要求承运人将货物从火车站运到仓库。

5. indicative mark 指示性标志

常见的指示性标志有：

Center of Gravity 重心点

Do Not Drop 请勿投下

Fragile 当心破碎

Glass 小心玻璃

Handle With Care 小心轻放

Keep Away from Cold 勿放冷处

Keep Away from Heat 勿放热处

Keep Dry 保持干燥

Maximum Stack 重叠数量

Open Here 由此打开

Sling Here 由此吊索

This Side Up 此边向上

Use No Hooks 请勿用钩

mark (n. v.) 标志、刷唛

On the outer packing, please mark wording, "Handle with Care".

在外包装上请标明"小心轻放"字样。

Every 100 dozen should be packed in a wooden case marked TM and numbered from No. 1 upward.

每 100 打装一箱，刷上唛头 TM，从第一号开始往上循序编号。

Please cable packing and marks.

请电告包装及唛头式样。

We have no objection to the stipulations about the packing and shipping mark.

我们同意关于包装和运输唛头的条款。

10.3 Specimen Letters

10.3.1 Describe a Container Service

Dear sirs

Thank you for your inquiry of 20 November regarding our container service.

The shipping containers we provide are of two sizes, namely 20ft. and 40ft. They can be opened at both ends, thus making it possible to load and unload at the same time. For carrying goods liable to be spoiled by damp or water they have the advantage of being both water-tight and air-tight. Containers are loaded and locked at the factory, rendering pilferage impossible.

When separate consignments are carried in one container if their ports of destination are the same, there will be a saving on freight charges, and an additional saving on insurance because of the lower premium charges for container-shipped goods.

We enclose a copy of our tariff and look forward to receiving your instructions.

Yours sincerely

● **Activities for comprehension**

1. What are the basic advantages of container shipment?
2. Search for some information about the categories of containers.

10.3.2 Express Concerns about the Packing Method

Dear sirs

We thank you for your proposal of 2 April and wish to inform you that we have discussed the matter with our salesmen and some of the clients. The reactions are:

(1) They fear that there will be more pilferage from goods packed in cartons than from goods packed in wooden cases, as it is easier to cut open such cartons.

(2) They fear that the insurance companies will say, in case of damage or pilferage, that the goods are not packed for ocean transportation and will not pay compensation for such losses.

(3) They fear that if and when the goods are transshipped at Hamburg, the package will stand in the open on the wharf and, in heavy rains, be subjected to damage, as the cartons will surely be soaked.

(4) They fear that such cartons will be more easily broken, and the goods damaged through careless handling at the wharf; for example heavy wooden cases being piled on the cartons.

However, if you will guarantee, and state such guarantee in all your sales confirmation you will pay compensation in all cases wherein the buyer cannot get indemnification from the insurance company for the reason that the goods are not packed in seaworthy wooden cases, we are sure that our clients will have no objection to your packing the goods in cartons.

We look forward to your early reply.

Yours truly

10.3.3　Give Explanations on the Choice of the Packing

Dear sirs

We thank you for your letter of April 24. In regard to your fears over packing in cartons as expressed in your letter, we have taken up this matter with the competent departments here, and wish to give you our comments as follows:

(1) Packing in cartons prevents skilful pilferage. As the traces of pilferage will be more in evidence, the insurance company may be made to pay the necessary compensation for such losses.

(2) Cartons are quite fit for ocean transportation, and they are extensively used in our shipments to other continental ports to the entire satisfaction of our clients. Such packing has also been accepted by our insurance company for WPA and TPND.

(3) These cartons are well protected against moisture by plastic lining. The very fact that they are made of paperboard induces special attention in handling and storage. Thus, shirts packed in such cartons are not susceptible to damage by moisture as those packed in wooden cases.

(4) Since cartons are comparatively light and compact, they are more convenient to handle in the course of loading and unloading. Besides, they are not likely to be mixed with wooden cases while in transport or storage, so that the rate

of breakage is lower than that of wooden cases.

The comments given above are based upon a comparative study of the characteristics of the two modes of packing, as well as upon results of shipments already made. Of course, occasional mishaps under peculiar conditions are not to be excluded. As long as we work closely with each other, it is believed that your clients will find the improved packing in cartons satisfactory and their fears unwarranted.

We assure you of our continued cooperation, and await your further comments.

Yours truly

10.3.4 Accept the Seller's Explanation
Dear sirs

Thank you for your letter of May 12.

With regard to the packing for ready-made garments, you say that you have taken up the matter with the competent departments and are of the opinion that packing in cartons will prevent skillful pilferage; such cartons are well protected against moisture; they are light and convenient to handle, etc. After discussing the matter with our clients, we find that your comments sound quite reasonable. However, we cannot be sure how things will prove to be until the first lot of goods packed in such cartons arrives.

We are of the opinion that if the result packing in cartons turns out to the satisfaction of our clients, you may continue using this packing in future. However, in case of the result not being so, we are afraid that this will considerably affect the development of business between us.

You may rest assured that in our mutual interest we shall do everything possible to give you our full cooperation.

As soon as the goods reach us, we shall not fail to communicate with you.

Yours truly

● **Activities for comprehension**

1. Why the buyer was reluctant to adopt the new packing method at first?

2. What requirements did the buyer make for the seller to use carton packing?

3. How did the seller persuade the buyer to accept the new packing method?

10.4 Summary

Outer packing serves for the shipment of goods, which is of utmost importance in international trade. The goods should be packed in a way according to the importer's instructions or the trade custom, without violating the import country's regulations on outer packing materials, length and weight.

外包装是运输包装,在国际贸易中有很重要的意义。应该根据进口商的要求或贸易管理选择货物的包装方式,不要违反进口国对外包装材料、长度和重量的规定。

When quantities, weights or contents of the various packing cases in an export shipment vary, it is usual to prepare a separate list (packing list) for each case indicating its contents, weight and measurements. It also often includes the outside dimension of each case and the total cubic content and total weight of the shipment.

如果每一个出口货物的包装箱的盛装数量、重量或物品不同,往往需要为每一个包装箱准备一个清单(箱单),说明每一箱所装货物类型、重量和尺码等。箱单中还会写每个箱的外部尺寸、全部货物的总容积和总重量等。

The exporter or his/her agent—the customs broker or the freight forwarder—reserves the shipping space based on the gross weight or the measurement shown in the packing list. Customs uses the packing list as a check-list to verify the outgoing cargo (in exporting) and the incoming cargo (in importing). The importer uses the packing list to inventory the incoming consignment.

出口商或其代理人——报关代理人或货运代理人应按照装箱单上所写的毛重或尺码预订舱位。海关把箱单用作检查清单以核对进出口的货物。进口商将进口货物入库时也要根据箱单的内容。

10.5 Useful Expressions

1. All export orders will be packed in single kraft paper bags laminated with PE wovenbag, 25 kgs net each.

所有出口订单下的货物都用内衬塑编布包的单层牛皮纸袋装, 25 公斤/包。

2. The consignment shall be packed in wooden case with 2 reels inside and each reel is wrapped with Poly-Membrane and kraft paper. It was bound with iron belts externally.

所有货物应用木箱包装, 内装 2 卷。每卷用塑料薄膜牛皮纸包裹, 箱外铁带捆扎。

3. Partial strapping of the carton will not only save freight, but give full protection to the contents.

如果采用在纸箱外打箍的方式, 不仅可以节省运费, 而且可以实现对箱里的货物充分的保护。

4. As the boxes are likely to receive rough handling at this end, you must see to it that packing should be strong enough to protect goods.

由于在这里可能会发生对箱子进行野蛮搬运, 你方务必确保包装足够结实以保护好货物。

5. As the goods will probably be subjected to a thorough customs examination, the cases should be of a type which can be easily made fast again after opening.

因为海关可能会对货物进行彻底检查, 所以货箱应该是打开后能够很容易地就密封的那种。

6. Please pack this machine in a strong wooden case and wrap and pad generously all polished parts of the machine to avoid scratches and knocks against the container.

请将这台机器装在结实的木箱里, 必须多用些东西将机器上抛光的部分衬垫、包裹, 以避免划伤及与集装箱壁碰撞。

7. Please stencil our shipping marks five inches high and give gross and net weight, port of destination, country of origin and a B in the rectangle as the main mark of each case.

请将我们的唛头印成 5 英寸高,每个箱子上的主标志包括的内容有毛重、净重、目的港、原产国以及一个长方形里面写一个 B 字母。

8. Drugs with different batch numbers should, by no means, be mixed and packed in the same cases or container. Each package should contain drugs of only one batch number.

批号不同的药品绝对不可以混放在同一个箱子或集装箱里。每一个包装中的药品应该是同一个批号的。

9. The goods should be packed in tin-lined waterproof wooden case, each piece wrapped in oilcloth, and 30 pieces packed in one case.

这些货物应该装在内衬锡箔的防水木箱里,每件货物用油布包裹,30 件装入一个箱子里。

10. Please put the machine in a case of about 10 cubic meters covered with waterproof cloth and strapped vertically and horizontally with metal bands and cut vent holes in the case to minimize condensation.

请将机器放入容积约为 10 立方米的箱子中,机器用防水布盖好,并用铁皮条纵横捆扎,箱子上要开出一些通风孔以减少冷凝水的产生。

10.6　Reading Materials

10.6.1

Dear Sir

Thanks for your letter of July 1. As requested, we will make packing arrangements as follows:

Women's leather shoes are first packed one pair in a polybag, then in a paper box. 10 boxes to a carton lined with water-proof paper, bound with straps outside, and 10 cartons on a pallet. Each carton contains S/1, M/6, L/2 and XL/1. You may rest assured that our cartons are strong enough and seaworthy.

We hope the above arrangements will turn out to your satisfaction and await your early confirmation, so that we may have the goods prepared.

Yours faithfully

10.6.2

Dear sirs

We are in receipt of your letter November 11 enquiring us about the packing requirements.

As the ordered goods are fragile, we require these articles to be wrapped up in corrugated paper and packed in wooden cases with excelsior.

Please limit the weight of any one of the wooden cases to 50 kg and metal strap all cases in stacks of three.

We look forward to your shipping advice.

Yours faithfully

10.6.3

Dear sirs

The shipping date is near and we would like to reiterate our packing requirements so as to avoid any future problems in regard to packing.

All the crates must not exceed an overall length of 10 meters. The crates are to be marked with an A in the square and number them consecutively from No. 1 to No. 5.

All marks other than our company's are to be removed from the crates before shipment.

We thank you for your cooperation and hope to have your shipping advice without any delay.

Yours faithfully

10.6.4

Dear sirs

The 12 000 cycles you ordered will be ready for dispatch by 17th December. Since you require them for onward shipment to Bahrain, Kuwait, Oman and Qatar, we are arranging for them to be packed in seaworthy containers.

Each bicycle is enclosed in a corrugated cardboard pack, and 20 are banned together and wrapped in sheet plastic. A container holds 240 cycles; the whole cargo would therefore comprise 50 containers, each weighing 8 tons. Dispatch can be made from our works by rail to be forwarded from Shanghai harbour. The freight charges from works to Shanghai are US $80 per container, totally US $4 000 for this consignment, excluding container hire, which will be charged to your account.

Please let us have your delivery instruction.

Yours faithfully

 Exercises

I. Choose the best answer to complete each of the following sentences.

1. We do not mind whether the goods are _____ in cartons or in wooden cases, as long as the packages are seaworthy.

    a) packing   b) packed   c) packaged   d) pack

2. We are sure that the _____ is strong enough to withstand rough handling.

    a) packing   b) packed   c) packaged   d) pack

3. _____ instructions are stated accurately in the captioned contract.

    a) Packing   b) Packed   c) Packaged   d) Pack

4. Exporters should be aware of the demands that international shipping puts on _____ goods.

    a) packaging   b) pack   c) packaged   d) packing

5. Buyers are often familiar with the port systems overseas, so they will often specify _____ requirements.

    a) packaging   b) pack   c) packaged   d) packed

6. All the mountain bikes are packed on wooden pallet _____ with four iron belts externally and the packing is sound.

    a) bind   b) binding   c) bound   d) bounding

7. The cotton goods are packed in kraft paper _____ with Polyethylene film of 25 kgs net each.

    a) lining   b) lined   c) line   d) liner

8. We are afraid that we shall have to charge more for the designated packing, as it _____ more labor and cost.
   a) calls for   b) calls at   c) calls on   d) calls out

II. Put in each blank the proper word or phrase from the following list.

| comments | opened and fastened | separated | packed | lining |
| turned out | as well as | | precaution | marked | secured |

1. As the goods will be checked up at the customs, the cases must be of a type which can be easily _____ at once after check.

2. We will pass your _____ on packing on to the manufacturers concerned for their consideration.

3. All the sacks have an interior water-proof _____ to protect goods.

4. Our scissors are _____ in boxes of one dozen each, 200 boxes to a wooden case.

5. The packages should be _____ with the lot number as given in the order sheet.

6. You will note that our packing has been greatly improved with the result that our recent shipments have all _____ to the satisfaction of our clients.

7. We understand your concern about packing, and can assure you that we take every possible _____ to ensure that our products reach our customers all over the world in prime condition.

8. The crates are lined with waterproof, airtight material and the lids are _____ by nailing.

9. In the case of consignments being sent to you, transshipment at Buenos Aires will be necessary, so each case will be marked with details required by the Argentinian authorities, _____ with your own mark.

10. The boxes are then packed into strong cardboard cartons, twelve into a carton, _____ from each other by corrugated paper dividers.

III. Translate the following letter into Chinese.

Dear Sirs,

We thank you for your packing arrangements, at the same time, please note our shipping marks as follows:

Please mark our initials BOB in a circle, under which the quantity and port of destination should be indicated. In addition, warning marks such as "Fragile", "This Side Up" etc., should also be stenciled on the outer packing.

Please follow our instructions strictly so as to facilitate our taking delivery of the cargo.

Yours faithfully

● **Skills Practice**

Write a letter to your customer, telling him about the packing of your Trip Scissors.

Particulars: 1. 每盒装一打,每一纸板箱装一百盒。
2. 尺码是高 17 cm、宽 30 cm、长 50 cm,体积约 0.026 m³。
3. 毛重 23.5 公斤,净重 22.5 公斤。
4. 唛头除包括毛重、净重和皮重外,还须印刷"中华人民共和国制造"字样。

Unit 11 Insurance

Learning Objectives

After learning this unit, you should:

✍ Know the risks coverage for sea, air, overland transportation and parcel post under C. I. C. Clauses(了解中国人民保险公司货物运输保险中海运、空运、陆运和邮包运输险的险种)

✍ Know the Institute Cargo Clauses(了解协会货物条款)

✍ Know how to write letter concerning insurance(了解有关保险问题的信函写作方法)

✍ Master typical sentences and expressions in writing such letters(掌握此类信函中常用句型和短语)

11.1 Introduction

When goods have to be shipped to a foreign country, there is always the risk that they may be damaged, destroyed, or stolen and may vary, according to the country of destination, the route and method of shipment.

当货物运往海外时,总会存在货物破损或失窃的风险,这种风险的大小与运输的目的地、运输路线和运输方式等都有关系。

To be protected from financial loss as a result of this risk, either the firm that sells the goods or the firm that buys them, arrange for insurance. It is to the exporter's advantage to be responsible for placing the insurance on the shipment. Such insurance cannot prevent accidental losses but can provide reimbursement for financial loss should the exporter's shipment somehow fail to arrive or arrive intact.

为了避免由于这类风险而遭受经济损失,卖方或买方都会安排货物保险。由卖方安排保险对卖方是有利的。保险并不能防止意外损失,但可以在货物不能到达目的地或不能完好地到达目的地而遭受经济损失时提供一些补偿。

In insurance business the insured is one who pays the insurance company for the coverage of risks of the cargo. The insurer is the insurance company that agrees to make payment in case of loss or damage occurred to the insured. The insured and the insurer are bound by a contract known as the insurance policy. The marine insurance policy forms part of the shipping document. When goods are sold on CIF basis, the seller is under obligation to present a marine insurance policy or an insurance certificate at the time of negotiation.

保险业务当中,向保险公司支付保险费而得到货物的保险的人是被保险人。同意当被保险人的货物受损或灭失时向被保险人进行赔付的保险公司是保险商。被保险人和保险商受保险单这一合同的约束。海运保险单是货物运输单据的一个组成内容。如果货物是按 CIF 价格售出的,卖方有义务在议付时交出海运保险单或保险凭证。

Very often, the exporter will quote a CIF price to its foreign customer. This is an export price that includes the cost of the goods, the insurance and the freight, to a named point of destination. If the quotation is accepted, the exporter will automatically be responsible for arranging the marine insurance.

通常,出口商向国外的客户报 CIF 价格。在这个价格中包括了货物的成本、货物运到指定目的地的运费和保险费。如果买方接受报价,出口商就要承担对货物投保海运保险。

Even though the export price may be F.A.S. (free along side, named point of shipment), the exporter may still be responsible for arranging the marine insurance. This would be so if the exporter has made it one of the terms of the "export sales contract". In this case, the cost of the insurance would be billed as a separate expense, additional to the FAS or FOB sales price. Such insurance might include war risk insurance as well as straight marine insurance.

即使是装运港船边交货价,如果在出口销售合同中规定由出口商负责办理保险手续,出口商也可以办理。此时,保险的费用是在装运港船边交货价或装运港船上交货价之外单独收取的。投保的险种除了一般海运保险险种以外也可以投保战争险。

If it is stipulated that payment to be by letter of credit, the issuing bank in the foreign importer's country will insist on having marine insurance-even though the export price quoted is FAS or FOB Because the bank will wish to protect its own financial interest should the goods be damaged or destroyed in transit.

如果规定采用信用证方式付款,即使出口价格是 FAS 或 FOB 价,进口国的开证行也会坚持要求货物要保险。因为银行希望如果货物在运输途中发生部分或全部破损时自己的经济利益得到保障。

The Institute Cargo Clauses, shortened as I. C. C. were set forth by the Institute of London Underwriters. They have exerted great influences in the development of international insurance. Most countries in the world have referred to them more or less in making their own insurance clauses.

伦敦保险商协会制定的保险条款被称为协会货物条款,简写为ICC。它对国际保险事业的发展产生了很大影响。大多数国家在制定自己的保险条款时都或多或少地参考了协会货物条款。

Insurance coverage under I. C. C. falls into six clauses: Institute Cargo Clauses A; Institute Cargo Clauses B; Institute Cargo Clauses C; Institute War Clauses—Cargo; Institute Strike Clauses—Cargo; Malicious Damage Clauses.

协会货物条款分六种:协会货物条款(A)、协会货物条款(B)、协会货物条款(C)、协会战争险条款、协会罢工险条款和恶意损害险条款。

The People's Insurance Company of China has its own insurance clause, known as China Insurance Clause (CIC), which is different from ICC The principal perils which the basic marine policy of the PICC insures against under its Ocean Marine Cargo Clause are:

a) Free from Particular Average (FPA)

b) With Particular Average (WPA)

c) All Risks

中国人民保险公司有自己的保险条款,被称为中国保险条款(CIC),它不同于协会货物条款。中国人民保险公司海运保险条款承保的基本险种包括平安险(FPA)、水渍险(WPA)和一切险。

An insurance claim, if any, should be submitted to the insurance company or its agent as promptly as possible. In order to substantiate an ordinary average claim, the following documents must be presented: insurance policy or certificate, bill of lading, original invoice, survey report, master's protest and statement of claim.

如果需要进行保险索赔,应该尽快向保险公司或其代理人提出。索赔时,需要提交下列单据以支持你的索赔请求:保险单或保险凭证、提单、原始发票、检验报告、海事报告和索赔说明。

11.2　Model Letters Comments

11.2.1　Ask the Buyer to Cover Insurance

China National Import & Export Co.
15 Chifeng Road
Shanghai, China
Tel: 021-78493940
Fax: 021-78454930

30 March 2003

Lee Clothes Store
22 West Road
London, U.K.

Dear sirs

　　We refer to your order No. K756 for 20 cases of silk blouses.

　　We have booked shipping space for the consignment on S.S. Bright which sails for your port on or about 14 April.

　　We would be grateful if you would please arrange insurance cover for the consignment at your end.

　　Please fax your confirmation as soon as possible.

Yours sincerely

Comments

Paragraph 1: identify the reference

Paragraph 2: state what action has been taken

Paragraph 3: ask the buyer to arrange insurance

Paragraph 4: ask for confirmation

The letter describes the current situation regarding the order. It goes on to ask the buyer to arrange insurance and send confirmation.

Notes

1. insurance (n.) 保险

We usually effect insurance against All Risks for the invoice value plus 10% for the goods sold on CIF basis.

对于以 CIF 价售出的货物,我们通常按发票金额的 110% 投保一切险。

According to our usual practice, insurance is to be effected for 110% of the invoice value.

按照我们的惯例,是按照发票金额的 110% 投保。

The rates quoted by us are very moderate. Of course, the premium varies with the range of insurance.

我们所收取的费率是很有限的,当然,保险费用要根据投保范围的大小而有所不同。

insure (vt.) 给……保险

The shipment is to be insured against All Risks and War Risk.

这批货要投保一切险和战争险。

We agree to your request to insure the shipment for 130% of the invoice value, but the premium for the difference between 130% and 110% should be for your account.

我们同意你方的请求,对货物按照发票金额的 130% 投保,但是你方应该承担保险费超过按发票金额 110% 投保的保费那部分。

The cargo is to be insured warehouse to warehouse against All Risks.

按仓至仓条款对货物投保一切险。

2. cover （*vt. n.*）保险

We regret being unable to comply with your buyer's request to cover the goods against All Risks.

很遗憾,我们不能按照你方买主的要求对货物投保一切险。

Please let us know immediately whether we can cover marine insurance elsewhere at a more reasonable rate.

请立刻告知我方是否可以在其他地方以更合理的费率投保海运保险。

We are pleased to inform you that we have covered the shipment with the People's Insurance Company of China.

很高兴通知你方我们已经在中国人民保险公司对货物投保了。

The underwriters are responsible for the claim as far as it is within the scope of cover.

只要是在保险责任范围内,保险公司就应负责赔偿。

We require immediate cover and shall be grateful if you will let us have the policy as soon as it is ready.

我们要求立即投保,如果你们能够让我们尽快拿到保险单我们不胜感激。

The cover is limited to 60 days upon discharge of the insured goods from the sea-going vessel at the final port of discharge before the insured goods reach the consignee's warehouse.

所投保的货物在最终卸货港卸船后,如果在 60 天内没有到达收货人仓库,则保险责任终止。

coverage （*n.*）保险险别,保险范围

The loss in question was beyond the coverage granted by us.

损失不包括在我方承保的范围内。

WPA coverage is too narrow for a shipment of this nature. Please extend the coverage to include TPND.

针对这种性质的货物只保水渍险是不够的,请加保偷盗提货不成险。

The coverage is WPA plus Risk of Breakage.

投保的险别为水渍险加破碎险。

If coverage against other risks is required, such as breakage, leakage,

TPND, hook and contamination damages, the extra premium involved would be for the buyer's account.

如果要加保其他险别,例如破碎险、渗漏险、盗窃遗失险、钩损和污染险等,额外保险费由买方负担。

3. at your end 在你地

With the approach of the rain season at your end, there surely will be an increasing demand for high quality raincoats.

在你地,随着雨季的来临,对高品质雨衣的需求一定会增加的。

Since the market at your end is still firm, there is little chance to make further reduction in prices.

由于你地市场坚挺,再降价的可能性不大。

11.2.2 Inquiry about Insurance Rate

Flight Electronics Co.
1 East Road
Beijing, China
Tel: 010-80304430
June 10, 2007

China Insurance Company Beijing Branch
No. 12 Fuxing Road
Beijing China

Dear sirs

We are writing to inquire about your insurance rate as we have 200 CTNS of ladies' dresses, valued at USD 500 000, ready for dispatch to New York on S. S. Tian Ma 2010 before the end of June.

We should be pleased if you would send us your particulars of it and quote us for a 20″ container with total weight of 2 000 kgs covering All Risks and War Risk from Tianjin to New York as soon as possible.

Yours faithfully

Comments

Paragraph 1: explain the purpose of writing the letter and give the particulars of the consignment

Paragraph 2: make a polite request for insurance rate quotation

The letter gives a clear and definite description of the consignment to be insured to enable the insurer make a quote for the insurance coverage.

Notes

1. value (*vt.*) 估价,估值

Please clear through the customs, making entry in our name and declaring weight at 75 metric tons, valued at USD6 000.

该批货物重量为 75 公吨,价值 6 000 美元,请以本公司名义向海关报关。

20 bales of cotton piece goods, valued at USD4 000, are over-shipped and we are waiting for your instructions on how to dispose of them.

你方多装了 20 包棉布,价值约 4 000 美元,我们现在正听候你方的处理安排。

2. particular (*n.*) 细节,详细情况

Please provide particulars of your rate for the coverage.

请提供该险别费率的详细资料。

All the particulars about the consignment are given on the packing list.

有关货物的详细情况都写在箱单上了。

3. cover (*n. vt.*) 保险,投保

Please confirm that you hold the consignment covered.

请确认你方投保了这批货物。

The value of the stock varies with the season, but does not normally exceed USD10 000 at any time. Please arrange cover in this sum for All Risks.

这批货的价值随季节波动,但从来没有超过 10 000 美元,请按这个价值保一切险。

We require immediate cover as far as New York and shall be glad if you will let us have the policy as soon as it is ready.

我们要求立刻得到货物到纽约的保险,如果能尽快让我方得到保单,不胜感激。

11.2.3　Answer a Request for Excessive Insurance

Flight Electronics Co.
1 East Road
Beijing, China
Tel: 010-80304430

26 March 2007

Gregory Inc.
2 Flint Street
Sydney, Australia
Dear sirs

　　Thank you for your letter of 14 March referring to your order No. 234 for 10 000 DVD players.

　　In your letter you ask us to insure the order for an amount 25% above the invoice value. Our normal practice is to insure shipments for the invoice value plus 10%. We are, however, prepared to comply with your request and obtain cover for 125% of the invoice value. In the circumstances, the extra premium will be for your account.

　　We trust that you will find this arrangement acceptable.

Yours faithfully

Comments

　　Paragraph 1: identify the reference and the order

　　Paragraph 2: accept the request and point out that the customer will have to pay the extra premium

　　Paragraph 3: end with a polite message

　　The letter makes it clear that the seller thinks that the insurance requested is excessive. The proposal will only be accepted if the buyer agrees to meet the extra cost.

Notes

1. 25% above the invoice value 意思是指发票金额的125%

类似的表达方式有:invoice value plus 25%,125% of the invoice value。

We've covered insurance on these goods for 10% above the invoice value against All Risks.

我们已经将这些货物按发票金额加10%投保一切险。

2. be prepared to do 愿意做……

We are prepared to give you a 5% reduction in price to help you occupy the market.

为了帮助你方占领市场,我们愿意给你方5%的降价。

We are prepared to take any risk arising from this.

我们愿意承担由此造成的任何风险。

3. comply with 遵照,按照,与……一致

To comply with your request, we insure the goods against All Risks.

按照你方的要求,我们已经为货物投保了一切险。

We are in a position to promise you that the goods supplied comply with the sample in both the quality and design.

我们可以向你方承诺,所供应的货物品质与设计与样品完全一致。

4. in the circumstances 在这种情况下

Please let us know what settlement you consider fair in the circumstances.

请问你方认为在这种情况下什么解决方案是公平合理的。

In these circumstances, would you be satisfied if we were to take over 50% of the cost of reshipping the goods?

在这样的情况下,如果我方承担一半的货物重装费用你方是否满意呢?

5. premium 保险费

The premium varies with the extent of insurance. Should additional risks be covered, the extra premium would be for buyer's account.

保险范围不同,保险费则不同。如果投保了附加险种,额外的保费由买方负担。

Could you find out the premium rate for porcelain?

您能查一下瓷器的保险费率吗?

6. for one's account 由某人支付

类似的表达方式有：be credited to one's account, be charged to one's account, be borne by sb。

The packing charges will be credited (charged) to your account.

包装费用由你方支付。

As our usual practice, insurance covers basic risks only, at 110 percent of the invoice value. If coverage against other risks is required, such as breakage, leakage, TPND, hook and contamination damages, the extra premium involved would be for the buyer's account.

按照我们的惯例,只保基本险,按发票金额110%投保。如果要加保其他险别,例如破碎险、渗漏险、偷窃提货不着险、钩损和玷污险等,额外保险费由买方负担。

11.3 Specimen Letters

11.3.1 Request Seller to Arrange Insurance

Dear sirs

We would like to refer you to our order No. 1289 for 500 cases of toys, from which you see that this order is placed on CFR basis.

As we now desire to have the shipment insured at your end, please insure the same on our behalf against All Risks at invoice value plus 10%.

We shall of course refund to you the premium upon receipt of your debit note, or, if you like, you may draw on us at sight for the amount required.

We sincerely hope that our request will meet with your approval.

Yours truly

● Activities for comprehension

1. How is the insurance value calculated?

2. As far as foreign trade is concerned, what risks are covered under an insurance policy?

11.3.2 Reply

Dear sirs

This is to acknowledge receipt of your letter dated 20th July requesting us to effect insurance on the captioned shipment for your account.

We are pleased to inform you that we have covered the above shipment with the People's Insurance Company of China against All Risks for US $2 200. The policy is being prepared accordingly and will be forwarded to you by the end of the week together with our debit note for the premium.

For your information, we are making arrangements to ship the contracted goods by S.S. "Yoming", sailing on or about the 11th of August.

Yours truly

● **Activities for comprehension**

1. What is insurance policy?
2. What is the difference between insurance policy and insurance certificate?
3. At what time is the seller under obligation to present a marine insurance policy when goods are sold on CIF basis?

11.3.3 Request the insurer to cover the consignment

Dear sirs

We wish to insure the following consignment against All Risks for the sum of US $5 000, 4 cases of VCRs, Marked AD-1-4.

These goods are now lying at Albert Dock, Liverpool, waiting to be shipped by S.S. "RAJIA", due to leave for Bombay on Friday, 26 March.

We require immediate cover as far as Bombay and shall be grateful if you will let us have the policy as soon as it is ready. In the meantime please let us have your confirmation that you hold the consignment covered.

Yours sincerely

● **Activities for comprehension**

1. What information should be included in a letter of insurance application?

11.3.4 Reply

Dear sirs

Thank you for your letter of 4 March asking us to cover the consignment of four cases of VCRs from Liverpool to Bombay.

The premium for this cover is at the rate of 90% of the declared value of US $5 000. The policy is being prepared and will be sent to you within a day or two. Meanwhile, we confirm that we hold the consignment covered as from today.

Yours sincerely

11.3.5 Request the Seller to Make a Claim

Dear sirs

Thank you for your prompt shipment of our order No. JK-9673 by S. S. "Huanqiu".

After unloading the goods, however, we found that one side of case No. 2 containing DVD players was split. We informed the local insurance surveyor immediately who opened the case in question and examined the contents in the presence of the shipping company's agents. Eight of the 20 DVD players contained were found to be badly damaged.

As you hold the insurance policy, we should be grateful if you would take the matter up for us with the insurer. We are enclosing the shipping agent's statement.

Meanwhile, please arrange to supply eight replacement DVD players and charge to our account.

We hope no difficulty will arise in our insurance claim and thank you in advance for your trouble on our behalf.

Yours truly

● **Activities for comprehension**

1. Whom should an insurance claim be submitted to?

2. What documents must be presented in order to substantiate an ordinary average claim?

11.4 Summary

In international trade, most of the goods are transported by the sea. During transportation over the long distance, due to miscellaneous perils of the sea and extraneous risks, loss of or damage to the goods, that is losses, may occur in transportation, loading and unloading or warehousing. To get financial reimbursement when losses occur, we need to insure the goods against transport risks according to the international trade practice. The cost of marine insurance is quite small compared with the cost of the goods shipped and the freight charges involved. Therefore, the benefit of the marine insurance, in terms of financial reimbursement if disaster strikes, is usually well worth the cost. It is now an indispensable part to the import and export practice.

People's Insurance Company of China, referring to the realities of China's insurance business and the usual practice in international insurance market, set forth Ocean Marine Insurance Clauses, Overland Transportation Insurance Clauses, Air Transportation Insurance Clauses and Parcel Post Insurance Clauses as well as additional risks coverage for insurance under these different transportation modes. Even if we conclude business with foreign importers on terms of CIF or CIP, our export companies and insurance companies can, as the foreign partners request, accept coverage under Institute Cargo Clauses of the Institute of London Underwriters.

在国际贸易中,货物大多经由海上运输。在长途海运中,货物可能会因各种海上风险或意外事故,在运输、装卸、储存等环节上发生灭失、损伤,即所谓损失。为了保障货物一旦发生损失后能取得经济上的补偿,根据国际贸易惯例,通常都要对货物进行运输保险。海运保险的成本比货物本身的价值和运输成本要低得多。所以,从如果发生灾难获得的经济赔偿这个角度看,支付一些费用投保海运保险是值得的。现在,保险已经是进出口业务中必不可少的环节。

中国人民保险公司根据我国保险业务的实际情况,并参照国际保险市场的习惯做法,分别制订了海洋、陆上、航空、邮包运输方式的货物运输保险条款以及适用于上述各种运输方式货物保险的各种附加险条款。但在我国按CIF或CIP条件成交的出口交易中,国外商人有时要求按伦敦保险业协会货物险条款投保,我出口企业和保险公司一般均可接受。

11.5　Useful Expressions

1. The cover paid for will vary according to the type of goods and the circumstances.

保险费用按照货物类别和具体情况会有所不同。

2. Insurance brokers will quote rates for all types of cargo and risks.

保险经纪人会开出承保各类货物的各种险别的费用。

3. If buyers require additional risks to be covered, the extra premium is for buyers' account.

如果买方要求加保更多的险种,他就需要承担额外的保费。

4. We may cover special risks at buyer's request, but buyers are to bear the premium.

我们可以按照买方的要求投保特殊的险种,但买方需要自己承担保险费。

5. Please hold us covered on the goods listed on the attached sheet.

请承保附件中所列的货物。

6. We enclose a proposal form as requested. You should fill out and then return it to us by the end of March, otherwise we may find it difficult to issue the policy in time.

按照你方的要求,我们随信寄上一份投保申请单,请填写后于3月底之前寄回我方,否则我们难以及时发出保险单。

7. The policy is under preparation and will reach you within this week, along with our debit note for the premium.

保单正在制作中,你将于本周收到,同时还会收到保险费借记通知。

8. We take it that you wish us to insure the goods against the usual risks, for the value of the goods plus freight. Unless we hear from you to the contrary, we shall arrange this.

我们认为,你方希望我们按照货物价值加运费对货物投保一般险种。如果你方没有不同意见,我们就这样安排了。

9. Please send us all the documents necessary to support your claim for Particular Average Loss on the five packages lost in the S. S. Brightness.

就你方对光明号轮船上灭失的 5 包货物提出的按单独海损赔偿的要求,请你方寄给我们一切必要的单据证明你们的索赔权。

10. As our insurance company is a state-owned enterprise enjoying high prestige in settling claims promptly and equitably, you are advised to do business with us on CIF basis and leave the insurance to be effected by us.

我们的保险公司是一家国有公司,因理赔及时、公正而享有很高的声誉。所以,我们建议你方按 CIF 条件与我们交易,以便由我方办理保险事宜。

11.6 Reading Materials

11.6.1

Dear sirs

Re: Your Order No. 1023 for 300 Cases Toys

We have received your letter dated 26 June requesting us to effect insurance on the captioned shipment for your account.

We are pleased to inform you that we have covered the above goods with the People's Insurance Company of China against All Risks for US $9 000. The policy is being prepared accordingly and will be sent to you by the end of this month together with our debit note for the premium.

For your information, we are making arrangements to ship the 300 cases of toys by S/S Tai Da sailing on or about 12 August.

Yours sincerely

11.6.2

Dear sirs

Additional Risk of Breakage

We have just received your L/C No. 234 covering artistic porcelain.

Please note the insurance item in Contract No. AD124, because we do not cover Breakage for this article. Please delete the word "Breakage" from the insurance clause in the credit.

Furthermore, we would like to emphasize that Breakage is a special risk. For the above goods as well as window glass, wall tiles, etc., even if they have been insured, the coverage is subject to a franchise of 5%. That is to say, if the breakage is surveyed to be less than 5%, no claims for damage will be considered.

We believe that everything is clear now. Please fax the amendment at once.

Yours sincerely

11.6.3

Dear sirs

We wish to invite your attention to the fact that the subject goods are purchased on CFR basis, while your L/C calls for CIF. This is not in conformity with the contract.

We would have advised you for amendment, but on second thoughts we didn't think it necessary. In order to avoid any delay in shipment, we think, the simplest way for us is to arrange the necessary insurance in our district and deduct the premium, which would amount to US $100, from the 2% commission payable to you. Any remaining will be remitted to you as soon as the proceeds have been collected from the letter of credit.

We hope the above will be acceptable to you.

Yours sincerely

11.6.4

Dear sirs

We have received your letter of credit No. ASL235 covering your order No. 3092.

On examination, however, we find the L/C requires insurance against ICC (A). you will no doubt recall that there is an understanding between you and us that we quote CIF price on the basis of ICC(B), with additional clauses for the buyer's account. This means that ICC(A), War Risks, and SRCC Risks are to be borne by the buyer.

In view of our long-standing business relations, we will absorb the differences between ICC(B) and ICC(A) for this time as an exceptional case. But we hope you will understand that in our future business, any additional coverage other than ICC(B) shall be for the account of the buyer.

Yours sincerely

Exercises

I. Fill in the blanks with your choices.

1. Please insure the goods _____ F. P. A. for US $100 000.

 a) against   b) with   c) for   d) at

2. Please effect insurance _____ the cargo for US $50 000 by S. S. Bright from Tianjin to Seattle.

 a) by   b) at   c) with   d) on

3. We have opened insurance you ordered for US $9 000 _____ the shipment by S. S. East Sun.

 a) by   b) on   c) in   d) of

4. We wish to renew the above policy _____ the same amount and _____ the same terms as before to cover our consignment to be shipped by S. S. Bright next month.

 a) on...for   b) on...on   c) for...on   d) for...for

5. As requested, we have covered insurance _____ 20 000 DVD players _____ 10% above the invoice value _____ All Risks.
    a) on... at... for   b) on... at... against
    c) with... at... for   d) with... at... against

6. Unless we hear from you _____ the contrary before the end of this month, we shall arrange to cover the goods against F. P. A. for the value of the goods plus freight.
    a) to   b) on   c) with   d) for

7. Any additional coverage other _____ ICC (B) shall be for the account of the buyer.
    a) to   b) than   c) in   d) against

8. We confirm that we hold the consignment covered as _____ today.
    a) of   b) per   c) to   d) from

9. We have arranged _____ the surveyor to investigate the extent of the damage and shall forward his report together with our claim.
    a) for   b) with   c) of   d) in

10. We understand that these terms will apply _____ all our shipments of bottled sherry by regular liners to West European ports.
    a) in   b) with   c) to   d) for

II. Complete the sentences with the appropriate words given below.

cover, covered, covers, covering, coverage, insure, insurance, effected

1. Please _____ against All Risks.

2. This insurance policy _____ us against TPND.

3. We will _____ WPA insurance.

4. The documents will be sent to you under separate _____.

5. We have to point out that our letter of March 11 has fully _____ this matter.

6. We send you herewith a copy of B/L _____ shipment of 20 metric tons Walnuts.

7. We have pleasure in advising shipment of your order No. 07896 _____

30 tons of walnuts.

8. Insurance on the goods shall be _____ by us for 110% of the CIF value.

9. We have arranged the necessary _____ cover.

10. Regarding insurance, the _____ is for 110% of invoice value up to the port of destination.

III. Combine each group of sentences into ONE paragraph

A.

The insurance shall terminate when the goods are delivered to the consignee's warehouse at the destination named in the policy.

If broader coverage is required, the extra premium involved will be for buyer's account.

In reply to your letter of March 1 inquiring about the insurance on your order, we wish to inform you that for goods sold on CIF basis, insurance is to cover All Risks & War Risk for 110% of the invoice value.

The cover, however, is limited to 60 days upon discharge of the insured goods from the sea-going vessel at the final port of discharge before the insured goods reach the consignee's warehouse.

B.

Claims against the ocean carriers will usually become time barred one year after discharge of the cargo from the sea-going vessel.

Our underwriter—The People's Insurance Company of China has agents in practically all the big cities in the world to handle claims.

An insurance claim should be submitted to the Insurance Company or its agent as promptly as possible so as to provide the latter with ample time to pursue recovery from the relative party in fault.

C.

The policy is being prepared accordingly and will be forwarded to you by the end of the week together with our debit note for the premium.

We are pleased to inform you that we have covered the above shipment with The People's Insurance Company of China against All Risks for US $10 000.

This is to acknowledge receipt of your letter of 10 July requesting us to effect insurance on the captioned shipment for your account.

● **Writing skills**

A. Translate the following letter into English.

你方五月十八日函悉。根据你方要求,我们已于今日上午按 CFR 条件给你方报去 100 吨羊毛。

至于中国人民保险公司承保范围及一些情况,兹介绍如下:当客户无明确要求时,我们一般投保水渍险和战争险。若你方愿投保一切险,我们可以办理,但保费稍高一些。投保货值:按照惯例我们按发票金额的 110% 投保。因此,额外保费(如有要求)由买方负担。

我们还可以安排投保一切险及战争险以外的险别,但额外保费也应由买方负担。

相信以上所述将能满足你方要求。

B. Write a letter for Vision Corp. to its client notifying them that their ordered goods 1 000 sets of DVD Player are going to be shipped at the end of the month and you are going to insure the goods against All Risks unless you receive their contrary instructions.

● **Practice**

根据下列所提供的信用证条款的主要内容及有关制单资料,填制海洋运输货物保险单中(1)—(5)项内容。

Irrevocable documentary credit

Number:LC123-786

Date:August 4,2007

Date and place of expiry:October 20, 2007, Qingdao, China

Advising bank:Bank of China

Beneficiary:China XYZ import and export corp.

Applicant:ABC corporation.

Total amount:USD9 000 (SAY US DOLLARS NINE THOUSAND ONLY)

Shipment from:Qingdao China

To:Osaka Japan

At the latest: October 5, 2007

Description of goods: 100% Cotton Towel as per S/C No. 1232

Total quantity: 8 000 pieces packing: 800 Cartons

Total gross weight: 20 000 kg

Total measurement: 30CBM

Price term: CIF Osaka

Following documents required:

+ Signed commercial invoice in three copies.

+ Full set of clean on board ocean bill of lading made out to order and endorsed in blank and marked "freight prepaid" and notify applicant.

+ Insurance policy for 110 PCT of the invoice value covering the Institute Cargo Clauses (A), the Institute War Clauses.

Ocean Vessel: "Golden Star" Voy. No. : 018E

Container No. GSTU3156712/20′

Marks & Nos: ITOCHU OSAKA NO. 1-800

Laden on board the vessel: October 4, 2007

B/L date: October 4, 2007

B/L signed by BBB shipping agency

Carrier: AAA Shipping Co.

中 保 财 产 保 险 有 限 公 司
The People's Insurance (Property) Company of China, Ltd.

发票号码	保险单号次
Invoice No.	Policy No.

海 洋 货 物 运 输 保 险 单
MARINE CARGO TRANSPORTATION INSURANCE POLICY

被保险人: (1)

Insured: _____

中保财产保险公司(以下简称本公司)根据被保险人的要求,及其所缴付约定的保险费,按照本保险单承担险别和背面所载条款与下列特别条款承保

下列货物运输保险,特签发本保险单。

This policy of Insurance witness that the People's Insurance (Property) Company of China, Ltd. (hereinafter called "the Company"), at the request of the Insured and in consideration of the agreed premium paid by the Insured, undertakes to insure the undermentioned goods in transportation subject to the conditions of this Policy as per the Clauses printed overleaf and other special clauses attached hereon.

保险货物项目 Description of Goods	包装　单位　数量 Packing Unit Quantity	保险金额 Amount Insured
(2)	800cartons	(3)

承保险别　　　　　　　　　　　　货物标记
Conditions (4)　　　　　　　　　Marks of Goods

总保险金额:
Total Amount insured:＿＿＿＿＿＿＿＿＿＿＿＿＿＿＿＿＿＿＿＿＿＿＿
＿＿＿＿＿＿＿＿＿＿＿＿＿＿＿＿＿＿＿＿＿＿＿＿＿＿＿＿＿＿＿＿＿

保费　as agreed　　载运工具　　　　　　开航日期
Premium ＿＿＿＿＿Per conveyance S.S ＿＿＿＿＿Slg. On or abt ＿＿＿＿＿
起运港　　　　　　　　　　目的港
From ＿＿＿＿＿＿＿＿＿＿＿＿＿＿＿＿To ＿＿＿＿＿＿＿＿＿＿＿＿＿＿＿

所保货物,如发生本保险单项下可能引起索赔的损失或损坏,应立即通知本公司下述代理人查勘。如有索赔,应向本公司提交保险单正本(本保险单共有 2 份正本)及有关文件。如一份已用于索赔,其余正本则自动失效。

In the event of loss or damage which may result in a claim under this Policy, immediate notice must be given to the Company's agent as mentioned hereunder. Claims, if any, one of the Original Policy which has been issued in Original (s) together with the relevant documents shall be surrendered to the Company, if one of the Original Policy has been accomplished, the others to be void.

中保财产保险有限公司
THE PEOPLE'S INSURANCE (PROPERTY) COMPANY OF CHINA, LTD.

赔偿地点　Osaka, Japan
Claim payable at _____

日期（5）　　　　　　　　　　　　在 Qingdao, China
Date _____ at _____

地址
Address：

Unit 12　Shipment

Learning Objectives

After learning this unit, you should:

✍ Know the basic modes of foreign transportation(了解国际货物运输的基本方式)

✍ Get familiar with the shipping clauses in a contract and kinds of shipping documents(熟悉合同中的装运条款和各种运输单据)

✍ Know how to write letters to urge shipment, to request amendment to the shipping clauses and to advise shipment(掌握催装函、装运条款修改函以及装船通知的写作方法)

✍ Master typical sentences and expressions in writing such letters(掌握这些信函中的常用句型和短语)

12.1　Introduction

The business of foreign trade transport is complicated. Although most of the shipment is often effected by forwarding agents, businessmen will find it helpful to have a fairly good knowledge of the details regarding the procedures of shipment and the relative shipping documents in order to fulfill an export transaction and effect shipment in a safe, speedy and economical way.

国际货物运输是一件相当复杂的工作。尽管大部分货物运输工作现在都由货运代理人完成,但对于贸易商来说,掌握有关货物运输程序及运输单据等知识还是有助于实现安全、迅速和经济的货物运输,保证出口交易的顺利实施。

In shipping goods abroad, the exporter has various alternative methods. These include ship, truck, rail, air and parcel post. The choice will depend on the nature of the product (light or heavy, fragile or sturdy, perishable or durable, high or low in value per cubic meter, etc); the distance to be shipped; available means of transportation; and relative freight costs.

在将货物向海外运输时,可供出口商选择的方式有多种,包括水运、公路运输、铁路运输、空运和邮包运输等。具体选择什么运输方式取决于货物的属性(轻重、结实还是易碎、耐存放还是易变质、单位体积的价值高低等);运输距离的长短;可选择的运输方式以及运输成本。

Goods having high weight or cubic capacity or value ratio, the usual method of shipping overseas is by ocean cargo vessel. However, when speed is essential, air cargo may be preferred, although more expensive. For example, ski jackets are shipped from Germany to Japan by sea but towards the end of the ski season, air cargo is used.

如果货物的重量或体积价值比较高,通常就采用海运作为国际运输方式。但如果运输速度是首要问题时,就选择空运了,即使成本要高很多。例如,将滑雪服从德国运到日本,可以选择海运,但如果滑雪季节就要过去了,这时就要选择空运了。

One popular method of shipment is to use containers obtained from carriers or private leasing companies. These containers vary in size, material, and construction and accommodate most cargo, but they are best suited for standard package sizes and shapes. Also, refrigerated and liquid bulk containers are usually readily available.

现在一种常见的装运方式是利用从承运人或私营的租赁公司那里得到的集装箱进行装运。集装箱的尺寸、材质和构造各有不同,能够装载大部分类型的货物,但是最适用于包装尺寸和形状标准化的货物。现在,也有冷藏集装箱和液体散装货集装箱。

The ocean bill of lading is an essential document in making a shipment. It presents three aspects. First, it is a receipt of the goods. Second, it is a contract for the performance of certain services upon certain conditions. Third, it serves also as evidence of ownership of the goods described, and when made out "to order", it becomes in practice a negotiable instrument, used as security for loans and other purposes. When drawn in this way, it is known as an order bill of lading. The straight bill of lading, on the other hand, is made out to a specific consignee.

海运提单是海运工作中一个重要单据。它有三个作用,一是货物收据;二是在一定条件下完成货物运输服务的合同;三是作为货物所有权凭证。如果出具的是指示性提单,那就是一种可转让的票据,可以作为抵押用于贷款或其他目的。而记名提单是指提单的收货人是确定的人。

After making shipment, the seller should promptly advise the buyer of its effectuation, no matter whether the transaction is concluded on FOB, C&F or CIF basis. For FOB and C&F transactions, the buyer will have to effect insurance to the shipment upon receipt of shipping advice from the seller. It has been a customary practice that in the case of FOB transactions, the seller, before shipping, should ask the buyer to name the vessel on which the goods are to be shipped unless otherwise specified in the contract or L/C.

无论是以 FOB、C&F 或 CIF 成交,货物装运后,卖方应该立即通知买方货物已经装运。如果是以 FOB 或 C&F 成交,买方收到装运通知后要立即对货物投保。如果是以 FOB 成交,习惯做法是除非信用证另有规定,卖方在装运前要请买方指定装运船只。

Letters regarding shipment are usually written for the following purposes: to urge an early shipment; to amend shipping terms; to give shipping advice; to despatch shipping documents and so on.

有关运输内容的信函包括催促尽快装运、修改装运条款、发出装船通知以及寄送运输单据等。

12.2 Model Letters Comments

12.2.1 Request Early Shipment

John Hills Clothing Co.
20 King Street
London, U.K.

2 February 2003

China Textiles Import & Export Co.
10 Guanghua Road
Beijing, China

Dear sirs

We refer to our order No. LG 769.

Under the terms of the order, delivery is scheduled for June/July. We would now like to bring delivery forward to March/April.

We realize that the change of delivery date will probably inconvenience you and we offer sincere apologies. We know that you will understand that we would not ask for earlier delivery if we did not have compelling reasons for doing so.

In view of our longstanding, cordial business relationship, we would be grateful if you would make a special effort to comply with our request.

We look forward to your early reply.

Yours truly

Comments

Paragraph 1: identify the reference
Paragraph 2: make the request
Paragraph 3: apologize for any inconvenience caused by the request
Paragraph 4: politely urge acceptance of the request
Paragraph 5: ask for a reply

The letter politely requests early shipment. It backs up the request by reminding the seller the business relationship is a longstanding one and that there are strong reasons for it.

Notes

1. delivery (n.) 交货

There's still another possibility to ensure a prompt delivery of the goods.
还有另一种可能可以确保即期交货。

You expect us to make delivery in less than a month, right?

您是希望我们在不到 1 个月的时间内交货吗?

With the bill of lading, the buyer may take delivery of the goods at the port of destination.

有了提单,买方就可以在目的港提货了。

delivery date 交货期

The delivery date is drawing near and we have not yet received any shipping instructions from you.

交货期临近了,可我们还没有得到你方的装船指示。

The unexpected bad weather makes it difficult for us to meet the delivery date.

没有预料到的坏天气使我们很难按期交货了。

2. inconvenience (v. n.) 不便,麻烦

This delay has put us to great inconvenience by holding up our shop display.

交货延迟给我们带来很大麻烦,因为这耽误我们进行店面展示了。

We are extremely sorry for any inconvenience this clerical mistake may have given you, and wish you to know that we have taken adequate steps to preclude any similar errors.

对由于我方笔误给你方带来的麻烦我们深表歉意,希望你方明白我们已经采取了很多措施防止类似事情再发生。

Any delay in shipment will greatly inconvenience us, since we have promised our customers the date of delivery.

装运工作中的任何延迟都会给我们造成很大麻烦,因为我们已经向客户承诺了交货期。

3. comply with 与……一致,遵照

The goods must comply in every respect with our specifications.

这些货物必须在各个方面与我们的规格要求一致。

To comply with your request made in your letter of April 12, we have much pleasure in sending you the samples and price list.

按照你方 4 月 12 日来函的请求,我们很高兴地寄去样品和价格单。

12.2.2 Proposal for Partial Shipment

Maceetosh Co.
20 Arthur Street
Singapore
Tel: 65744932

24 January 2003

China Nonferrous Metal Import & Export Co.
2 Anhua Road
Beijing, China

Dear sirs

Thank you for your letter of January 16 regarding your order No. LG769 for 10 sets of M463 punches.

In your letter, you ask for earlier shipment of the whole order. I regret to say that we are unable to comply with your request.

When the sale was agreed, we expressly stated that shipment would be made in June/July. If you wish to have earlier delivery, the best we can do is to make a partial shipment of 7 sets in April and ship the remaining 3 sets in June. We hope this arrangement will meet with your approval.

Should you agree to the new arrangement, please fax an amendment to the relevant letter of credit allowing us to effect partial shipment.

We expect your prompt reply so that we can ask the manufacturer to expedite delivery.

Yours sincerely

Comments

Paragraph 1: identify the reference
Paragraph 2: give the answer to the proposal
Paragraph 3: propose partial shipment as a compromise

Paragraph 4: remind the buyer that the L/C will have to be amended to cover the new arrangements

Paragraph 5: urge a prompt reply

Although the seller is under no contractual obligation to agree to the proposal, he does his best to help. By taking extra trouble, the seller is building up goodwill with the buyer.

Notes

1. shipment (n.) 运输

You are requested to inform us immediately when shipment can be effected so that our customer may plan their production schedule.

请你方装船后立即通知我方以便我们的客户安排生产计划。

We will be able to make shipment of your order within 20 days after receipt of your L/C.

收到你方信用证后20天内我们将装运你方订购的货物。

In case of transshipment, we have to pay extra transportation charges.

货物如果转运,我们得多付运费。

Partial shipment is allowed, so we can ship the goods in three lots.

准许分批装运,所以我们可以将货物分成三批装运。

ship (v.) 装运

We have shipped your order today.

我们今天装运了你方订购的货物。

Please inform us with certainty when you can ship the goods so that we can promise a definite time of delivery to our customers.

当你方能够装运货物时,请给我方发一个确切的通知,以便我们向客户承诺确定的交货期。

The goods we ordered are urgently required and we request you to ship them by the first available vessel.

我们订购的货物是急需的货物,所以请你方尽快装运。

shipping (n.) 装运

Please let us have your shipping instructions immediately so that we can arrange to make shipment.

请立即做出装船指示以便我方安排装运。

The shipping date is coming near and please open your L/C urgently.

装船期临近了,请立刻开立信用证。

In order to book shipping space, we have to take a shipping order from the shipping company.

为了订到舱位,我们需要拿到船公司的装货单。

On finishing shipment, we will fax you the shipping advice.

一完成装运,我们就将装船通知给你方传真过去。

A full set of shipping documents are required for negotiation.

议付时需要全套运输单据。

2. amendment 修改(通知)书,改正

Upon receipt of your amendment to the L/C, we shall immediately make the shipment of the goods.

收到信用证的修改通知书后,我们就会立即装运。

When you find anything to the contrary in the L/C, please tell us so that we can make amendments accordingly.

若发现信用证的内容与此不符,请告知我们以便做相应修改。

12.2.3 Postpone Delivery Date

Flight Electronics Co.
1 East Road
Beijing, China
Tel: 010-80305043

20 September 2003

Gregory Co.
20 Flint Street
Sydney, Australia

Dear sirs

We refer to your order No. 356 for 10 000 DVD players.

Owing to the problem at the port, we will not be able to meet the agreed delivery date of 1 October.

We are doing everything possible to ship your order but the contracted date has now become unrealistic.

We believe, however, that we will be able to meet a December 1 delivery deadline.

We apologize for the inconvenience, but the delay is due to circumstances beyond our control.

                Yours sincerely

Comments

 Paragraph 1: identify the reference

 Paragraph 2: state the problem and the reason for it

 Paragraph 3: describe the current situation

 Paragraph 4: give the likely delivery date

 Paragraph 5: offer apologies

The letter frankly states why a delivery date cannot be met. The seller assures the customer that everything possible has been done to ship the goods and gives a realistic delivery date.

12.2.4 Shipping Advice

                Lawton & Sons plc.
                7 Kenya Street
                Birmingham
                U.K.

                2 March 2003

Top Printing Ltd
3 Shanghai Road
Hongkong, China

Dear sirs

 We are now pleased to inform you that we have shipped the goods you ordered for 1 000 sets of sewing machines against your L/C No. 2432 on board S. S. "Winner" which sails for your port tomorrow.

 We enclose one set of the shipping documents covering this consignment, which includes:
  (1) one copy of non-negotiable B/L;
  (2) commercial invoice in duplicate;
  (3) one copy of Certificate of Quality;
  (4) one copy of Insurance Policy.

 The originals of these documents are being sent to you through our banker. We are glad to have been able to execute your order as contracted and trust that the goods will reach you in good time to meet your urgent need and that they will turn out to your entire satisfaction.

 We avail ourselves of this opportunity to assure you of our prompt and careful attention in handling your future orders.

Yours faithfully

Comments

 Paragraph 1: identify the reference and make the shipping advice
 Paragraph 2: state the documents enclosed
 Paragraph 3: assure the buyer of satisfactory execution
 Paragraph 4: hope for future orders

 The letter advises the buyer of the delivery and the seller assures the customer that everything possible has been done to execute the order satisfactorily.

Notes

1. original (*n. adj.*) 正本,正本的

The forwarding agent issued the bill of lading in 3 originals and 6 copies.

这个货运代理人签发的提单是 3 份正本,6 份副本。

Our bank only negotiates original documents.

我方银行只议付正本单据。

2. execute 执行

We assure you of our best attention in executing your order.

我们保证非常认真地执行你方订单。

The heavy backlog of orders makes it impossible for us to execute any new ones.

订单大量积压使我们不能执行新订单。

3. in good time 准时

The goods have been ready for shipment and your shipping instructions have not yet reached us. If there is any further delay, we can not ensure the arrival of the goods at your port in good time.

货物已经备好待运多时了,但仍未收到你方的装船指示。如果再耽搁,我们就不能保证货物准时到达你方港口了。

Your L/C arrived here in good time, which enabled us to effect prompt delivery.

你们的信用证及时到达,使我们能够立即装运货物。

4. avail oneself of 利用

We can avail ourselves of their good knowledge of the China market and with their help we can surely increase our market share there.

我们可以利用他们对中国市场的全面了解,在他们的帮助下,我们一定能提高市场份额。

I think we can avail ourselves of their policy of easier payment terms for old clients and request for D/A collection on this order.

我认为我们可以利用他们给老客户便利付款方式的政策,要求这个定单以承兑交单方式托收。

12.3 Specimen Letters

12.3.1 State Marking Requirements

Dear sirs

We enclose the countersigned copy of contract No. LX246 of June 3 of 2003 for 5 cartons of children's shoes.

The letter of credit is on its way to you.

Please mark the cartons with our initials, with the destination and contract number as follows:

LT

Liverpool

LX246

This will apply to all shipments unless otherwise instructed.

Please advise us by fax as soon as shipment is effected.

Yours truly

● **Activities for comprehension**

    1. What is the use of marking?

    2. Which parts does shipping mark consist of?

12.3.2 Urge an Early Shipment

Dear sirs

Referring to our previous letters and faxes, we wish to call your attention to the fact that up to the present moment no news has come from you about the shipment under the contract No. LX246.

As we mentioned in our last letter, we are in urgent need of the goods and we may be compelled to seek an alternative source of supply.

Under the circumstances, it is not possible for us to extend further our letter of credit No. 223, which expires on 3 June.

As your prompt attention to shipment is most desirable to all parties concerned, we hope you will let us have your shipping advice by fax without further delay.

Yours truly

● **Activities for comprehension**

    1. How to remind the supplier of the late delivery in a letter?

12.3.3　Advise Shipment

Dear sirs

    We are very much pleased to advise you that we have dispatched by S. S. Bright to Liverpool the goods under your order No. SG-145, and trust that the shipment will prove to be satisfactory to you.

    It is a pleasure to go into business with you. We very much appreciate the efforts you have made in introducing our commodities into your market. We sincerely hope that the successful execution of your first order will lead to more business in future.

    You will observe that the goods will suit the need of your market very well. Nevertheless, we still welcome any comments from you so as to be better informed of the situation of your market and see what we can do to cooperate with you.

Yours truly

● **Activities for comprehension**

    1. To what kind of buyers is such an advice addressed?

    2. Besides shipment advice, what is the purpose of such a letter?

12.3.4　Inquiry for Freight Rate

Dear sir

    At the beginning of next week, we shall have a consignment of motorcar spares for delivery from Shanghai to Hongkong. The spares will be packed in two wooden cases, each measuring 2 × 2 × 3 feet and weighing about 100 pounds.

We would be glad if you would let us know your rate for freight and send us details of your sailing and the time usually taken for the voyage. We should also like to know what formalities are involved.

We are looking forward to your early reply.

Yours faithfully

● **Activities for comprehension**

1. How is ocean freight determined?

2. What kind of information should be included in an inquiry letter for freight rate?

12.4　Summary

In international sales, the contract referring to shipment should stipulate the mode of transportation and obligations of each party concerning transportation. There are several ways to carry the goods to their destination, including truck transport, rail transport, air transport, sea transport and multi-modal transport, etc. Among them, sea transport is widely used in international trade. Shipping clauses in contract between importers and exporters should stipulate time of shipment, port of loading, port of destination, mode of transport, partial shipment, transshipment and shipping advice etc.

在国际货物买卖中,凡是涉及运输的买卖合同,都需要就货物的运输方式以及当事人双方在有关货物运输方面的责任做出安排。运输方式包括公路运输、铁路运输、航空运输、海洋运输、多式联运等等。其中,海洋运输在国际贸易中是使用广泛的运输方式。出口商和进口商签订的合同中的装运条款必须明确装运时间、装运港、目的港、运输方式、分批装运、转船、装运通知等。

The shipping advice is a notice to the importer on summary of the shipment.

Foreign importer may arrange the cargo insurance on time based on the shipping advice (if buyer is to arrange the insurance). Moreover, importer may know when to receive the goods and arrange with a customs broker for the cargo clearance.

装运通知是将货物装运的整体情况通知买方。

根据装运通知,买方可以安排货运保险(如果是由买方投保的话)。此外,买方可以知道什么时候准备接货并与报关代理人商议货物清关事宜。

The shipping advice is particularly important in short-sea trades, for example within the Asian countries where the goods may arrive at the port of destination before the shipping documents, and in the ports of destination where theft and pilferage of the imported goods is rampant.

在近洋运输中,装运通知特别重要,例如,亚洲国家之间的贸易,可能会出现货物先于单据到达目的港,而目的港可能又是盗窃活动猖獗之地,所以装运通知就非常重要了。

12.5　Useful Expressions

1. We take pleasure in notifying you that the goods under your order No. SFT-54 have been dispatched by S.S. Wilson sailing on May 3 for Liverpool.

欣告你方,你方SFT-54号订单下的货物已经由Wilson号货轮装运,5月3日启航开往利物浦。

2. We wish to advise you that the goods under S/C 45CWS went forward on the steamer Welsh on June 4. They are to be transshipped at New York and are expected to reach your port in early July.

我们现通知你方,45CWS号售货确认书项下的货物在6月4日装上了Welsh号轮船。货物将在纽约转运,预计在7月初到达你方港口。

3. For the goods under S/C No. 789, we have booked space on S.S. Easter due to arrive in London around 14 June. Please communicate with our shipping agent, Lambert Co. London, for loading arrangements.

我们已经为789号售货确认书项下的货物在Easter号轮订好了舱位,预计在6月14日左右到达伦敦。有关装运安排事宜,请与我们的运输代理人伦敦的Lambert公司联系。

4. We acknowledge receipt of your confirmation that your consignment should be sent by air freight, and have accordingly forwarded the goods.

我们已收到你们要求空运货物的确认函,并按照要求发运了货物。

5. Your delay has caused us considerable inconvenience and we request you do your utmost to dispatch the overdue goods with the least possible delay.

你方的耽搁给我们造成了极大的不便,我们请你方尽最大努力尽快发运迟交的货物。

6. Your failure to deliver the goods within the stipulated time has greatly inconvenienced us. Please take the matter up at once and see to it that the goods are delivered without any further delay.

你方未能在规定的期限内交货已给我们造成极大不便。请立即办理此事,不要再有任何耽搁。

7. Please inform us, 10 days before the contracted time of shipment, of the name of the carrying vessel, its expected time of arrival at the port of loading and the name of the shipping agent so that we can contact the shipping agent to make arrangement for shipment.

请在合同规定的装运期前10天告知船名、预计抵达装运港时间以及运输代理人的名称,以便我方与代理人联系安排货物装运事宜。

8. Owing to the increase of consignment arriving at Ningbo port, discharge of the cargoes seems to be much delayed, and we must ask you to change the port of destination to Wenzhou port and there should be no alteration in shipping date.

由于宁波港到货数量大增,似乎卸货时间会耽搁很多,我们必须要求你方将目的港改为温州港,装运时间不变。

9. We are sorry for the delay in shipment, as there is no direct steamer available. We should be grateful if you would be kind enough to grant us a few days' grace for shipment.

由于租不到直达船,因此装船延误,我们对此表示歉意。如果你方能给我们几天宽限期,我们将十分感激。

10. In compliance with the terms of the contract, we forwarded you by airmail a full set of non-negotiable documents immediately after the goods were loaded.

按照合同条款的规定,我们在货物装船后立即给你方航空邮寄去了全套不可转让的单据。

11. The goods ordered in May are ready for dispatch and as the transaction is concluded on FOB basis, you are to arrange the shipment. We should be glad to have your immediate shipping instructions.

你方 5 月份订购的货物已经备妥待运,由于此次交易是 FOB 成交,由你方安排订舱,请立刻发出装船指示。

12.6　Reading Material

12.6.1　Adjust a Delivery Date

Dear sirs

We refer to your order No. 875 for 1 000 metric tons of steel bars.

There has been an unusually heavy demand for such goods. Consequently, we are currently out of stock and will have to order more from the manufacturer.

The lead time for delivery to us is normally 13 weeks. We will, however, place our order for delivery by air freight. We should then be able to ship the goods before the end of this month.

Please accept our sincere apologies for the delay. We will be in touch as soon as we have a firm delivery date.

Yours truly

12.6.2　Request Early Shipment

Dear sirs

With reference to Contract No. 252/F1001 covering the captioned goods, we believe that amendment to the relative letter of credit has been made and has reached you already. We should like to solicit your cooperation to expedite shipment.

Yesterday our clients came to us with the request that 20 metric tons of mild steel flat bars be shipped during February and the remainder in March, as they are in urgent need of them.

We presume that you must have received a lot of bookings for this commodity from abroad, resulting in a tight shipping schedule; nevertheless, we venture to write to you, hoping that you will see your way to accommodate us. Thank you in advance for your kind cooperation.

Yours faithfully

12.6.3 Reject a Request for Early Shipment
Dear sirs

With reference to your letter of Jan. 12, we wish to inform you that we have just received your amendment to the L/C.

Immediately upon receipt of your above letter, we approached our mills with the request that they hasten their production of your contracted bars, but much to our regret, they are not in a position to advance deliveries as they are heavily booked with orders for months ahead. Under the present condition, the best the mills can do is to ship the whole quantity of 31 metric tons in one lot with the contracted time of shipment, i. e. March of 2004.

While we are extremely sorry for our inability to advance the date of shipment of 20 metric tons to February to meet your urgent need, we can assure you that special care will be given to your order and that we shall do everything possible to ensure smooth shipment of the contracted goods.

Yours truly

12.6.4 Advise Shipment
Dear Sirs

    Contract No. 8901/6

We are pleased to inform you that the Panasonic fax machines Model Panafax UF-990 you have ordered from us have been shipped on 17 April on S. S. Commander scheduled to sail for Liverpool on 20 April. Please find the details as follows:

    Commodity: Panafax UF-990

    Quantity: 2 000 sets

Contract No.: 8901/6

L/C No.: LC1122

B/L No.: BLA0033

Name of Vessel: Commander

Voy. No.: H-136

ETD: April 20, 20××

ETA: May 20, 20××

Shipping Agency at port of destination:

China Railway United Logistics Co. Ltd, Liverpool Branch

Royal Liver Building

First Floor

Liverpool L3 1PS

United Kingdom

Tel: +44 151 2247255

Fax: +44 151 2363453

We hope the said goods will reach you at the due time and will find a ready market at your end. Meanwhile we are enclosing the copies of shipping documents of the above goods consisting of a shipped clean bill of lading(No. BLA0033), invoice(No. EH3314), and insurance certificate(No. AR119358). Also enclosed is a catalogue of our new models and we believe you will be very interested in the machines illustrated on pp. 103-110.

We look forward to hearing from you again at the due time.

Yours faithfully

 Exercises

I. Choose the best answer.

1. In our letter of May 10, we make _____ clear that shipment be effected in June.

  a) you   b) them   c) us   d) it

2. As the shipment was delayed, the buyer _____ the seller for an explanation.

  a) forced   b) pressed   c) hastened   d) expedited

  3. I wonder if you could advance the shipment by one month _____ we need it urgently.

  a) as   b) provided   c) or   d) because of

  4. Please make serious efforts to get the goods _____ promptly.

  a) dispatch   b) dispatched   c) dispatching   d) to dispatch

  5. Your order will be delivered on October 15 _____ you requested.

  a) like   b) since   c) as   d) when

  6. Sometimes, transshipment and partial shipment are _____ by the buyer.

  a) permission   b) permitting   c) prohibited   d) prohibiting

  7. We wish to receive your shipping advice soon for the goods under the captioned _____.

  a) letter   b) cable   c) contract   d) communication

  8. The importer will go to the wharf and _____ delivery of the goods.

  a) make   b) effect   c) fulfill   d) take

  9. Please do your best to ship our order _____ S.S. "Dongfeng".

  a) by   b) of   c) to   d) at

  10. Your letter of credit failed to reach us at the stipulated time. This has caused us much _____.

  a) convenience   b) convenient   c) inconvenience   d) inconvenient

  II. Fill in the blanks.

  1. Owing _____ the delay _____ the part of the suppliers, we must ask you to extend the date _____ shipment _____ September 15 _____ October 15.

  2. We wish to draw your attention _____ the fact that the date _____ delivery is approaching, but up _____ the present moment we have not received any news _____ you.

  3. The packing must be strong enough to withstand _____ handling.

4. Please take the matter _____ consideration at once and see to it that the goods are delivered _____ further delay.

5. We shall appreciate it if you will inform us _____ the condition of packing as _____ as the consignment arrives _____ your end.

6. We could not deliver the total quantity _____ one shipment.

7. Shipment is to be made from April to June _____ three equal lots.

8. We shall be obliged _____ you will effect shipment as soon as _____.

9. As the manufacturers cannot get all the quantity ready at the same time, it is necessary _____ the contract stipulations to be so worded as to _____ partial shipment.

10. In view _____ the difficult situation faced by us, you are requested to amend the L/C to allow transshipment of the _____ in Hongkong where arrangements can easily be made _____ transshipment.

III. Combine each group of sentences into ONE paragraph

A.

You may expect to receive the goods by the 10th.

We have received your letter of September 1 and very much regret the delay which has occurred in the execution of your order of August 1.

And we can assure you we will lose no time in the prompt delivery of the goods.

The damage, however, has been repaired.

This was occasioned by a serious breakdown in our machinery.

But we trust this unavoidable accident will not influence you unfavorably in the matter of future orders.

We regret the inconvenience you have sustained.

B.

We have no explanation to offer yet, but will give a full account as soon as we can.

We have been in touch with our packers and we have asked them to send a detailed report.

We apologize for any inconvenience caused by the error.

We shall ensure that similar mistakes do not occur again.

In the meantime, we have arranged for the dispatch of four replacement crates, and we have asked our packers to carry out the packing instructions carefully.

C.

We shall be much obliged if you will keep case No. 23 and contents until called for by the local agents of our forwarding agent.

Relative documents will be mailed as soon as they are ready.

We have already faxed to inform you of this, and we enclose a copy of the fax.

On going into the matter we find that a mistake was indeed made in the packing, through a confusion of numbers, and we have arranged for the right goods to be dispatched to you at once.

D.

Under the circumstances, it is not possible for us to extend further our letter of credit which expires on 12 September.

As we mentioned in our last letter, we are in urgent need of the goods and we may be compelled to seek an alternative source of supply.

We wish to remind you that we have had no news from you about shipment of the goods.

● **Skills Practice**

1. Translate the letter into English.

敬启者：

我方已收到贵公司4月15日往伦敦巴克莱银行开出的第D303号信用证。

经审阅后我们发现该信用证规定的货运目的港贝尔法斯特，已不允许转船，由于大连至贝尔法斯特的直达船，每月只有一二次航次，我们经常在香港转船。为确保货物按时发送，请修改信用证允许转船，这对双方均有利。

若贵公司不同意这一修改，亦可将目的港贝尔法斯特改为利物浦。由大连至利物浦的直达船较多。

敬请首肯。

2. The buyer of ABC Corp. complained that the delayed shipment had caused their client to refuse the ordered goods. You are writing for ABC Corp. to the buyer telling them that although you have tried your best to meet the shipping date, you could not finish the production and failed to make delivery on time. To be worse, the following long New Year Holiday made it impossible for you to deliver the goods. But now, the goods are waiting for shipment in Keelung and you request the buyer not to decline the ordered goods.

Unit 13 Claim

Learning Objectives

After studying this unit, you should:

✎ Know the disputes apt to occur in sales contract(了解合同执行中易发生的纠纷)

✎ Know how to lodge a claim in a specific situation(知道在特定情况下如何提出索赔)

✎ Know the essential points to be included in a claim(知道索赔函的要点)

✎ Know how to adjust and decline a claim(知道如何受理或拒绝索赔)

13.1 Introduction

In ideal business conditions, everything should be done so carefully, with details of offers and orders checked, packing supervised, handling of goods carried out expertly, that no mistakes are made and nothing is damaged. Unfortunately, complaints or claims may sometimes arise in spite of out well-planned and careful work in the performance of a sales contract. When the buyer finds the wrong goods delivered, the quality below the requirements as specified in the contract, the price higher than as agreed, or the goods delivered damaged or late, and so on, he will be unsatisfied and make complaints. Sometimes, however, for various reasons, the buyer may intend to escape from his contractual obligations and he may likely find fault with the goods and make complaints not based on facts.

如果贸易活动开展顺利,一切环节都应该是认真完成的,双方会检查发盘或订单的每一个细节,会监督货物的包装工作,货物的搬运工作也是非常专业地处理,所以不会发生什么差错,货物也不会损坏。但不幸的是,尽管我们在履行合同时周密安排、认真操作,还是会发生索赔或投诉。当买方发现收到的货物有误,或者品质低于合同中的规定,或者价格高于双方的约定,或者收到的货物破损或晚收到货物等,买方都会感到不满,因而提出索赔。但有时,因种种原因,买方可能不愿履行合同义务,也会故意挑毛病,不顾事实地提出索赔。

If a claim has to be made by buyers, the matter should be investigated in detail, and these details should be laid before the party charged. When making a complaint, plan your letter as follows:

(1) Begin by regretting the need to complain;

(2) Mention the date of the order, the date of delivery and the goods complained about;

(3) State yours reasons for being dissatisfied and ask for an explanation;

(4) Refer to the inconvenience caused;

(5) Suggest how the matter should be put right.

如果买方需要做出索赔,他应该进行详细地调查,并将详细的调查结果通知给处理索赔的当事人。索赔函的内容应该包括以下内容:

(1) 信的开头应对提出抱怨表示遗憾;

(2) 说明订单的日期,交货的时间以及货物的情况;

(3) 说明不满的原因,并要求予以解释;

(4) 提及由此造成的不便;

(5) 提出纠正建议。

A claim is written to inform the company of the problem and suggest a fair compensation. No matter how infuriating the nature of the problem or how great the inconvenience, the purpose of a claim is not to express anger, but to get results. Therefore, it is important to avoid a hostile or demanding tone. A claim must be calm and polite though, of course, also firm.

索赔函的目的是告诉卖方发生的问题以及提出公平的赔偿建议。不管问题性质多么令人气愤不安或者是造成多大的麻烦,索赔函都不是要表达你的气愤,而是要得到结果。所以,在信函中要避免不友善的话语或者咄咄逼人的态度。索赔函必须是语气平稳、礼貌,但又不减力度。

To settle the claim made by the buyer, the seller need first investigate the claim. When the facts of a claim have been confirmed, one of three fair solutions is possible:

(1) The requested adjustment is granted;
(2) A compromise adjustment is proposed;
(3) Any adjustment is denied.

Responsibility for the problem, reliability of the customer, and the nature of the business relationship are all considered in determining a fair adjustment. But the ultimate settlement must always be within the bounds of company policy.

为了处理买方提出的索赔要求,卖方首先应该调查索赔问题。如果证实了买方的索赔情况属实,可以采取的解决办法就是:

(1) 同意买方提出的赔偿要求;
(2) 对买方提出的赔偿要求做出改动建议;
(3) 拒绝买方的赔偿要求。

在确定公平的解决方案时,既要考虑到责任问题,买方的诚信,也要考虑双方业务关系的性质。但最终的解决方案一定是符合公司政策要求的。

The company, responding to the claim, will write a letter of adjustment. Acknowledgement of a complaint should be prompt to restore the customer's goodwill and confidence in the company. When agreeing to the buyer's request, the letters often begin with good news. Then express the apology for causing inconvenience and give the explanation of how the firm is making every effort to prevent the problem from being repeated and even to ensure satisfactory future orders. However considerate the seller may wish to be to the claims of the buyer he can not assume responsibility for errors which he did not make, or offer compensation where no compensation is due. If the complaint is unreasonable and must be rejected, the letter should point out politely why it is settled in this way, why the settlement is fair, and what the firm's policy is. Such unwelcome news as rejecting a claim partly or completely, are likely to cause disappointment. The opening paragraph of this kind of letter should not begin with the bad news but be cautious of terms that prepare the receiver for what is coming and soften the blow when it does come. Remember, your company's image and goodwill are at stake when you respond even to unjustified claims.

处理函是对对方索赔函的回复。对于顾客的索赔函回复应该及时,这样才能恢复顾客对公司的善意和信任。如果答应买方的请求,回复函开头应该告诉买方这个好消息,然后对于给买方已经造成的不便表达歉意,并解释公司为防止类似事件再次发生采取了哪些措施,或者向买方保证将来订单的执行一定会令其满意。但不管卖方多么希望对买方的投诉和索赔做出周全的处理,他也不可能对自己没犯的错误承担责任,或者对于不该赔偿的情况做出赔偿。如果买方的投诉索赔是无道理的,就一定要严词拒绝。这种信函应该客气地指出为什么会这样处理,为什么这样处理是合理的以及卖方公司的政策是什么。部分或全部拒绝买方索赔要求的信函是令人不愉快的信息,甚至令人失望。所以信函开头措辞一定慎重,使收信人有思想准备接受这样的安排。记住,即使是对不合理的索赔要求的答复都会影响公司的形象和声誉。

13.2　Model Letters Comments

13.2.1　Claim for Poor Packing

Gregory Co.
20 Flint Street
Sydney, Australia
Tel: 612-53892934

3 June 2003

Flight Electronics Co.
1 East Road
Beijing, China

Dear sirs

　　We refer you to our order No. LNG 347 for 550 units of DVD player.

　　The goods were shipped per S.S. Bright. On examining your goods, we found the cartons to be badly damaged. Consequently, we feel that we must make a claim against you.

Of the 100 cartons, 20 had burst open due to poor packing. The rest were in a damaged condition.

We have repacked the whole consignment in new cartons for delivery to our customers. The expense involved amounted to US $200.

In view of the tight profit margin on this consignment, we must insist that you compensate us for the repacking.

You will be aware that customers are likely to get a false impression of the quality of goods that are poorly packed. We suggest that in future you make sure that the goods are properly packed.

We look forward to hearing from you.

Yours truly

Comments

Paragraph 1: identify the reference

Paragraph 2: make the complaint and state what action you require

Paragraph 3: give details of the complaint

Paragraph 4: state what action you have had to take and the cost involved

Paragraph 5: ask for compensation

Paragraph 6-7: state your future requirements and urge a reply

The letter clearly sets out the claim and the reasons for it. The tone of the letter is firm but polite. The supplier is left in no doubt that compensation is expected.

Notes

1. per 经,由,靠

Enclosed you will find the invoice for the cotton fabrics, shipped per S. S. "Sea Dragon" from Hongkong to Yokohama.

随函附上棉布的发票一份,该货已由香港开往横滨的海龙号货轮装运。

2. S. S. 为 steam ship 的缩写,轮船

3. on examining the goods, on 或 upon 在……后立即

We shall make payment on arrival of the goods.

货物一到我们立即付款。

We shall effect shipment upon receipt of your L/C.

一收到你方的信用证,我们立即装运。

4. claim (*n. vt.*) 索赔

claim for... 或 claim on account of... 由于……索赔

claim for (amount) 索赔……(钱)

claim on sth 对……(货)索赔

claim against sb 向……索赔

raise (put in, file, lodge, make) a claim 提出索赔

Buyers have lodged a claim on this shipment for USD500 on account of short weight.

由于短量,买方对此批货物索赔500美元。

We have made a claim against the exporter for the damages of the goods caused by poor packing.

由于包装不善导致货物受损,所以我们向出口商索赔。

We will settle the claim to our mutual satisfaction.

我们会采取令我们双方满意的措施处理你们的索赔。

The insurance company dismissed the claim and the buyer did not get any compensation.

保险公司拒绝受理买方的索赔,买方没有得到任何赔偿。

The buyer claimed a compensation of US2 000 for the damaged goods.

买方因货物破损提出了2 000美元的索赔要求。

The insured party has the right to claim US5 000 on the goods.

被保险人有权对该货索赔5 000美元。

5. due

(1) 适当的,按时的

After due consideration, we have decided to grant your request.

经过适当考虑,我们决定答应你方的要求。

We trust the shipment will reach you in due course. 我们相信这批货会按时到你处。

(2) 到期

The time of shipment falls due next month.

装船期将于下月到期。

(3) 预定的,应到的

The steamer is due next Wednesday.

该船应于下星期一到达。

Fresh supplies are due to arrive early next month.

新货应于下月初到达。

(4) 所欠的

This remittance is in payment to all commissions due to you up to date.

这笔汇款是迄今为止欠你方的所有佣金。

due to 由于

The flight was cancelled due to the fog.

班机因雾停航。

She arrived late due to the storm.

由于暴风雨天气,所以她来迟了。

6. involve (vt.) 卷入,陷入,包含,牵连到

This company is involved in a scandal.

这家公司卷入到一个丑闻事件。

Building this road will involve the construction of ten bridges.

修这条路要建造10座桥。

This is a task which involves much difficulty.

这项任务有许多困难。

7. amount to 合计,总共达

The annual output of the steel plant amounts to 1 000 tons.

这家钢铁厂的年产量达到1 000吨。

These three lots of shipment amount to USD5 000 in value.

这三批货总值达到5 000美元。

8. tight (or narrow) profit margin 利润很低

还可以用 nominal insignificant 表示利润几乎为零

In anticipation of a large order from you we have cut our price to a point where the margin of profit is almost insignificant.

我们期待着你方大量的订单,所以我们将价格压到了很低的水平,利润几乎为零了。

As we expect larger orders from you, our price has been cut down to where our profit margin is but nominal.

9. compensate *vt.* 赔偿,补偿

The shipping company compensated the buyer USD 200 for the damages to the goods caused by their rough handling.

船公司野蛮搬运货物导致货物受损,所以赔偿了买方200美元。

The excellent performance in the contest compensates his efforts in exercises.

比赛中的优异表现是对他在训练过程中的付出的补偿。

compensation (*n.*) 赔偿,补偿

Buyers claim a compensation of USD200.

买方索要200美元的赔偿。

We shall remit to you an amount of US $2 000 in compensation for the loss arising therefrom.

我们给你方汇去2 000美元以赔偿你方在这件事中遭受的损失。

Compensation trade is a roundabout way to solve the problem of acquiring foreign exchange to finance essential imports.

补偿贸易间接地解决了进口业务的外汇融资问题。

13.2.2 Accept a Claim

China National Nonferrous Metal Import & Export Co.
10 Anhua Road
Beijing, China
Tel:010-80830008

3 April 2003

B. Greenwood Co.
21 Maple Street
London, U.K.

Dear Sirs

Thank you for your letter of 24 March referring to your order No. L89. We are glad to hear that the goods were delivered promptly.

We regret, however, that case No. 2 did not contain the goods you ordered. We have investigated the matter and find that we did make a mistake in putting the order together.

We have arranged for the correct goods to be dispatched to you at once. The relevant documents will be mailed to you as soon as they are ready.

Please keep case No. 2 and its contents until called for by our agents who have been informed of the situation.

We sincerely apologize for the inconvenience caused by our error.

Yours sincerely

Comments

Paragraph 1: identify the reference

Paragraph 2: apologize for the mistake

Paragraph 3: state what action is being taken

Paragraph 4: give instructions about the wrong goods

Paragraph 5: apologize for the inconvenience caused

The supplier frankly admits to the mistake and apologizes. Steps are set out to remedy the mistake. The tone of the letter is apologetic yet businesslike.

Notes

1. refer to 谈到，涉及，依照

We have received your letter of May 4th referring to the packing details.
我们收到你方5月4日来函,信中谈到包装细节问题。

Referring to our telephonic message of today, please deliver the above ten cases tomorrow.
根据我们今天的电话交谈,请于明日运来上述货物10箱。

Referring to our conversation of this morning, we enclose a pamphlet describing our new articles.

依照今天上午的谈话,随函呈上本公司新产品的小册子一本。

2. investigate 调查,同义词有 examine,还有一个常用短语 look into

We at once investigated the matter, and we frankly admit that in this particular instance your order did not get our usual careful attention.

我们立即调查了此事,我们得坦白地承认此次情况特殊,我们没有像往常那样认真执行你方订单。

We received your consignment yesterday which we found in order except that it contained only 40 doz. of Art. 444 Table Cloth, whereas we ordered and invoiced 50 doz. Please examine the matter and dispatch the missing 10 doz. by air freight.

我们昨天收到了你方发运的货物,除货号为 444 的桌布外,其他货物均正常。我们订购了 50 打货号为 444 的桌布,发票也是按此开立的。但只运来 40 打。请你方调查此事,将另外 10 打空运过来。

We immediately looked into the matter, and yet we are unable to explain the shortage and damage since all the goods underwent a thorough inspection at the time of shipping, which you may be sure of from the inspection certificate we obtained.

我们立即调查了此事,但无法对这次的货差货损做出解释,因为在装运时,所有的货物都经过了彻底检查,而且你们从我方提供的检验证明中可以看到这一点。

3. put the order together 这里表示将订购的货物备妥

4. arrange for 安排

As we need the articles we ordered to complete deliveries to our own customers, we must ask you to arrange for the dispatch of replacement at once.

由于我们需要所订购之货物来完成对我方客户的交货,因此我们必须要求你方立刻安排发运替代货物。

5. dispatch ($v. n.$) 运送

As instructed by you in your letter of June 20, we have dispatched to you by fast freight the goods, the invoice of which is enclosed.

遵照你方 6 月 20 日来函指示,我们已经将货物快运发出,货物发票同函寄上。

We are dispatching you today the goods ordered last week, and hope you will find them satisfactory.

本日发出上星期贵公司所订购的货物,希望贵公司对该货感到满意。

We have 10 containers of ladies' dresses for dispatch to New York before the end of June.

我们有10个集装箱的女士服装需要于6月底前发往纽约。

6. call for 要求,需要

The occasion calls for prompt action.

情势所迫,必须立即采取行动。

Any orders we place with you call for immediate delivery.

我们向你方订购货物都要求即刻交货。

7. inform sb of sth 通知某人某事

As soon as the goods are loaded, please inform us of the name of the vessel and date of sailing.

货物一旦装船,请告知船名和开航日期。

Please inform us, 10 days before the contracted time of shipment, of the name of the carrying vessel, its expected time of arrival at the port of loading and the name of the shipping agent so that we can contact the shipping agent to make arrangement for shipment.

请在合同规定的装运期前10天告知船名、预计抵达装运港日期以及船运代理人的名称,以便我方与该船运代理人联系安排货物装运事宜。

You are kindly requested to inform us of ocean freight for container shipment.

请告知集装箱运输的海洋运费。

8. apologize for 对……表示歉意

With reference to your fax of June 20, claiming for a short delivery of 13 tons of chemical fertilizer, we wish to apologize for the unfortunate incident.

关于你方6月20日就13吨化肥短量而发来的传真,我们对这一不幸事件深表歉意。

We sincerely apologize for any inconvenience you may have suffered as a result of this mistake, and wish you to know that the necessary steps have been taken to prevent its recurrence.

对由此错误给你方造成的任何不便我们深表歉意,并且我们已采取一切必要措施防止类似事件再次发生。

13.2.3 Reject a Claim

China National Textiles Import & Export Co.
10 Guanghua Road
Beijing, China
Tel: 010-85495770

30 May 2003

Lee Clothing Inc.
3 High Street
London, U.K.

Dear sirs

Thank you for your letter of May 21 referring to the consignment of cotton goods sent to you per S.S. Bright. We regret to note your complaint.

We have investigated the matter thoroughly. As far as we can ascertain, the goods were in first class condition when they left here. The bill of lading is evidence for this.

It is obvious that the damage you complain of must have taken place during transit. It follows, therefore, that we cannot be held responsible for the damage.

We therefore advise you to make a claim on the shipping company, Wilson Line, who should be held responsible.

We are grateful that you have brought the matter to our attention. If you wish, we would be happy to take issue with the shipping company on your behalf.

We look forward to resolving this matter as soon as possible.

Yours sincerely

Comments

Paragraph 1: identify the consignment and acknowledge the complaint

Paragraph 2: state the results of the investigation

Paragraph 3: reject the claim

Paragraph 4: advise the buyer on what steps to take to get compensation

Paragraph 5: as a goodwill gesture, offer to take up the matter yourself with the shipper

The letter acknowledges the claim but rejects it, giving reasons for doing so. It advises the buyer about making a claim against the shipper. In order not to antagonize the buyer, the seller volunteers to take the trouble of sorting out the claim.

Notes

1. complain of (about) 抱怨

The buyers complained of the poor quality of this shipment.

买方抱怨该批货物质量较差。

We have never experienced such damage to the packing as was complained of in this particular instance.

这次受到投诉的包装损坏情况是我们从未遇到过的。

We have again to complain about the non-delivery of the goods ordered by us for immediate delivery, which you stated were in stock.

我方不得不再次对你方未能立刻交付我方订购的货物进行投诉,你方原来告知是现货供应。

2. hold sb responsible for 某人应对……负责

We appreciate your fairness in informing us that you hold yourselves responsible for the part of the damage done.

我们十分感激你方能够客观公正地承诺对货物的损失承担责任。

Upon checking on arrival of the goods, we found goods in case No. 10 damaged, due to improper packing, for which the suppliers should be held responsible.

货物到达后,我方立刻检查发现由于包装不良,导致 10 号箱内货物受损,供货商应对此负责。

We shall not be held responsible for any damage which happened during transit.

对于运输途中发生的任何损失,我们不承担责任。

3. on your behalf 代表你方

There is a considerable demand for your products here, and we would do our utmost to push the sale on your behalf if you are disposed to entertain our commission rate.

最近本地客户对贵公司的产品有大量需求,如果贵公司愿意考虑我们的佣金比率要求,我们乐于倾力推销。

We requested Bank of China to collect due payment on our behalf.

我们请中国银行替我们收取应付款。

We hope to have the consignment insured at your end, and we will be appreciative of your kind arrangement to insure them on our behalf against All Risks for invoice value plus 10%.

我们希望这批货物在贵地投保。我们将非常感谢贵方代我方为这批货物投保一切险,保险金额为发票金额的110%。

13.3 Specimen Letters

13.3.1 Buyer's Complaint of Poor Quality

Dear sirs

We duly received the documents and took delivery of the dress materials supplied to our order No. LNG-521. We are much obliged to you for the prompt execution of this order.

After careful examination, however, we are both surprised and disappointed to find that the quality of these materials is certainly much below that of the samples you sent us.

We are enclosing a cutting sample from the goods we received. You will admit that these materials do not come up to the sample on which we passed you the order.

As the materials are quite unsuited to the needs of our customers, we hold the goods at your disposal.

Please look into the matter and let us know what you can do about it as soon as possible.

Yours truly

● **Activities for comprehension**

1. How many kinds of complaints are frequently made by buyers?
2. In what way is a letter of complaint written?

13.3.2 Exporter's Reply

Dear sirs

We very much regret to learn from your letter of March 21 that you are not satisfied with the dress materials supplied to your order No. LNG-521.

Tracing our records, we find that there has been some mistake in our selection of the materials meant for you.

We are very sorry for this carelessness on our part. To settle the problem, we would like either to replace the inferior materials as soon as possible or to give you a special allowance of 30% for the invoice amount.

We apologize once more for any inconvenience our mistake may have caused you and look forward to your decision as to which of the above two adjustments is preferable to you.

Yours truly

● **Activities for comprehension**

1. What points should be included in a letter accepting a claim?
2. What is the tone like in such letters?

13.3.3 Importer's Claim for the Loss

Dear sirs

We have received your shipment of 500 cameras on our order No. W-174.

While appreciating your prompt shipment, however, we are surprised to find that two cases labeled as C/No. 2 and C/No. 5 were broken with the result that 40 cameras contained were damaged to various degrees.

We think the packing is not strong enough to protect the goods and the wooden materials should have been 7/8″ thick.

We informed an authorized surveyor at once, who examined the goods in the presence of the shipping company's agents, and we are sure the enclosed surveyor's report will prove our view to be right.

Under such circumstances, we shall have to dispose of the damaged cameras at a greatly reduced price below 50% of their invoice cost. Therefore, we suggest you make us an allowance to make up for the loss accordingly, say, US $50 for each damaged camera.

We are looking forward to your comments.

Yours sincerely

13.3.4 Exporter's Reply

Dear sirs

We are very sorry to have learned from your letter of March 4th that 40 cameras were damaged. After careful consideration of your claim for damages, we wish to reply as follows.

Firstly, the cases we used for packing cameras are specially fit for export as you may see that they are all labeled "Export Packing" by the authorized surveyor.

Secondly, the clean bill of lading proves fully the goods in question to have been loaded in perfect condition. Therefore, it is evident that the damage of wooden cases has been caused by rough handling in voyage or when discharging at your port.

Under such circumstances, we could not be responsible for the damage. As the shipment is covered against All Risks, we would rather advise you to file the claim with the insurance company as soon as possible. We would, of course, do anything in our power to help you in your insurance claim.

Yours sincerely

● Activities for comprehension

1. How to avoid antagonizing the buyer when rejecting his claim?

13.4　Summary

In international trade, disputes may arise between the seller and buyer over their respective rights and obligations and complaints, claims, adjustments and arbitration, sometimes even litigation, will ensue. The causes of disputes between the seller and buyer are various, including the quality of goods inferior to the contract stipulations, short delivery, damages to the goods, or late delivery, etc.

国际贸易中,买卖双方会因彼此间的权利和义务的问题引起争议,从而导致投诉、索赔、理赔、仲裁,甚至诉讼等情况发生。买卖双方发生争议的原因很多,如货物的品质与合同规定不符,货物的数量短缺或货物受到损毁,不按期交货等等。

Don't delay to make a complaint. Failure to make a complaint effective usually occurs as a result of inadequate presentation of the complaint. The more specific the letter is, the better it will be for the seller to treat the complaint. A vague complaint will almost always come to the end of failure. The complaint letter should be firm but reasonably worded. Rudeness will create ill-feeling and cause the seller to be unwilling to resolve matters. Complaints must be well founded and diplomatically, tactfully put forward with care and restraint so that future business relationship are not harmed.

应该及时投诉。如果投诉内容没有表达清楚,那么往往难以达到效果。投诉函内容越详尽,越有利于卖方处理投诉事宜。如果投诉函内容模棱两可,往往会导致失败的结果。投诉函必须内容肯定、措辞合理。如果信函中表现出态度粗鲁,那么会让对方产生反感,从而不愿意解决问题。所以,投诉时一定要做到证据充分、态度诚恳、灵活务实,并且为避免影响日后业务往来，一定要审慎克制。

Replies to complaints should always be courteous. If the complaint is justified, you have to admit it readily, express your regret and promise to put matters right; if the complaint is not justified, point this out politely and in an agreeable manner; if you cannot deal with a complaint promptly, acknowledge it at once and explain that you will send a full reply later.

对投诉函的回复要礼貌。如果对方的投诉是正当的,就应该诚恳地承认,表达歉意并承诺改正。如果对方的投诉是无理的,也应该礼貌地指出。如果不能立即处理对方的投诉,那就先承认错误并说明日后会给对方圆满的答复。

In this unit, we learn how to write letters of complaint, claim and adjustment.

本单元介绍了投诉函、索赔函以及投诉或索赔处理函的写作方法。

13.5　Useful Expressions

1. On checking the goods received, we find that several items on your invoice have not been included; we enclose a list of the missing articles for your inspection.

一经查验,我们发现有几项你方发票中的货物并没有运过来;我们随函寄去缺失货物的清单以供你方查对。

2. Your shipment arrived here today and has been found correct with the exception of T/412 of which 200 bales were ordered and invoiced, while the shipment totaled only 130 bales.

你方发运的货物今天已经到达,除了 T/412 号货以外,其他均正常。我们订购了 200 包 T/412 号货,你方发票也是按 200 包开出的,但装运的数量只有 130 包。

3. The packing inside the case was too loose with the result that there was some shifting of the contents and several cups and plates have been broken. The attached list will give you details.

箱子内的包装太松了,所以导致箱子内的货物晃动,有一些杯子和盘子就破碎了。附寄的清单是货损的详细说明。

4. After inspection of the shipment we found 5 pieces of the cups contained in the case No. 5c broken. Apparently, this was attributable to improper packing.

查验货物后,我们发现5c箱子中所装的5只杯子破碎了。显然,这是由于包装不当造成的。

5. In your acknowledgement of our order you stated that the consignment would be dispatched within a fortnight and we are therefore very surprised that we have had no Advice of Dispatch yet.

在你们确认我方订单的信函中,你们说在两周内发货,但我们至今未收到发货通知,甚为惊讶。

6. We are enclosing a cutting sample from the goods we received. You will admit that these materials do no come up to the sample on which we passed you the order.

随函附寄从收到的货物上剪下的样品。你方会承认这些布料与我方下订单依据的样品不符。

7. In order to settle the claim, we make you an offer of USD5 per piece as allowance for inferiority of the quality, which we trust you will see your way to accept.

为解决索赔案,每件品质有瑕疵的货物给你方5美元的补贴。相信你们会接受。

8. We were very sorry to receive your complaint that the material you received was not of the quality expected. What you complained about is now under investigation, which, however, will take some time; we shall let you know the result at the conclusion of it.

很遗憾地从收到的你方的投诉函中得知你方收到的材料与预期的品质有差异。我们现在正在调查此事,这需要一些时日,一旦我们得出结论将会立即通知你方。

9. The goods, though not the very ones you ordered, are of good quality and in attractive designs, and we think you can sell them out at our price.

这些货物虽然与你们所订购的货物不是完全一样,但同样是品质优良、设计新颖,所以我们认为按照我们的价格你方能够将货物售罄。

10. Such color deviation existing between the products and the samples is normal and permissible, therefore, the compensation claimed is impracticable.

产品与样品之间的这种色差是正常的,也是允许的,所以你方索要赔偿是不合理的。

11. Should you insist on an allowance of 20% for the damaged goods, we shall have to put the matter before the Chamber of Commerce for arbitration.

如果你方坚持我们对破损的货物让价 20%,我们将就此向商会提请仲裁。

12. In view of this, you will fully agree that we are in no position to assume any responsibility as the shortage and damage occurred during transit. We suggest, therefore, that you file a claim with your insurance company.

鉴于此,你方应该同意,我们对于货损货差不应承担任何责任,因为这都是在运输途中发生的。所以,我们建议你们向保险公司索赔。

13. We see no reason on our part to meet your claim. But we are not unaware of your difficult situation. As a compromise, we have decided to allow a discount of 10%, and cabled you accordingly. We hope you will find this solution agreeable.

我们不认为自己需要对你方进行赔偿。但我们也了解你们的困境。所以,作为折中意见,我们决定给你们 10% 的让价,并已电报通知你方。希望你们觉得这种解决办法可以接受。

14. We are no longer responsible for the goods once they have left us. Nevertheless, we are most anxious to help you out of the trouble. We will seek redress from the carrying company. In the meantime, if you will please reship the faulty parts to us, we will send you replacements by air.

货物一装运走,我方就不再承担任何责任了。但是,我们非常想帮助你方解决这个困难,所以我们会向承运公司索赔。同时,如果你们愿意,请将有瑕疵的部件退回给我方,我们将更换的部件给你们空运过去。

13.6 Reading Material

13.6.1 Make a Claim for Short Weight

Dear sirs

We refer to sales contract No. 546 covering the purchase of 200 metric tons of white cement.

We telexed you on 7 November informing you that the consignment arrived on

20 October.

On inspection, we found that 180 bags had burst and that the contents, estimated at 1 000 kg, had been irretrievably lost.

We proceeded to have a survey report made. The report has now confirmed our initial findings.

The report indicates that the loss was due to the use of substandard bags for which you, the suppliers, are responsible.

On the strength of the survey report, we hereby register our claim against you as follows:

Short delivered quantity	US $280
Survey charges	US $100
Total claimed	US $380

We enclose survey report No. TS4678 and look forward to early settlement of the claim.

Yours truly

13.6.2 Accept a Claim for Short Weight

Dear sirs

Thank you for your letter of 11 November in which you lodge a claim for short delivery of 9 000 kg of white cement.

We wish to express our deep regret at this incident. We have checked with our warehouse and discovered that part of your consignment was not packed in 5-ply paper bags as specified in the contract. This was due to a negligence of our warehouse staff.

We are most concerned to maintain our long-standing trading relationship. We therefore enclose a cheque for US $380 in full and final settlement of your claim.

We trust that this unfortunate error will not adversely affect our future relations.

Yours truly

13.6.3　Request More Information on A Claim

Dear sirs

　　Thank you for your letter of 20 June with a claim for breakages.

　　Your claim is for US $1 000 on the shipment delivered on 2 June to your order No. 2343.

　　The goods were in perfect order and properly packed in cardboard boxes. They were then placed in a sealed container at our factory. It is difficult to imagine how any breakages could occur.

　　Fortunately, the goods were fully insured under our standard policy with Smart Insurance Co. of Austria, but in order to make a claim we shall need much more information.

　　Please make a complete inventory of the broken items and send it to us. We shall then contact our insurer. Their agent will probably call on you to check the consignment.

　　I apologize for the inconvenience caused.

Yours truly

13.6.4　Request Replacement of Defective Equipment

Dear sirs

　　At the beginning of March this year we took delivery of one of your LS500 laser colour separation machines on order No. 3456.

　　Since then, the machine has broken down six times. The breakdown have led to the loss of 12 days' production time while we waited for your local agents to fix the machine.

　　The scanner has now broken down again. Although service is included on a one-year warranty, we do not want it serviced again. Instead, we want you to replace it with a new machine.

　　It is clear that the machine is defective. We can no longer permit the interruptions caused by repeated breakdown.

　　We bought the machine because of your company's reputation for quality and service. We do not want to lose confidence in you.

Please let us know when we can expect delivery of a replacement machine.

Thank you for your cooperation.

Yours truly

13.6.5 Answer a Complaint

Dear sirs

Thank you for your letter of 15 June regarding the colour separation machines bought by your company on 12 February.

As leading manufacturers in this field, we are deeply concerned when a customer is dissatisfied with one of our products. We take great pride in producing top quality machines.

Judging by your report, the machine you purchased is well below our usual high standard. I have contacted our agent in your area and they will be calling on you with a replacement machine in the near future.

Please accept my sincere apologies. We are very sorry that you have been inconvenienced in this way.

Yours truly

13.6.6 Deal with a Claim

Dear Sirs

We have just received your letter of May 1, and we are very sorry that the goods we shipped were not in good condition.

The defective goods which you mentioned must have been overlooked by our inspector. Kindly let us know what arrangement you think is fair and satisfactory in this matter, so that we can consult with our manufacturer and inform you of the result as soon as possible.

Yours sincerely

Exercises

I. Fill in the blanks with your choices.

1. The goods you delivered are below the standard we expected _____ the sample.

   a) from   b) to   c) on   d) in

2. We are sorry for our mistake in the number, _____ resulted _____ your receiving the wrong goods.

   a) that...of   b) this...from   c) which...in   d) it...as

3. It is most essential that the delivery _____ punctual, otherwise our summer sales cannot be carried out.

   a) will be   b) would be   c) has been   d) should be

4. None of the articles in this case is of any use to us, and we hold them _____ your disposal _____ your instructions.

   a) for...waiting   b) by...awaiting

   c) under...depending   d) at...pending

5. Case No. 11 was found to be 3 packages _____.

   a) too short   b) shortage   c) to shorten   d) short

6. With reference to our Order No. 142 executed by you, we have to inform you that owing to negligent packing, several bales were damaged to such an extent that we were _____ to dispose of them at a greatly reduced price.

   a) compelled   b) forced   c) pushed   d) troubled

7. You will recognize that we are accordingly in a _____ to repudiate the whole contract, but such a drastic step would be most unwelcome to us.

   a) site   b) status   c) position   d) ability

8. After unpacking the case we found the goods did not _____ with the original sample.

   a) agree   b) match   c) compare   d) measure

9. After inspection of the above shipment we found 5 cases _____.

   a) missed   b) missing   c) lost   d) losing

10. Fifty cases of Green Tea you sent us were found to be badly damaged. This was apparently attributable to _____ packing.
   a) faulty   b) large   c) inner   d) outer

II. Put in each blank the correct word or phrase from the following list.

concession	arrange for	informed	claimed	make a complaint
replace	unsalable	compensation	exception	recur
due to	discrepancy	on account of	redress	

1. Such colour deviation existing between the products and the samples is normal and permissible; therefore, the compensation _____ is impracticable.

2. This is the maximum _____ we can afford. Should you not agree to accept our proposal, we would like to settle by arbitration.

3. The merchandise seems to be in good order with the _____ of Case No. 2, which appears to contain goods of a type completely different to our order.

4. There is a clear _____ between the packing lists which arrived together with the consignment and your invoice.

5. We must ask you to _____ the dispatch of replacements for the missing cabinets at once, as we must make a delivery to our own customers.

6. Inform us about steps you are taking to make sure this problem does not _____.

7. I'm sorry to have to _____ in writing about a recent purchase of a defective laptop computer because my repeated complaints by word of mouth have not produced the desired result up to now.

8. We reserve the right to claim _____ from you for any damage.

9. The defect may be _____ a fault in a machine, and we are now checking up all the machines.

10. Owing to your failure to keep us _____, we have not been able to obtain cover and the goods are carried at your risk.

11. We are sorry to have received your letter of October 5, requesting us to make a 20% allowance _____ the quality not being the same as the sample.

12. Meanwhile, if you will please return to us the defective parts, we will _____ them and ship them to you by air freight.

13. The goods have proved to be _____ and we suggest that you make us a reduction of 10% in price.

14. Although our responsibility ceases as soon as the goods have left us, we are most eager to help you out of your difficulties. We shall try to obtain _____ from the carriers.

III. Put the following sentences into Chinese.

1. According to contract stipulations, we are not liable for the damage, but, as there was evidence of rough handling on our part, we are willing to allow you half the amount of your claim.

2. This is the first time in all our dealings with you that any mistake has occurred. We hope you will do all that you can to remedy the trouble.

3. We regret to have to return these goods and shall be glad if you will substitute the right goods for them as early as possible.

4. You will remember that we stressed the importance of punctual shipment, and you will understand that your delay in the circumstances give us a right to sue for the losses caused.

5. As the demand for these goods is seasonal, we shall be forced to cancel this order unless we can get immediate shipment.

6. With regard to the loss in weight, we are enclosing a surveyor's report in order to prove to you that the loss could only have occurred in transit.

7. In our opinion, the export cases were not sufficiently strong to protect these instruments.

8. With regard to the loss in weight, we would suggest that you make your claim with the forwarding agent as, in a case of this kind, we really cannot accept any liability.

9. As you consider our proposals unacceptable, we suggest that the matter be submitted to arbitration.

10. As your complaint does not agree with the results of our own test, we suggest that another thorough examination be conducted by you to show whether there is any ground for claim.

● **Skills Practice**

A. Write an English letter in proper layout for BURGESS furniture Co. 5 Aston Road, Birmingham, U. K., to China national Import & Export Corp., Shanghai Branch, complaining that the wrong quality were sent. This letter should be written according to the instructions below:

1. 5月6日订购的434号家具装饰订单现已运到。

2. 经查验后发现货物质量与商定的不符,极为失望。

3. 货色与样本质量相差悬殊,部分质量极为差劣,怀疑订购过程可能出现错误。

4. 要求退货,换为订单要求之货色。

5. 若接受上述安排,则从贵公司确定能供应合格货物之日起计算交货日期。

B. The account manager of Foundation Import & Export Co. ordered US $ 30,000 worth of cotton piece goods with Elegance Fabrics Corp. on June 4 and asked for delivery by August 4. But the delivery was not made a week after the anticipated latest date. Write a letter for this account manager to Elegance Fabrics Corp. to lodge a complaint.

C. You are the manager of Stylish Office Furniture. You placed an order with Office Furniture Wholesalers for twenty filing cabinets and eight executive chairs. The delivery deadline for the goods was yesterday. But you received only twenty filing cabinets yesterday, while the eight executive chairs are missing. You called them and talked to their assistant manager. However, all she told you was that the chairs are unavailable and she could not specify a date as to when the chairs will be in stock. Write a letter to complain about the situation and extend your delivery date to 20 August.

教辅申请说明

　　北京大学出版社本着"教材优先、学术为本"的出版宗旨，竭诚为广大高等院校师生服务。为更有针对性地提供服务，请您按照以下步骤在微信后台提交教辅申请，我们会在1~2个工作日内将配套教辅资料，发送到您的邮箱。

◎手机扫描下方二维码，或直接微信搜索公众号"北京大学经管书苑"，进行关注；

◎点击菜单栏"在线申请"—"教辅申请"，出现如右下界面：

◎将表格上的信息填写准确、完整后，点击提交；

◎信息核对无误后，教辅资源会及时发送给您；如果填写有问题，工作人员会同您联系。

温馨提示：如果您不使用微信，您可以通过下方的联系方式（任选其一），将您的姓名、院校、邮箱及教材使用信息反馈给我们，工作人员会同您进一步联系。

我们的联系方式：
北京大学出版社经济与管理图书事业部
北京市海淀区成府路205号，100871
联 系 人： 周莹
电　　话： 010-62767312 /62757146
电子邮件： em@pup.cn
Q Q： 5520 63295（推荐使用）
微信： 北京大学经管书苑（pupembook）
网址： www.pup.cn